£1

Niall Mackenzie
the autobiography

Niall Mackenzie

the autobiography

Niall Mackenzie
with Stuart Barker

CollinsWillow

An Imprint of HarperCollinsPublishers

First published in Great Britain in 2002
by CollinsWillow
an imprint of HarperCollins*Publishers* London

Copyright © Niall Mackenzie and Stuart Barker 2002

1 3 5 7 9 8 6 4 2

A CIP catalogue record for this book is
available from the British Library

The HarperCollins website address is:
www.**fire**and**water**.com

ISBN 0-00-714489-X

Typeset by Rowland Phototypesetting Ltd
Bury St Edmunds, Suffolk
Printed and bound in Great Britain by
Clays Ltd, St Ives plc

Picture acknowledgements
All photographs supplied by the author with the exception of the
following: **ASL Photography** p.15; **Stephen Davison/Pacemaker**
p.8 (bottom); **Hero Drent** p.3 (top); **Empics** p.9 (bottom), p.12
(bottom); **GeeBee Photographic** p.14 (centre); **Gold & Goose** p.5
(centre), p.6 (top), p.7 (centre), p.9 (top and centre right), p.10 (top);
Dan Jess Photography p.2. (centre); **Don Morley** p.3 (centre and
bottom), p.4 (top and bottom), p.5 (top and bottom), p.6 (centre),
p.8 (top); **Original Double Red Ltd** p.10 (centre and bottom),
p.11 (centre), p.12 (top and centre); p.13 (all), p.14 (top and
bottom); **Sportfoto** p.7 (top)**; Peter Wileman** p.2 (bottom).
Every attempt has been made to credit the
pictures used in this book

With love for my mum, Amelia, who sadly
passed away just before this book was completed.
1929–2002

Contents

Acknowledgements

The unsung heroine of this whole story is my wife Jan. She put up with my moods when I had bad results, dealt with the uncertainty of the off-seasons, waited in countless medical centres around the world and generally sacrificed her life to accommodate my selfish obsession with racing motorbikes.

Jan never once complained or put me under pressure to retire – the final decision was mine alone. And as if that wasn't enough, she gave me the two most precious sons a dad could ever ask for in Taylor and Tarran.

I have my mum to thank for keeping me on the straight and narrow after we lost my dad and for teaching me to work hard. She has always given me her unconditional love.

I had my dad for thirteen good years and he left me with an interest in all things mechanical as well as a great sense of adventure and a desire to be a little different. But I hope he hasn't always been watching me from that great paddock in the sky!

Robert Fearnall from Donington Park has helped me self-lessly throughout my career from 1983 to the present day and he even found my wife for me! Without his guidance, I wouldn't have gone half as far in life as I have and I count him as one of my best and most loyal friends.

This book would never have materialised if Stuart Barker hadn't convinced me that I had a story worth telling. I've enjoyed the process of working on this book and I appreciate Stuart's talent, hard work and enthusiasm.

A big thank you to all at HarperCollins*Publishers* for giving Stuart and myself the opportunity to tell my story. The help and personal attention we've received has been first class and made our job so much easier.

The last personal thank you is to Mick Doohan for his kind words in the foreword but, more importantly, for being a good friend to me over the last thirteen years. Mick's success was unimaginable for most people but I was fortunate enough to witness at first hand the effort he put in and the hurdles he overcame to win five world titles, although I believe it could so easily have been eight.

Finally to all my family, friends, team staff and fans, you are the people who put me first. I dedicate this book to you.

Foreword

by MICK DOOHAN
Five Times 500cc World Champion
1994–1998

Niall Mackenzie was one of the first people I got to know when I started Grand Prix racing with Rothmans Honda in 1989 and since then we've always had a friendly relationship. He was one of the few guys against whom you could race and then go and have a coffee with at the end of the day without any worries. It was good to have him and his wife Jan around the GP paddock and they were very popular with everyone.

Back then we used to do some training together and would often go out running, which was something I couldn't do any more after I broke my leg at Assen in 1992.

In my first season, I sometimes used to ask Niall about the weather in the various countries in Europe. I was straight out of Australia and had never been to most of those places, whereas Niall knew his way around. Before my first GP at Spa Francorchamps, I remember I mentioned to Niall that the weather in Belgium wasn't so flash and he replied that he'd never been in a dry Grand Prix at Spa in all the years he'd raced there! Niall beat me in the 1989 championship when he was seventh and I was ninth.

That season, and the next, we were often racing each other closely and he was always a very fair sportsman in the way he rode.

Over the years that we've been friends he has visited me in Australia and we've been out on boats together and spent lots of time just relaxing away from the Grands Prix.

Niall started GP racing a year or two before me and around that time there was plenty of strong competition with riders such as Eddie Lawson, Wayne Rainey, Kevin Schwantz, Wayne Gardner, Christian Sarron and others.

It was a really quality field in those days but Niall had a pole position, seven podiums, and a total of twenty-eight top five finishes between 1987 and 1993.

The results don't always tell the whole story, but on this occasion they show that Niall was a very competitive motorcycle racer and Britain's best rider in 500cc Grands Prix at that time.

Since then he has raced in a variety of championships at world level and in Britain, mostly on Superbikes, and not surprisingly, he's always done well relative to the capabilities of his equipment.

Another of Niall's strengths is his character. We all have our ups and downs in this sport, but Niall was one who enjoyed his success without getting too carried away with it and could also take setbacks in his stride. He's a guy who always seems to bounce back.

Niall obviously enjoys riding and racing motorcycles, otherwise he wouldn't have had the motivation to keep going for as long as he did. Motivation is everything if you're going to have some success in racing; you really have to want to ride the thing, and Niall did that for many seasons.

I can't think of a better role model for young British riders than Niall. He's got talent, determination, and most importantly he's a good guy. I'm sure this publication will give a good insight into how his career unfolded.

I'm fortunate to have Niall as a friend and I look forward to catching up with him again soon.

Mick Doohan
Australia, March 2002

CHAPTER ONE

Chip Shops and Railway Tracks

I remember having a conversation with Wayne Gardner and Randy Mamola about how we all got started in bike racing.

At the time, the three of us were at the peak of our careers racing in the 500cc Grand Prix World Championships. Wayne had won the title in 1987, Randy had been runner up four times and I was a full factory rider for Honda, and had set pole position in my first ride for the team at the Japanese GP.

We were sitting around a campsite having a barbecue somewhere on the continent and their stories of biking childhoods seemed so exotic to me. Randy had been riding children's dirt track bikes round purpose-built tracks all over California since he was about four years old and Wayne had been doing the same thing in Australia. I, on the other hand, made my two-wheeled debut on a knackered old scooter dragged off a scrap heap at the ripe old age of thirteen and didn't even think about racing until I was nineteen. So I was wondering what to say when I had to reveal my racing pedigree because it sure as hell wasn't going to stand up next to Wayne and Randy's.

When Randy turned to me and said 'What about you Niall? How did you get started in racing?' I decided to lie. Instead of telling them how it really was, I concocted a story that I

1

thought would make them laugh. I said that I'd been working for the electricity board in Scotland (which was true) when I got caught in a woman's house doing a job dressed from head to toe in her underwear that I'd taken from her bedroom drawers. I added that I was sacked from my job and thought I might as well try my hand at racing bikes professionally since I had been thinking about it anyway.

Wayne Gardner erupted. He was actually crying with laughter. I still don't know if he was laughing so hard because he thought it was a funny story or because he thought it was true. But either way, there's still nasty rumours kicking around the paddocks of the world that I have transvestite tendencies and I still blame Wayne for spreading them so I think he probably did believe me. I suppose he had even more reason to believe my story after I dressed as Grand Prix racer Rob McElnea's girlfriend just so we could get into an all night couples bar in Italy.

Just for the record, it's absolutely not true – I'm not a transvestite. In fact, my wife's clothes don't even fit me.

But making up that story to raise a laugh was an indication of just how completely out of place I felt in the company of Grand Prix superstars like Wayne and Randy, even though I was giving them a good run for their money in the GPs at the time.

I simply couldn't get my head around the fact that Wayne Gardner and Freddie Spencer were my team-mates or that I had become friends with people I'd only previously known from seeing on television. But most of all, I couldn't believe that someone like me, who came from a small, unremarkable village in Central Scotland, could be mixing with the best riders in the world in the 500cc Grand Prix World Championship.

Everyone accepts that GP racers come from Italy, America,

Australia or somewhere equally exotic, so being born in Fankerton seemed to rule me out of a career in GPs straight away. Somehow, it just doesn't have the same ring to it as Modesto, California or the Gold Coast, Australia. In fact, my home town is so small that it's not even listed on most road maps.

So let me just put the record straight. Fankerton is situated about a mile from Denny in Central Scotland and it's just a tiny village of around sixty houses, most of which were built to provide homes for the local papermill workers.

I was brought home there to a council house at 3 Myot View after being delivered at Stirling Royal Infirmary at 3.15pm on 19 July 1961 and my parents called me Niall Macfarlane Mackenzie – a name as suited to Grand Prix racing as my background was.

My father Neil, chose the Gaelic spelling of his own name for me since he came from Inverness, the capital of the Scottish Highlands and a city steeped in Gaelic tradition. The pronunciation, incidentally, is the same as with the standard spelling of the name, although that fact has been lost on many TV commentators who have who persisted in pronouncing it 'Nyall.'

Dad was a qualified engineer but spent twenty-three years working in India as a tea plantation manager before returning to Scotland in the late 1950s and marrying my mum, Amelia Macfarlane. I was an only child but I've got three half-brothers, John, Brian and Colin, from my dad's first marriage.

Dad lost most of his savings from India in a succession of ill-advised business investments and he returned to engineering work to support my mum, who worked as a secretary, and myself. We weren't exactly on the breadline but there wasn't a lot of extra cash for luxuries and from a very early age, I knew that if I wanted something extra, I was going to have to work for it.

So, straight from primary school I helped on a farm carrying milk from the milking parlour to the tank. I was paid ten bob (50p) a week and I loved it. I knew there was no money in paper rounds so as soon as my parents allowed me to, I got up before school and did a milk round for £8 a week and also worked on the farm. It was good fun as well as being an earner, and me and my mate Beefy thought we were the sharpest milkmen in Scotland.

My mum opened a bank account for me with my christening money when I was very young and I was fascinated by how money could just grow if you left it there. To me, interest was money for nothing and I thought that was great. I'm not tight, you understand, but I've just always been a good saver. I don't know if it's a security thing but it definitely came from my mum. She was always good with money and that grounding has stood me in good stead throughout my career.

I suppose my childhood was much the same as any other kids growing up in rural Scotland at the time. Cash may have been tight but as long as there were rivers, forests and glens to play in, boys could be boys, knees could be muddied and everyone was happy. Having a friend who lived on a farm helped too. All the kids congregated at the farm and if you wanted to work there you could. I suppose it was slave labour in a way but we loved it all the same.

The farm seemed more like an adventure playground than a workplace with all the tractors and machinery to play on and the tunnels that we explored in the haysheds.

Some of the funniest times I experienced as a kid was when I played 'The Grand National' and 'Chap Door Run' with my pals. There was a big square of council houses that had all their gardens backing onto each other and the aim of 'The Grand National' was to make a run for it and throw yourself over all the hedges while being chased by the people who lived in the houses. It was a particular favourite with me and my mate Hammy. 'Chap Door Run' is just one of a thousand names for every kid's other favourite game – knocking on doors and running away! Well, at least we were getting exercise.

But while my childhood was relatively carefree, and even financially productive to a certain extent, my teenage years were more trying. In 1975 when I was just thirteen, my father died after a long history of health problems. He had a heart condition mainly due to working too hard and playing too hard; he had just hammered himself when he lived in India. He'd been teetotal ever since I was born but the damage had already been done after years of playing too much polo and drinking too much whisky – not a good combination.

My father's death not only affected my teenage years, it also affected my career prospects as having a motorbike when dad was alive just wasn't an option. He actually had a 350 AJS at one point and used to ride it fifty miles to and from work every day as my uncle Alick still reminds me. But when it came to me having a bike, he gave me the usual speech about money and safety like most parents do. So if my dad hadn't died, I might never have become a bike racer because he really wasn't keen on the whole motorbike thing. Maybe because he'd owned one he was more aware of the dangers than most.

I know that lots of kids who lose a parent can be psychologically scarred for life, but somehow I quickly accepted the reality of the situation. To be honest, it was almost a relief when he died because he'd been ill for three years and it was so sad to watch him deteriorating. I loved him to bits and was probably closer to him than to my mum but in a way I was prepared for his death. I shed a few tears with my mum that night but went back to school a week later and tried to carry on. There were a few tears at school too because kids can be so cruel about things like that, but after a few weeks I was fine and just got on with my life. In fact I received a lot of attention for having lost my father and quite enjoyed it.

As a rule, I wasn't a bad kid but I was definitely given more of a free rein by my mum and my teachers because my dad was dead. It sounds terrible but I actually loved the freedom of not having a father figure around. I didn't completely abuse that freedom but there was a lot less discipline in my life than some of my mates had to put up with. I was never one to hang around the graveyard smoking fags, doing drugs and getting drunk all the time – it just wasn't my thing – but I had a few Strongbow Cider experiences and generally goofed around a bit more than before.

Like I said, I didn't abuse my new-found freedom but like most young boys, I overstepped the mark on a few occasions and faced the wrath of the law as well as that of my mum, particularly when I stole my friend's dad's car.

I had learned to drive tractors when I was very young so I could drive a car with no problem, long before I was old enough to drive legally. My mates and I didn't go to school much in our final year and we thought it would be a good idea to 'borrow' a car to cruise around in to pass the time and show off. So the four of us, me, Shanksy, Stoney and Bunny (Stoney would come back to haunt me on the other side of the world years later when I was racing in GPs), started to drive around in the car quite regularly. I suppose it was only a matter of time before we got caught. We eventually got too cocky and once when we were parked behind the ice cream van at the school gates, a flashing blue light came up behind us. I floored the accelerator and took off, getting chased round the streets until I finally got some distance between us and the police, ditched the car and made a run for it. I got out and ran off as did Shanksy who was in the passenger seat, but the child locks were on in the back and Stoney and Bunny couldn't get out. They were sitting ducks for the cops to nab and were taken straight down to the police station and photographed and fingerprinted like real criminals. They eventually 'squealed' and told the cops everything and I got fingered as the driver.

Up to that point, my mum had never hit me, and my dad had never laid a finger on me when he was alive, but that night my mum attacked me, pulling my hair and kicking and screaming like a banshee. I didn't like seeing her in such a state and I realised I'd made a mistake that I didn't want to repeat so I tried to behave myself a bit more after that.

Apart from gaining a bit of disciplinary leeway, the most significant effect of losing my dad was that I was free to pursue my interest in motorcycles, which had been sparked off by a friend's dad who raced bikes. He was called Jimmy Rae and he used to race at the Isle of Man TT and in the Scottish championships. Bob MacIntyre's old mechanic, Pim Fleming, used to spanner for him and Jimmy had known Bob too so that always impressed us as kids, as Bob Mac was Scotland's most famous bike racer and the first man to do a 100mph lap at the TT.

Hanging around that garage was my first real exposure to bikes but I wasn't mad on them at that point; I was just interested like most young lads would be.

It was only when I actually got to ride a bike that I became hooked, even though my introduction to powered two-wheel transport was less than glamorous, as I've already explained. While my future Grand Prix rivals were learning their trades on expensive children's racing motorcycles as soon as they could sit on them, I had to wait until I was thirteen before I sat on a bike and even then it was more of a push-bike than a motorbike. And rather than riding on a purpose built school-boy motocross track my debut was on an old railway line.

The first bike I ever rode was a Raleigh scooter and it relied on good old pedal power more than the power of its minus-cule combustion engine. It was basically a push-bike with a little engine and some of my mates had dragged it off a dump and managed to get it going so we ended up on the old railway line that used to serve Carron Grove Papermill with it. I was the youngest one there and was given a go and I just couldn't believe that this push-bike thing was moving without me having to peddle – well, sometimes at least. It must have made about 3bhp but I was just blown away with the whole concept and that was the start of it for me: I had to have a motorbike.

It's debatable whether my first two-wheeled purchase could actually be described as a motorbike however as Honda's C90 is probably the most basic form of two-wheeled transport there is. But its reputation for reliability and its ease of use have made it the biggest selling bike of all time with some thirty million of them having been sold to date, mostly to grannies and pizza delivery boys.

I paid about £40 for my second hand C90, which was quite a lot of cash back then but I had saved up enough money from my milk round and I just had to have it. I mostly rode it round the fields with my old orange helmet on but some-times I would have to ride it on the road to get to the fields even though it had no tax or insurance and I hadn't passed my test. My mates were mostly older and had Yamaha FS1Es and Suzuki AP50s so I was always playing catch up.

After the C90, I bought a Honda TL125 trials bike from Lloyds Brothers in Hamilton. I don't really know why I wanted one because I certainly didn't do any trials on it. It cost £330 brand new, which was a fortune to me, and I had to save everything I earned for six months to get it since my mum still didn't want me to have a bike and wouldn't let me use any of the money she'd put away for me.

As soon as I turned seventeen, I naturally wanted a proper bike for the road and the coolest thing a seventeen year old could have in the late 1970s was a Yamaha FS1E or 'Fizzy' as they became affectionately known. So I sold the Honda TL125 to raise cash to buy a 'Fizzy' and I was ready to rock. But first there was the minor inconvenience of passing a bike test. I could have ridden the little pedal-assisted Fizzy on a provisional licence indefinitely but I had aspirations of moving onto bigger bikes so I took my test at the first opportunity.

Fortunately, for me at least, riding standards were not quite as strict in the 1970s as they are now and I passed my test at the first attempt even though my examiner disappeared before the test was over! Nowadays, you take your test on a bike with a radio link to the examiner, who's on another bike. But in those days, the examiner just used to watch you riding round the streets as he stood on the pavement. At one point, I was asked to ride round the block and the examiner said he would hide behind a car and jump out holding his hand up for me to do an emergency stop. I went round the block but got lost and by the time I found the right street again he was gone – nowhere to be seen. I somehow managed to find my way back to the test centre and he was already there, waiting to give me my licence. I think he just wanted to go home as it was half past four on a dark and drizzly winter afternoon in Falkirk and he was just going through the motions, but that was fine by me as I still got my licence.

If there is one downside to motorcycles it's that they can be dangerous. Whichever way you dress up the facts and figures, the truth remains that a lot of people both on the road and on racetracks, get hurt or killed riding bikes. But anyone who rides a bike has weighed up the risks and decided they're worth taking. After all, you can't live your life wrapped in cotton wool trying to avoid every possible danger. Taking risks and getting the adrenaline pumping is what makes people feel alive and, when all's said and done, bikes are great fun and that's why we ride them.

Even so, I had a grim early lesson in the dangers of motor-cycling. I had bought the Fizzy from a friend called Craig Feeney who had just bought a bigger 250cc Ham Yam (a customised Yamaha with bolt-on racing parts) which was con-sidered the bees' knees at the time. A few months later, Craig was paralysed from the chest down after a road accident. I was gutted for my friend but never thought about selling up and quitting bikes. It was a big shock because he was in a wheel-chair but it didn't put me off and I actually bought a Ham Yam similar to Craig's not long after his accident. Craig eventually received a big compensation pay out and he helped me out financially when I started racing.

In those early days, I still didn't harbour any ambitions to be a racer. In fact, I had no ambitions at all except to enjoy myself. It's not that I was totally stupid. I was actually quite good at school. I managed to get seven 'O' Levels (the equiva-lent of GCSEs), and I even stayed on at school to study for four Highers (the Scottish version of English 'A' Levels). However a crash on my Fizzy resulted in a damaged knee which in turn resulted in several weeks off school. I missed a lot of the groundwork for the new term and I was fed up with trying to catch up so I just left school and went to work full time on the farm. I still had my milk run in the morning and I helped at a haulage firm at night so I was making enough cash to get by.

My mum would have supported me financially through college if I had wanted to go but the idea of studying for four years at that age just didn't appeal to me. I wanted to be having a good time and anyway I liked driving tractors at the farm, doing all the harrowing and rolling and the like, so why would I want to be stuck in a classroom?

However, the glamorous world of motor sports seemed something that only other, more privileged children could aspire to. In fact, the closest I ever got to considering racing as a career was dreaming of being a rally car driver as a kid but I never considered that as a realistic option – it was just day-dreaming stuff. As for bike racing, it never even entered my head. I wouldn't have had a clue where to start for one thing. Where I came from, you were considered lucky just to get a trade apprenticeship and the highest you could aim for was getting in with the big companies like BP or ICI in Grangemouth. I certainly wasn't encouraged to dream about alternative glamorous lifestyles so, like everyone else, I stuck with the jobs I had and just got on with things.

When I wasn't working, I started to discover the pleasures of girls and alcohol and I liked what I found. I knew from playing Postman's Knock at Sunday school at a very early age that I was definitely heterosexual! We used to organise snogging sessions in primary seven when I was ten. I'd cover myself in Old Spice aftershave and get stuck in and it was really exciting even though we didn't know what the hell we were doing.

I suppose my first proper girlfriend was Lorraine Binnie who came from a very good family of Baptists. I wasn't exactly religious, reliable or mature so I'm sure the Binnies were pleased to see the back of me when Lorraine and I drifted apart.

But by the time I was seventeen I'd popped my cherry and never looked back! I dated some nice girls over the years but never wanted a steady girlfriend because I was too busy with bikes and fooling around with my mates.

At seventeen, I also started going to pubs with my pals. I looked so young that I couldn't get served before that, so up until then we'd had to content ourselves by buying bottles of Pomagne or Buckfast from the off-licence and drinking them in the park. Pure class.

When I did go out drinking, it would be at The Pines in Denny or at various Young Farmers discos which were a big thing in rural Scotland at the time (and probably still are). I was already familiar with The Pines pub because of the chip shop of the same name next door. We all used to hang about at The Pines chip shop every night as kids then we graduated to the pub next door when we were old enough. We were there every night with push-bikes, motorbikes, cars or whatever we had. Everyone on bikes would try to show off doing wheelies and stunts and I was no exception. I had one go wrong once and ended up riding right in through the chip shop doors, landing on my backside in a heap, back wheel still spinning, saying 'Two steak pies and a fish supper please.'

It was a great atmosphere at The Pines. Everyone got on well together and the cops pretty much left us alone because we weren't doing any damage, chip shop doors notwithstanding. I was always good at socialising with different groups from the rough kids right through to the really academic types. I just seemed to blend in well with anyone.

By this time, my friends Alistair and Stewart Rae (Jimmy's boys) had started racing and I went with them to several meetings in Scotland and in the north of England. I still had no intention of going racing myself, I was chuffed just to be helping the lads. They had a Fiat van, which was always breaking down, and we went all over the place in it having a great time wherever we'd go.

There would be the Rae brothers, me and my best mate Wullie McKay, with whom I worked, and we always got drunk on Saturday nights and ended up fighting each other in the back of the van. We were all in sleeping bags battling for space to stretch out and once someone started kicking, all hell broke loose. It actually got pretty rough and there were some nasty cuts and bruises dished out but it was such a laugh that we didn't care.

I figured those boys were going to be world champions when they started finishing in the top six in club races. I believed they would go all the way.

But even attending race meetings and helping out where I could wasn't enough to inspire me to go racing myself. It was something entirely different which provided that inspiration. It was called an RD350LC and it was Yamaha's hot new street bike.

When the RD350LC was first launched in 1980, it was *the* bike for teenage boy racers and it still has a cult following to this day. With a top speed of 110mph, it was derived straight from the racetrack and I just knew I had to have one. Although I didn't know it at the time, that was the bike which launched my road-racing career and helped keep the wolves from the door for the next twenty years.

But before that happened, I still had to learn my trade on the streets of Denny with the newly acquired RD that, incidentally, cost me the princely sum of £1130. My mates and I had a circuit that ran round Denny and the official start line was at The Pines pub. On a flying lap, we'd ride past there at over 100mph and I did my first through-the-box wheelie on that circuit too, which was one of my best moments in biking. I'll never forget the feeling of changing right up into third gear on the back wheel. I was 'the daddy' that night and I remember stepping off the bike and passing all the girls going into the chippie trying to act all cool about it. But inside I was bursting with pride and I knew (or thought) that I was *the* man in Denny that night.

I suppose my propensity for speed was beginning to blossom on the little Yam although I didn't realise it at the time. I used to pass people on the brakes before the junction at the bottom of the road and didn't really know why I was faster than they were – I thought they were just braking early for some reason. But I was always nervous of traffic on the roads and never really felt that comfortable. I fell off the LC a few times on filthy, greasy roads but it was always at low speeds and I only ever skinned my knees. Falling off back then never did my confidence as a road rider any good – it just reminded me that too many things could go wrong on public roads. And if you don't want to ride your motorcycle on public roads, there's only one place left to go – the racetrack.

After all, Knockhill was only a few miles away and it would soon be hosting rounds of the all-new 500cc Scottish Production Championship. By lucky coincidence, most of the entrants would be on Yamaha's new RD350LC, the bike that I had been racing round the streets. Surely a track would be safer?

CHAPTER TWO

Tractor Racing

When I bought my Yamaha RD350LC at the end of 1980 I didn't actually have a driving licence. I'd lost it due to a series of stupid incidents which meant I accumulated enough points to have it taken off me, although I got it back soon afterwards.

On one occasion, when I just had my provisional licence, I got caught driving a car with someone beside me who didn't have a full licence either and we got nicked. I thought the chances of getting done again the same night for the same offence were zero so we drove on to Falkirk unperturbed but against all the odds, I got caught again!

But the clincher came when I was still working at my friend's farm; I was driving a tractor down a country road when I came across an old farmer in another tractor and thought I could overtake him, even though we were both maxed out at around 24mph. With everything in my Massey Ferguson 35 cab rattling and shaking, I squeezed every last mph out of the thing but, although I got alongside him, I had no power left to get past and there was a corner approaching fast. A car appeared and was heading straight for me but somehow the driver managed to stop and the old farmer grudgingly backed off and let me pull in in front of him. That was when another car came round the corner, skidded, and slammed into the first car.

I should have stopped but instead I kept my head down and pretended I didn't see anything even though the whole thing was visible in my mirrors. Anyway, I got my just rewards because the old farmer recognised me and reported me to the police so they caught up with me and added my driving licence to their collection.

As soon as I got my licence back, I started riding the RD everywhere. Then late in the winter of 1980 the SACU (Scottish Auto Cycle Union) announced that they would be running a 500cc production championship the next year – and my bike fitted that category perfectly. My mates who raced said I should have a go so I did a few practice sessions at Knockhill pre-season. I didn't even need to have a race licence, I just showed up, paid my money and went out on track. It cost a fiver for the morning and a fiver for the afternoon. Top value!

I really enjoyed it and decided that I might as well have a crack at racing just to see what it was all about. But I have to come clean here and admit that my first ever race wasn't actually at Knockhill as most people think and as I've told everyone over the years. I said I'd won my first ever race because it looked good on my CV and to a certain extent it was true because I did win my first race at Knockhill. But my first actual attempt at racing was at Carnaby racetrack just north of Bridlington in the north of England the weekend before my Knockhill debut. It was just a wee white lie that sounded good when I was trying to get sponsorship so I don't mind admitting it now. May I take this opportunity to apologise for any inconvenience or confusion this may have caused!

I went out in the first practice session at Carnaby which was for production bikes and race bikes together, and I soon started passing some of the proper race bikes through the corners on my little RD350.

Obviously, they would blast past me on the straights again because they were so much faster but then I'd get them back at the next corner. After a few laps of this I realised I was going okay. Strangely enough I wasn't nervous at all, even going into the first corner of my first race which should have been a very scary experience with everyone fighting for the same piece of track, elbows and knees everywhere. I was so pumped up that I didn't care if I crashed or died or anything. I suppose I must have had some kind of natural feel for it; either that or God was on my side because there was no reason why I should have known what I was doing. It just happened and I somehow managed to make it round to the finish and in a pretty respectable position too.

I finished third in the 500cc production class at Carnaby among some pretty hot riders and I knew who they were because I'd been to Carnaby with the Rae brothers before. There were riders like Geoff Crust (who'd later become my mechanic), Charlie Corner, Kurt Langan and Gordon Allott and they were all really hard racers.

I remember coming home with this little wooden plaque with 'Carnaby 3rd' written on it and I kept it in my pocket for a week. I don't know how many times a day I would get it out of my pocket at work and just look at it. I couldn't believe I had actually won something, even though I hadn't won the race. I've still got that plaque to this day and it's the best trophy I've ever won.

I didn't get any money for racing at Carnaby (in fact it cost me £15 to enter and £5 in fuel) and later that year they even stopped giving out those plaques and replaced them with certificates. No comparison. I loved my little plaque.

The effect of that first race meeting on me was incredible and very difficult to explain. I was on a high for a week afterwards and totally hooked. If I'd finished last it might have been a different story but then again, I'm really good at justifying things to myself so I'd probably have just thought 'Right, next time I'll try not to be last' and kept working away at it. But I got third place and was just over the moon.

I didn't race against my friends and travelling companions Alistair and Stewart because they were in the pukka racing classes but I'm not sure what they thought after I'd done so well in my first race. They sort of congratulated me through gritted teeth but even if they did feel a bit put out as I suspected, they could still fall back on the fact that they were riding in the pure racing classes while I was in the less prestigious production class. I suppose in a way, I stole a bit of attention away from them and after they had helped me so much they maybe had a right to feel a bit annoyed. I'd probably have felt the same had the situation been reversed.

Incidentally, I hadn't gone to Carnaby to avoid having my debut race in front of people who knew me, it's just that the Raes offered to take my bike in their van so it simply made sense to go. It was a bit too far too ride my RD all the way to England then hope it would be in good enough shape to race, but I used to ride it to Knockhill and race it because it wasn't too far from Fankerton. The sump of the RD was permanently wired up so all I did when I got to the circuit was take the indicators and number plate off, tape up the lights and it was ready to race. Sometimes I would ride my bike to the circuit, win a few races on it and then ride it home again! And at lunchtimes, I'd often take it for a practice session round the little roads that run past the circuit just to make sure every-thing was okay. I'm sure the police wouldn't have been too chuffed to see me with the lights taped up and no indicators but I never got caught.

The week after Carnaby I had my first of many races at Knockhill in Fife, where I finished second in my first event of the day, which was the 500cc production race. I then won the invitation race, which was for the top fifteen in each produc-tion class, later on in the afternoon. I was up against bigger bikes like Suzuki GSX1000s and I remember it was future world endurance champion Brian Morrison's first ever race day. He won the big production class and went on to have a successful career in the British championships and in World Superbike as well as in endurance racing.

I got £70 for that invitation win which was great money considering I was taking home about £80 a week from the electricity board, where I had been working since the begin-ning of 1981. And I got £40 for finishing second in the proddie race so I took home more than a week's wages. I mean, the thrill of racing was more than enough but to get money for doing it too? I couldn't believe it.

My mum was there to see me win that day. By then she had accepted that I was going to go racing anyway and she was never really against it in the way my dad probably would have been.

I actually got a bollocking from Jimmy Rae after that race because I started waving my arms and legs frantically over the finish line when I realised I had won and I suppose he must have thought it was dangerous. I don't think I was even aware that I was doing it though, because I was so ecstatic.

That night I went down to The Pines pub for a few drinks and danced the night away to Soft Cell and Simple Minds or whatever New Romantic music was being played at the time.

I did the full season of the 500cc Scottish Production Championship in 1981 and at one stage it looked as if I might actually win it. However, lack of experience caught me out a few times, especially in the wet, and I eventually finished second which I suppose was still pretty good for a first attempt.

The championship was only held over three circuits, because that's all Scotland had to offer. We raced at Knockhill, East Fortune and Beveridge Park in Kirkcaldy and that place was a total nightmare. Donnie McLeod, my future team-mate in the Silverstone Armstrong squad once said you can only sign the entry form for Beveridge Park once and then your hand won't do it again! He wasn't far wrong.

It's a left-handed circuit that runs through a couple of parks and it's pretty fast, certainly too fast for the state of the track and the number of trees and obstacles round about it. A lot of people got killed there and it just wasn't fit to race on. On one of the corners you had to stick your head through a hedge because that was the racing line. But the classic corner was the one that had the main road as the run off area! If you over-shot, you went onto the main road, round a roundabout and then back onto the track again. It was totally mad. I had always wanted to do that just for a laugh because I had seen lots of sidecars doing it but at the same time I was always after a decent result so I never got round to doing it. Knowing me I'd probably have got lost and gone right into town!

I also raced at some events in the north of England like Silloth, which was an airfield circuit about fifteen miles west of Carlisle and where Steve Hislop's brother Gary was tragically killed. I won the 500 Production Club Championship there in my first year, which I was pretty chuffed with. Croft was another English circuit I raced at and I actually won there on a proper racing bike. I rode a Yamaha TZ350 which belonged to a guy named Alex Beith who ran a car auction business in Glasgow and who I had gotten to know quite well. He was going to sell the bike and knew I was doing all right at the racing so he said 'What about racing it to help me sell it?' So I rode it at Knockhill and finished third, then I won on it at Silloth and then again at Croft so the year ended on a high note for me – and the bike sold straight after that race at Croft too.

It was a nice bike to ride because it had a Spondon chassis and it handled really well. After riding production bikes, I couldn't believe the power of the thing – I thought it was going to pull my arms off. A lot of riders feel like that when they get on a real race bike for the first time and I was no exception, it was just awesome. My Yamaha RD350 probably had a top speed of around 110mph and it didn't really accelerate very fast either so the lightness and the power of the TZ350 came as a real shock to me. I hadn't even sat on it until I got to Knockhill for the race meeting and in those days we only got ten minutes of practice to set the bikes up so that was all the time I had on it before I raced. I knew there and then that I had to get a proper racing bike for myself. They were just in a different league and made the RD feel really slow and boring.

That first year in 1981 I raced at about twenty meetings and got twelve wins, either in proper races or in qualifying heats so it was a pretty successful season for me. I also had my very first crash when a guy called Bernie Harrower hit me from behind and punted me off down Duffus Dip at Knockhill but I wasn't hurt. I ended up having numerous crashes that year but never got badly injured and it certainly didn't upset me mentally. In fact, I thought it was really exciting, like when you broke an arm at school and you could show off your plaster and get everyone to sign it. I started building up this idea of invincibility that was really dangerous I suppose. Even so, it lasted a long time, right through until 1986 when I broke my leg badly at Cadwell Park in Lincolnshire. That soon snapped me out of it. But then again, I had always wanted to have a steel plate in my leg too, so I eventually got my wish granted. And I've kept the plate to go with my little wooden plaque from Carnaby.

The social side of life in the paddock in those early days was also quite good because I didn't have any preparation to do on my bike. I filled it with fuel, kicked the tyres and that was about it unless there was any accident damage that needed to be repaired. Pim Fleming, Bob MacIntyre's old mechanic, took the engine apart halfway through the season and just put it back together again. The idea was to match the ports up but he said they were fine when he took it apart. It just ran all year without any problems, which is a good advert for the reliability of RDs.

As far as tyres went, I only changed them when they looked like they were really worn down to the canvas. I maybe got through three or four sets all season, which is much less than a top rider today would use in one qualifying session! The rules said we had to run treaded tyres so the more wear on them the better because then I thought they were more like proper racing slicks.

Depending on where the race was and when everyone finished work, the Rae brothers and myself would usually set off in the van on a Friday. We'd find a local pub, have a few beers and then fight in the back of the van over space and covers until everyone nodded off.

As far as food went, we managed to heat up simple things like tomato soup on a little stove but usually we just survived on bacon butties and chips from vans. Quality!

Despite the glamorous image of modern GP bike racing, being a racer at club circuits in the early '80s didn't exactly increase my bird-pulling power. I think the image then was still of black leather-jacketed, greasy-arsed bikers, but I did all right on the girl front anyway. Don't get me wrong, I was no Tom Cruise but I got by. My racing mates and I would sometimes tell girls that we were bike racers but then I'm sure they'd heard all sorts of bullshit like that before, like 'Hi, I'm an astronaut' or 'Hi, I'm a racing driver' so I don't think they listened to us anyway. There were a few stalker types who went to Knockhill every week wanting to get off with racers but they never seemed to come in our direction, which is probably just as well. If they had spent the night in the back of our van there would have been more chance of them getting a kicking than getting snogged!

People started buying me drinks when I started doing well so that was good. It got to the point where I was going out with money in my pocket but never had to spend it because everyone insisted on buying me drinks! Result. I was pretty well looked after that way and I even got sponsorship from a local Denny pub called Whispers. After my first year they gave me £500 in cash which was mega and I got free Bacardi and Cokes every time I went there. All I had to do in return was put the pub's name on my van.

I think everyone could tell I was getting really serious about racing as I was spending all my money on it.

I remember getting my name in the paper for the first time in 1981 which was quite cool too. It was the *Falkirk Herald* and they probably spelt my name wrong. Over the years I've been Neil or Nyall or Nail and MacKenzie or McKenzie or any other variation you could think of. I've even been called Niall Armstrong by TV commentator Chris Carter but that was understandable because I was riding an Armstrong bike at the time – or maybe he thought I was a space cadet!

The other thing is where I come from. I've read that I'm from Falkirk, Denny, Stirling, Dunblane, Doune, Scunthorpe and everywhere except where I'm actually from which is Fankerton. Once on TV, Murray Walker even said I was from Bolton in England!

But it was great to get in the papers anyway and I still have a scrap-book with all those early cuttings, most of which were collected by my mum. I think she was quite proud of me after that first season. She was a friend of the Rae family and they told her that I was pretty good and that she should be proud of me. Mum was particularly friendly with Jimmy Rae's sister Margaret as they had grown up together, and Margaret followed my career with great enthusiasm right up until my last race in 2001.

After I'd been racing bikes all day, I'd usually go straight to The Pines for a pint or three before going home. My mum always used to wait up for me after a race as I suppose she didn't know if she still had a son or not, yet I'd be down at the local pub without a care in the world.

Once the pub shut, I'd normally head home unless the Mackenzie charm had borne some fruit with the ladies. I didn't have a car and couldn't take girls home so I either had to borrow a mate's car or just walk them home via the bus shelter, but I'd normally get home about 11.30pm and mum would be waiting to see if I was still alive. More often than not, I'd be half-cut and would insist on talking her through the whole day. She'd sit there and listen patiently and I thought she was totally engrossed even though she probably just wanted to go to sleep! For years I thought she was sitting up to hear all my tales of derring-do on the racetrack but then I realised she had only waited up to see if I was still alive and in one piece. Bless her.

During 1981 I developed an interest in Grand Prix racing and my first hero was Kenny Roberts who had already been three times world champion at that point. I liked Randy Mamola too, and he would later become a good friend and even nicknamed me 'Spuds' Mackenzie after the dog in the Budweiser adverts. I had no negative feelings towards Barry Sheene but he was such a massive 'name' that it was almost difficult to think of him as a bike racer. As far as I was concerned, he was a mainstream celebrity. To me, Roberts and Mamola were just pure bike racers and I liked that. And at that time they were beating Sheene so they were the men for me. But Sheene later gave me some good advice when I got into the 500 GP scene in 1986. I met him in London at a dinner and I had just signed for Honda. He told me not to get involved with any management companies (who usually take around twenty per cent of earnings), just to deal with things myself and that was a good piece of advice that I adhered to mostly over the years. There's a lot of people in this game who just want to jump on the bandwagon as soon as you have a bit of success and Sheene knew that better than most because he had such a high profile so he was worth listening to.

He also told me to invest everything I had in property in London back then. I thought he was a bit off the mark with that one but it shows how wrong you can be.

It may not sound terrific, but I had another result in 1981 that I was particularly proud of; a fifth place in the national Yamaha Pro-Am Championship when it came to Knockhill. This was the series that would later help me to make a name for myself and it showed me that even in my first year, I had what it took to mix it with some very good national riders. As

I said, I finished fifth but I started from the back of the grid and I know I could have won that race if I hadn't run out of laps. There were some good riders in that championship like Kenny Irons and Kevin Mitchell so I knew I was doing something right. I must have been because I broke the record for losing my orange novice jacket (having competed in nine national races) quicker than anyone else in Scotland, and as far as I'm aware, I still hold that record.

For me, the high points of my first year of racing were the third place at Carnaby and then winning my first race the following week at Knockhill. It could have been bad for me, winning so early on, because I might have very easily gone downhill after that. But it just gave me the kind of jumpstart that I needed to know that I wanted to race and although I enjoyed the whole experience of racing because it was so much fun, for me the climax was winning. If that hadn't been the case, I might have given it ten years or so but winning is what makes it more special, and I knew inside that I wanted it more than those types of guys who just show up and race as a hobby. I realised I was getting serious when I started pretending to the other riders that I was just there to enjoy it but deep down I wasn't – I wanted to go further than that. I wanted to win. I also realised that I might be onto something financially because in one weekend I could make more money than I did all week working for the electricity board. I was beginning to envisage a career in racing.

With my first racing season over, I was still working my normal job labouring with the South of Scotland Electricity Board and trying to make plans for racing in 1982. But then something happened which I didn't expect and which upset me massively but with hindsight, it was actually good for me.

I thought I would be able to go racing with the Rae brothers again in 1982, using their van to get to meetings. But in November we were all sitting in their garage chatting and one of them asked me what my plans were for the next season. I told him I was going to race the RD again and maybe try and get a race bike. I presumed they would let me chuck my bike in the back of their van again but they flatly refused. They said their dad didn't want to take my bike again. They had helped me as a favour initially and I suppose I shouldn't have just presumed they would take me but I was absolutely devastated and nearly in tears when they told me. I knew I wasn't family or anything but at the same time, I had their garage logos on my leathers and stuff all that season so I felt I was giving something back, even if it wasn't that much. Who knows?

Anyway, it's probably fair to say that my relationship with the Rae family cooled for a while after they refused to take my bike to meetings, but I certainly didn't hold any grudges once I had gotten over the initial disappointment and we never actually fell out or anything daft. I walked home from their house that night with my tail between my legs and was very close to crying. But it all worked out for the best, as these things often do, because at some point I needed to get myself a van anyway and that was the incentive I needed to do something about it. There was no prospect of getting one at that point though, because I just didn't have the money.

At about the same time, my mate Craig Feeney had received compensation for his bike accident and we had already discussed the possibility of him buying me a race bike. But when his big brother Wullie heard about my transport problems he said he'd get me a van (a Bedford CF to be precise). Another brother Alan organised a sweep at work every week to raise some cash and he started bringing me back between £30 and £50 a week which was fantastic. I opened an account and paid everything in there and showed Alan the books so he knew I wasn't spending it on anything else.

His dad had a haulage business and he said I could use his premises to work on my bike and he also gave me some work with the firm to help make ends meet. They were all brilliant and in just a few weeks I had gone from an apparently no-hope situation to being pretty much sorted out for the coming season.

At this point, I was also learning a lot more about how a bike works, which would later stand me in good stead. I have always had a good understanding of how mechanical things work and although I'm no engine tuner and I don't claim to be able to set a bike up perfectly, I was learning all the time at that point. My dad was always interested in mechanical things, which helped, but I must admit I'm better with two-strokes than four-strokes. I only found out recently that the piston in a four-stroke bike goes up and down twice before it fires! Shame on me.

For the 1982 season, I also enlisted the help of a mechanic called Graeme Bell. I met him at Knockhill and we became friends and he did a lot of work for me in '82 with no financial reward so I owe him a big thanks for all his help.

I was all set to contest the Scottish 500 Production Champ-ionship again and I also had a 'proper' race bike as well; a Yamaha TZ250 loaned to me by Craig Feeney, complete with a spares kit, spare wheels, the lot. I also realised that I had to break out of the Scottish scene that year if my career was to progress any further. Too many talented Scottish riders get stuck in the routine of just racing at Knockhill and East Fortune. If they're happy with that then fine, but if you want to progress, you have to take on stiffer competition in a national championship so that's what I set out to do in 1982.

Only problem was, I was diabolical whenever I raced in England. I knew I needed to be out of my depth in order to raise my game but I didn't realise I'd have to bloody drown before I could learn to swim!

The English circuits were so much bigger and more professional than the ones we had in Scotland but that never really overwhelmed me. However I was positively underwhelmed with my results. To begin with I was finishing anywhere between twelfth and twenty-fifth though at the time I didn't realise that the TZ250 was crap. It was quite well prepared but it was an older model and it just didn't run very well. It handled awfully too because I had no idea how to set it up properly so some of the blame has to rest on my shoulders.

Back home though, I was doing pretty well and winning most of the races I entered on the RD350 and eventually I won the 500cc Scottish Production Championship. On the TZ250, I started off quite lowly but towards the end of the season I was winning races on it too. Those results reminded me that I could still actually ride after the hard lessons I had learnt while racing in England.

So many people had told me that going to England was the wrong thing to do but you have to race with superior riders to learn how to go faster. The proof is easy to see as most British riders who have competed at world level come back home to the UK and win races and titles. Jamie Witham, Neil Hodgson, John Reynolds and James Haydon are just a few examples.

One of the highlights of 1982 for me was to be during another Pro-Am round at Donington Park. It was a televised race and I finished second in front of the TV cameras which was great exposure for me. That was the first time I ever saw myself on television but my mum wasn't pleased about it, as I was actually off work for eight weeks at the time because I had crashed at Donington earlier in the year and torn my knee and couldn't walk. When my mum turned on the TV and saw me racing she was cringing because she thought everyone else back home would see me and not be too impressed that I was racing motorbikes when I should have been at work. And because we both worked at the electricity board she was beside herself about what our boss might say if he found out!

Anyway, I was so excited about getting second place in a national race that I ran to the phone box at Donington's Redgate Lodge to call my mum but someone was on the phone so I went to the lavatory while I waited. It wasn't until I'd got my leathers off that I discovered I was sitting in the ladies' loo. I heard women speaking and then realised there were no urinals so finally put two and two together. Very embarrassing, but I was so excited I didn't know what I was doing.

Throughout my career I always looked forward to seeing the TV coverage if I'd had a good race somewhere but that first time was a bit special. All the way home to Scotland in the van it was all I could think about.

I thought that the next round of the Yamaha Pro-Am Championship could work out even better for me. It was at Knockhill and I had been waiting for a whole year to take on the Pro-Am boys on my home turf again after finishing fifth from the back of the grid in 1981. This time I won the race and it was my first national win even though the TV cameras weren't there to record it. I suppose Knockhill must have been too far away for them. But it was enough to convince me that I could maybe challenge for the title in 1983 so I lined myself up for another full season of Pro-Am. By the end of that season, I wanted to prove I was a pro and not just another amateur.

CHAPTER THREE

No Van, Man

As usual, the off-season during the winter of 1982–83 had thrown up a few surprises and challenges and as usual, they mostly concerned money.

My mate Craig Feeney who had supplied my Yamaha TZ250 in 1982 had got married in the summer of '81 and needed to sell the bike to raise some funds which was fair enough. I had done all right on the bike in Scottish races but never really had a decent result in England so I wasn't too bothered about losing it. I used to be so embarrassed about getting blown away on the long straights of the English circuits because the bike was so down on power. I should have realised it was the bike but I honestly thought it was me and that was really demoralising. My only lifeline was that I was beating the same guys in the Pro-Am races who were beating me in the 250 races so that was at least some sort of encouragement.

By the start of 1983, my mum was beginning to think that I might actually be able to make a career out of racing and she was really supportive. She asked me what I wanted to do in the coming season and I told her that I needed a new bike. She said she would borrow what she could and I did the same and we put it all together. It was a real family effort and we raised

31

about £4000 between us. Wullie Feeney who had loaned me his van during the previous season needed it back to take Harpo, his son, motocross racing so I was then faced with the additional expense of buying a new van as well as a new bike. But Jock McGuire from Dean Plant Hire in Bathgate stepped in to help and sorted me out with the cash for a new van for the season and Alan Pirie from Clydesdale Electrical eventually helped out too which was great.

With the £4000 raised by my mum and myself, I decided on buying a 250cc racing Armstrong bike. Armstrong was a British company which was run by the same people who make CCM bikes today. Initially, the bikes were all-British although the firm later used Austrian-built Rotax engines in an all-British chassis. Armstrongs had been getting some great results on the short circuits with people like Alan Carter on board and Steve Tonkin had even won the Junior TT on one. And anyway, I liked the look of the bikes and that's just as important!

I spoke to Carter and he highly recommended the Armstrongs, so as soon as I sat on one at the Alexandra Palace bike show in London my mind was made up. It cost just short of £4000 which was quite a lot back then and that was most of my money gone but Jock McGuire again helped me out with some more cash so we were still looking pretty good for the season. The plan was to do the full Pro-Am Championship again on the Yamaha RD350LC and the full British 250 Championship on the new Armstrong.

The Yamaha Pro-Am challenge was the maddest race series ever held. Twenty years on, bike racing fans still talk about it with glee and the riders themselves wonder how they managed to survive it all.

The concept was simple. British Yamaha importers Mitsui took twenty-five identical RD350LC bikes to various tracks throughout the year, riders drew lots for ignition keys before practice and then raced whichever bike the keys happened to fit. The idea was to put the emphasis on rider skill rather than machine superiority and it worked brilliantly.

The series was introduced in 1981 and pitted young amateur riders under the age of twenty-four against seasoned professionals. It was a perfect stage for me to prove my abilities at national level and the timing of the series couldn't have been better as far as my career was concerned.

Having learned my trade in club meetings over the previous two years, I was ready to take another step forward or risk riding round in Scottish championship meetings for the rest of my career. That's not knocking Scottish racing, in fact there's a healthy little scene up there, but if you want to get to world level you have to keep moving on. By the start of 1983, I felt I needed a bigger stage to play on and the televised Pro-Am series even ran the same make of bike which I'd been racing since I started in 1981, so it seemed like the perfect opportunity.

I had ridden a Pro-Am race in 1981 and finished fifth, then won a round in 1982 but I was ready for a full-on title assault in 1983 and saw no reason why I couldn't win the championship.

The bikes used in the series were almost bog standard Yamaha RD350LCs. They had a few mods to make them more suited to a racetrack but these were not exactly performance enhancing. Naturally lights and indicators were removed, the sumps were wired up and racing number plates were fitted. To reduce front-end patter, 20mm spacers were inserted into the forks and the air filter elements were junked to allow the engines to breathe more easily. The gear change system was changed to one up and five down like a proper race bike (as opposed to one down and five up like a road bike) and the footrests were moved higher up to allow more ground clearance. But that was pretty much it and riders were not allowed to make any further modifications themselves, even if we had the time, which we didn't.

The Pro-Am series was mental and we got up to stuff that you'd never get away with in any other racing class. We used to dab each other's' front brakes going along the straights, pull on the pillion grab rail of the rider in front to get a tow, and even hold our own front forks to make a more aerodynamic shape on the bike. In fact, anything to gain another one mile an hour on our rivals. It was brilliant fun and helped by the fact that no one took it too seriously.

If you put your arm down on the fork it meant you could tuck your head in tighter against the clocks and you would notice the speedometer going up by about one or two miles per hour. It was German Grand Prix rider Martin Wimmer who started it. He raced in a one-off Pro-Am World Cup race at Donington (which I won, incidentally) and all the other British riders and myself copied him after that. But sometimes he would also put his right leg up flat over the pillion seat to make himself even more aerodynamic! I thought that must have been some weird German trick and it didn't take off in quite the same way as the old fork leg trick, but each to their own.

Because the bikes were relatively slow compared to proper racing bikes there was so much time on the straights to mess around. So when you already had your arm outstretched on the fork, it made sense to stretch it a little bit further and pull the guy in front back a bit. Sometimes we even hit each other's kill switches in practice, which would cut the other rider's engine completely dead! Pro-Am was definitely a full contact sport.

I've still got a Yamaha RD in my garage and I still love to ride it because it handles so well. It's not my original bike although I know who's got that and he keeps promising to give it to me but he still hasn't. So Graeme, if you're reading this . . . I want it!

The RDs were so light that you could change your line mid-corner and they were pretty good on the brakes too, so they made for great racing and I think that's why the series was such a success where other one-make championships haven't done so well. Big heavy bikes like Triumph Triples just aren't suited to close racing.

But the best thing about the series was the TV coverage because it was helping to get my name known and that wouldn't have happened if I'd stayed in Scotland where there was practically no television coverage of the races. I had a Freddie Spencer replica helmet at that time which was quite distinctive so I could stand out on television. Despite the fact that the brilliant American would be my team-mate a few years later (although if you'd told me that at the time I would have laughed at you), it wasn't hero worship that persuaded me to buy it. It was just my shrewd Scottish head for a good deal. Alan Carter was wearing AGV helmets at the time but Arai, who made the Spencer rep, wanted to send him a lid to try. But Alan was happy with AGV so he sold me the Arai at half price, which is the only reason I bought it!

I got on well with Carter and I really thought he was going to be a multiple world champ after he won the 250cc French Grand Prix in 1983 when he was just eighteen. At the time, he was the youngest rider ever to win a GP. He had come up to Knockhill at the end of 1981 and crashed his brains out all over the place but he was extremely fast when he managed to stay upright. We became good friends during 1982 and I stayed with him in his home town of Halifax sometimes to go out for a few beers. Alan was completely mad – very talented but completely mad. He was a really intelligent bloke but then sometimes he'd just whip his lop-sided privates out in public (he had one testicle much bigger than the other) and cause a scene for no apparent reason. Still, he made me laugh and I respected him because he was so fast and I think it's good to surround yourself with people you can learn from just by constantly talking about racing techniques and stuff. I think Alan's biggest downfall was that he really believed, along with everyone else, that he'd just walk into GPs and take over and when that didn't happen he couldn't understand why and went off the rails a bit. Top bloke though.

We had some great races together in the Pro-Am series and he cleared off a few times making the rest of us a bit suspicious about his bike. After all, he was riding for Yamaha in the 250cc class so some of us suspected favouritism but now I realise it was just because he was so good.

All the riders in that series got on really well and there was never any 'handbags at dawn' or falling out over crashes or on-track incidents. As long as no one got hurt then everyone was happy and we had a great laugh. Things turned sour for me in the last round though and it was nothing to do with the other riders. I was going to the final round at Brands Hatch with a chance of winning the championship. I'd had three wins in the series and needed to win the last race to take the title but my main title challenger, Graham Cannell only needed to finish ninth to win.

Every race that season had been a clutch start so we didn't have to kill our engines on the start line; we just engaged first gear and went. But at the final round at Brands, the marshal held up a board telling us to kill our engines. All the other riders ignored this board and kept their engines running except for Kenny Irons and myself. We obeyed the start line marshal and killed our engines and when the lights turned green, everyone else got away while we were sitting there with dead engines and no hope of catching the rest of the field even if we had fired up the bikes and chased after them.

The rules clearly stated that it should have been a clutch start so I lost any chance of winning the series because that marshal hadn't read them properly. I wasn't happy. Especially since my main rival Graham Cannell crashed during the race so I would only have needed a decent finish to win the series and I desperately wanted to win a national championship at that point.

Kenny Irons and I went straight to the officials to complain but we were basically told not to cause a fuss and given £500 each to shut up and back down. There was a lot of money changing hands and a lot of promotional deals hinging on it so the organisers didn't want any trouble or bad feeling. I was still hopping mad but realised there was no way they were going to re-run the race even though Kenny and I had sat on the grid for half a lap in protest until we were dragged off kicking and screaming. I suppose we could have got lawyers on the case and got all heavy but we eventually calmed down and accepted the cash. It was £500 after all.

That was the low point of the season for me and coming right at the end of the year made it worse. But there were high points and the best of all was finally being able to quit my job! In May 1983, I finally became a professional racer but it happened in the most bizarre circumstances.

Early in the season I had gone to my first race on the new Armstrong at Oulton Park and knew straight away that I had made a good choice of machinery. It just felt perfect for me and I was on the pace immediately in the British championship, which was a far cry from the year before when I was nowhere on the Yamaha TZ250. I was running fourth amongst top riders like Alan Carter, Phil Mellor and Paul Tinker and then the bloody bike just exploded. My new £4000 bike! I had a good guy called Rab Hardy who had prepared it for months making sure everything was perfect yet it still blew up first time out. I couldn't believe it. So I packed the bike up in the van, drove straight to the Armstrong factory in Bolton and threw the engine on the table. I shouted at them that I had spent all this money on their bike and it had let me down in its first race. I even gave them the sob story about it being my mum's money and everything but they said there was no warranty on race bikes and that I must have done something wrong to make it blow up. In the end I came away with a credit note for spares but I was nearly in tears because my mum and I had wasted so much money and didn't have any more to buy another bike with.

But going to the factory turned out to be one of the best things I had ever done and that's what eventually led to me turning professional in the middle of the season.

I had the bike rebuilt for the next race at Donington where Armstrong's official rider, Tony Head, had a huge crash in practice and was put out of action for a while leaving the team with no rider. As it happened, Alan Carter's former mechanic Doug Holtom was working at Armstrong and he suggested they try me out on their factory bike. As soon as he mentioned my name the Armstrong guys remembered this mad, raving Scotsman who had burst into their factory complaining and I suppose they agreed to give me a chance on their official bike in the hope that it would shut me up!

In this business, getting your face known can mean the difference between getting a factory ride and not getting one. In my case, it meant that I got one.

This happened midway through practice. It was a big international meeting but I immediately put the bike on the front row of the grid for the race. Then, when the race started, I was running at the front again when the bike blew up! I couldn't believe it. My private Armstrong had blown up in its first proper outing and then the official factory bike did the same the first time I rode it! What was going on?

Still, Armstrong were happy with the way I had ridden over the weekend despite the disappointment and I received a letter from them soon afterwards asking if I would be interested in working for them full time as a development rider/ racer. They were planning to develop the bike as it raced though I was a bit dubious about that because it could have been unreliable and kept on blowing up. After all, my experience showed they weren't the most reliable bikes on the planet.

The first thing I thought about when I got that letter was packing my job in but when I went in and told some of the guys at work they all said 'Don't do it. You've got a job for life here.' I'm glad they said that because it made me even more determined to make it as a racer. There was no way I wanted to be still working for the electricity board in Falkirk when I was sixty. I know my colleagues had my best interests at heart but that job just wasn't for me. My mind was made up. I was young and still living at home with my mum at that stage too so I didn't even have a mortgage to worry about and I didn't have a serious girlfriend either. Mum was fine about it too, because she knew I could always go back to my old job if I had to.

I asked Armstrong if I could continue doing Pro-Am if I

accepted their offer and they said yes so that was it; I finally quit my job at the electricity board and became a professional racer. I was over the moon. I knew I could survive on the Pro-Am prize money and I would get the chance to go racing properly for free, even if I did break down a lot. Armstrong also paid me £3500 for my services as a development rider so it couldn't have worked out any better.

Once I had left my job and started working with Armstrong however, I went to Blackburn and moved in with the family of a fellow racer called Geoff Fowler, so that I didn't have to travel up and down from Scotland so much.

We had some top laughs on Friday nights at a pub just outside Blackburn called The New Inns. The usual protocol was to get drunk in there and then go skinny-dipping in the nearby reservoir. A bit dangerous looking back on it but we all survived somehow.

Then on Saturday nights it was off for a boogie at The Peppermint Place where I was thrown out of more times than I can remember. I was once thrown backwards through a set of double doors and down a whole flight of stairs just for being Scottish and obnoxious!

At the same time, I must have been getting a bit more pro-fessional because I started running to get fit. There were still no special diets or anything, in fact we lived off whatever we could find in the local Spar shop and a regular diet of Lancashire corned beef hash which Geoff's dad seemed to make for us every night.

But at least I was running which I hadn't done when I was working, because I didn't really have the time or the energy. It goes to show how much the media informs us these days about diets and fitness because most people are quite clued up about it now but at that time I did some pretty strange things to try and get fit. One of the daftest was my 'sauna theory.' I thought sweating buckets in a sauna was an easy way to get fit but unfortunately, I didn't have a sauna so I had to improvise. I sat in my van with as many layers of clothing on as possible, all topped off with a big duffel coat then turned the heater on full blast for hours on end! I used to drive all the way to race meetings in England like that thinking I was a regular little Rocky Balboa! Six hundred-mile round trips in the mobile Mackenzie sauna. Man, that van must have smelt bad and unsurprisingly enough, it didn't do me much good in the fitness stakes either.

My diet of curries and lager almost got me into trouble as well that year and I was lucky not to lose my Armstrong ride soon after getting it. When I competed in my first race for the team at Knockhill, I missed morning practice because I was locked up in the police station! I had gone out on Friday night and got a bit carried away in the local Indian restaurant. I was dancing on the tables, and generally being a bit messy and noisy and the next thing I knew, the police arrived to take me away. I had become an Indian take-away! They locked me up overnight and didn't let me out until lunchtime on Saturday hence I missed Saturday morning practice and that obviously didn't impress the team too much. It was a very dodgy start to my Armstrong career and I was lucky, and grateful, not to get sacked.

The Armstrong deal aside, another big bonus for me in 1983 was winning the Pro-Am World Cup race at Donington which was shown on TV. It was weird because I was racing with Alan Carter again and he waved me through as a joke because he must have thought he would just come straight past me at the next corner. He didn't and I won the race, so it was a bit daft of him but that was Alan all over. I suppose he was just messing about but I was pretty serious and I certainly wasn't going to pass up the chance of winning a World Cup race on live TV.

I also rode in my first race abroad in 1983 in another Pro-Am World Cup meeting at Hockenheim in Germany and came fourth which I was quite happy with. All in all, it had been a pretty good year as I ended up with second place in the Pro-Am Championship and I had enjoyed occasional success on the Armstrong in the 250cc class although the bike broke down too often to allow me to have any consistent results. I won some races in Scotland on the Armstrong and had a win at Knockhill and a fourth at Donington on a 350cc Armstrong that the factory had built for me. But the most important development of the year for me was that I had become a professional racer and for the first time I could spend all week concentrating on the race ahead instead of having to go to work. Having said that, I actually went back to work at a plant hire company called Dundaff Draining along with my mate Wullie McKay during the winter because it was some extra cash in my pocket and I had too much spare time on my hands. I've always liked working anyway, just because it's a good laugh if you've got the right sort of mates around you and I don't like being idle.

Armstrong had committed to backing me for a full season's racing in 1984 rather than having me just as a development rider-come-racer. I knew they were serious about winning the British championship so things were looking better than they had ever done for me at the end of a season. For me, Armstrong was *the* team to ride for at that point because they had their own factory right here in Britain, they built their own bikes, and they could respond quickly to any changes I wanted made. I didn't even look anywhere else for the 1984 season, not least because I suspected Armstrong would provide my route into Grand Prix racing which was where I really wanted to be.

Also, I was going to be the sole UK-based factory rider for Armstrong in '84. Tony Head, who had recovered from his Donington crash which gave me my big break, was given bikes to run in his own private team rather than being the factory's official rider.

The other exciting thing about Armstrong at that time was that they had built a carbon-fibre-framed bike that I had tested in the second half of 1983 and would race in 1984. It was going to be the first bike of its kind to be raced and I was very much looking forward to it. In fact, that bike was largely the reason why Armstrong landed government funding to go racing in the first place. The British government had provided a grant to develop carbon-fibre-framed bikes and the big carrot for them was that Armstrong said they were going to build an all-British 500cc Grand Prix racer. With Barry Sheene still making head-line news in those days, there was a lot of support for the idea of a unique British bike that could take on the world so it was a shame it never really happened. I'll explain why a little later.

My salary for 1984 was increased to £6000 and on top of that I got prize money and bonuses for winning as well as any personal sponsorship which I could sort out but there wasn't much of that about back then, just a few quid here and there for wearing helmets and leathers.

Still, the new season was going to be another big step forward and as it turned out, my fourth year of racing would see me ride in my first ever Grand Prix. My dreams were coming true at last.

CHAPTER FOUR

Stealing Tomatoes

The aim for 1984 was to win the 250cc British title on the 250 Armstrong with the Austrian Rotax engine and to win the 350cc British championship on the 350 machine that housed Armstrong's own in-line twin cylinder engine.

The downside of those commitments was that I would have to give up racing my beloved RD350LC that I had raced since the beginning of my career. I didn't mind too much as the Pro-Am series had achieved its purpose as far as I was concerned, by getting my name known, and it was on the slide anyway. It had run its course, but the extra prize money would have been useful because it had become pretty easy money for me. It was great fun too but I needed to be more out of my depth again if I was to keep improving my riding and I knew I still had a long way to go in that department. Because Armstrong paid me £6000 for the '84 season I stopped working in the winter to supplement my racing – and I haven't had a proper job since!

As well as contesting the British championships in 1984, I also took part in my first ever road race at the North West 200 in Northern Ireland. The organisers approached me about racing there and I had a spare weekend in the calendar so I thought I'd give it a go. I didn't know much about the course but I'd heard that it wasn't as dangerous as some of the other pure roads circuits even though the lap record averaged around 115mph. It's mostly long straights and slow corners which isn't as bad as having lots of fast corners lined with trees.

Although I enjoyed the NW200, I was never interested in doing the Isle of Man TT. I thought it was a great event but it just didn't appeal to me as a rider. It's not because it was dangerous because at that point in my career I honestly didn't care about getting hurt – I never thought it would happen to me. It's just that I wanted to get into GPs and I knew the TT wasn't the way to go about it.

But the North West was great fun, or at least it was once the racing began as I almost spent the whole weekend in a police cell! I was walking down the street in Portrush when I spotted the guys from Dunlop tyres through the glass front of a restaurant. Instinctively, I dropped my trousers and pants and gave the boys a big moonie and then the whole world went dark. I didn't have a clue what was going on but it turns out that the local Royal Ulster Constabulary police saw me mooning, threw a blanket over my head and bundled me into the back of a police car. I thought it was the Ku-Klux-Klan or something, until I got to the station. Eventually, the Dunlop boys came down (after wetting themselves laughing) and vouched for my character so I was released in time for the races.

I remember being really bored in practice because there was too much time to think on those long straights. It was getting tedious just holding the throttle to the stop and going in a straight line. But apart from being boring, it also gave me too much time to think about things that could go wrong. What would happen if the gearbox seized? What would happen if the engine seized and I couldn't get the clutch in? I was think-ing about all that sort of stuff in practice but the actual races were great fun, slipstreaming all the other riders for miles, flat out. I treated the course like a big, short circuit because I didn't know any different. I didn't know how you were sup-posed to ride a pure road race properly and I suppose I still don't but I did all right, finishing second to Kevin Mitchell in the wet 350cc race then coming home fifth in the dry 250cc event. I had been in second place and was dicing with Steve Cull but landed in a hedge on the last lap and remounted for fifth

But the best thing about the North West was the atmos-phere. We practised in the evenings then we all went out and got drunk and slept in late in the mornings. It was brilliant and the Irish hospitality and the fans were just fantastic; everybody bought me drinks from the moment I arrived!

I got to know the king of all road racers, Joey Dunlop, that year too but it was at Snetterton and not at the North West. He was riding Honda's new RS250 and we had a great battle until I fell on the last lap. Our paths didn't cross very often but I had a few pints with him over the years and I think we had a mutual respect for each other. I certainly had huge respect for him.

It may have been my fourth year of racing in 1984 but I was still crashing quite a lot and we had some reliability problems with the Armstrong, which meant we didn't get the results we wanted in the 250 class. I still wasn't too hot on setting bikes up either, which didn't help matters. But even though I was crashing, I never seemed to get hurt and I didn't really miss any races because of injury right up until 1986.

Looking back, the crowds were very poor at British cham-pionship meetings in 1984 but I hadn't known any different so

I didn't particularly notice at the time. As far as I was concerned, winning a British title was another step forwards and that's all I was thinking about. One figure that was banded about was that for every hundred people that came to see a race in 1980, only twenty-eight were coming in 1984. But there was a lot of unemployment and people didn't have a lot of cash to spend on leisure pursuits like going to bike races. It shows how well the sport is doing in the UK now though with crowds of up to twenty thousand regularly turning out for British Superbike meetings.

However, one of the main reasons I have to remember 1984 is because I competed in my first Grand Prix at Silverstone on 5 August. The whole weekend was a bit of an emotional rollercoaster and I went from highs to lows more times than I can remember. When I showed up at the circuit, I didn't even have an entry to race so I sat in the organisers' office all day and finally got an entry at the last minute when a foreign rider didn't turn up. Back then, if riders didn't show by 8pm on Thursday night they were disqualified so that was how I got my entry and that alone felt like winning the race for me. It meant I was actually going to be on the same grid as my heroes like Carlos Lavado, Martin Wimmer and Christian Sarron. I knew GPs were where I wanted to be, especially 500 GPs, but I wasn't sure it would ever happen. All I could think was that if I kept telling myself enough times that it would happen, then it might just come true.

As well as being my first Grand Prix, it was also my first time at Silverstone so I had to learn the track as well. I remember being amazed that I was on the same track as the big boys but I had to force myself to concentrate and do the best job I could. I qualified for the race which I felt was an achievement in itself but joy soon turned to despair as I finished the race

47

twenty-eighth and dead last. It was the one and only time in my twenty-year career that I finished last and I was absolutely gutted.

I knew the bike wasn't nearly as fast as the others out there, and I was getting passed a lot on the straights. It didn't help that Silverstone was such a fast track either but it was still demoralising even if being last wasn't completely my fault.

After the British GP, I got an entry for the Swedish Grand Prix at Anderstorp on 12 August but I had to fund the trip myself as Armstrong would only supply the bikes but wouldn't pay for the trip. It did my confidence a power of good though because I rode much better there than I did at the British GP. The circuit's not so fast for one thing and I just liked the layout of the place. I qualified in twenty-fourth place and was on the pace in the race but my bike broke down after twenty-one of the twenty-five laps. Still, I had laid to rest the Silverstone demons by turning in a half decent performance and at least I didn't finish last again.

The last Grand Prix of the year was at Mugello in Italy so me and my mechanic decided to drive down from the Swedish GP to Italy and try to get an entry. Bad move. Every racer had turned up so I was refused an entry, which meant we'd wasted all the time, money and effort it had taken to drive there. Still, at least it was a little warmer.

The riders' representative at the event, Mike Trimby, just looked at me as if I was stupid (which I was) and couldn't believe I had travelled all that way without an entry. It was a ridiculous situation and I was really upset. Then to make matters worse, I was plagued with a medical complaint below the belt that had been quietly incubating since the British GP weekend and decided to flare up while I was already at my lowest ebb. I suppose it was punishment for being a naughty boy.

I tried to solve the problem by dousing my privates with Old Spice but it was a pretty itchy trip back to England all the same. And when I did get back and went for a consolatory pint, I saw fellow racer Kenny Irons who gave me a knowing look that told me he was suffering with the same problem. After all, we had both liaised with the same girl – though on separate occasions I hasten to add!

When you ride in GPs, you realise just how much faster all the riders are compared to the guys back home in the UK. The plus side of that is that when you get back to racing at home you realise you can push that much harder than everyone else.

As a result of this new-found confidence, I won my first national title – the Circuit Promoters 350cc British Championship. Although the 350cc class wasn't as prestigious as the 250 series, it was still a national title and proved I was still getting better and moving forward which was my main aim.

I didn't have such good fortune in the 250cc class partly because I did a bit of crashing and partly because we were tuning the bike so much to make it competitive that it broke down too often. But strangely enough, my best result of the season, and in fact the best result of my career to date came on the 250cc machine at the Super Prestigio race at Calafat in Spain at the end of the year. Many of the top 250cc Grand Prix riders were entered including Sito Pons, Martin Wimmer, Juan Garriga and Carlos Cardus but I won the three-leg 250 event overall with a win and two seconds. The track was tight and twisty unlike Silverstone's fast, flowing layout, which I liked and it also suited the Armstrong.

Unknown to me at the time, my performance pretty much

ensured I would get a factory Grand Prix ride with Armstrong the following year. Former GP racer and multiple TT winner Chas Mortimer was to manage the Armstrong effort in 1985 and he had a big influence over my career over the next few years, helping me to improve my riding and making me more streetwise too. He asked me before the last leg in Calafat what I was planning to do in the race. When I said 'Finish second and take the overall win' he realised I had finally matured from the crash-happy win or bust merchant he had seen me as and I think that persuaded him to sign me for '85.

Speaking of Armstrong, I have a confession to make regarding their three-cylinder, carbon-fibre-framed 500cc project bike. As I said before, the 500 was the real reason why the firm was getting money from the government and because of that, there was a lot of pressure to debut the bike before it was ready. I wheeled it out into the pit lane at Donington in 1984 and posed before the TV cameras. I did actually ride the bike in practice but there was no way it was going to be competitive in the race so we actually stuck yellow number plates (the designated colour for the 500 class) on the 250cc machine and raced that! Even the TV commentators were fooled into thinking it was the 500.

I did a few laps at Brands again at the end of the season on the 500 and that was the last time it was run. It's in a shed somewhere just outside Preston these days. Shame really, because it was a fantastic looking motorcycle and technically very interesting. Incidentally, it was designed and built by Barry Hart who was the guy who'd built the bike for the 1980 movie *Silver Dream Racer* starring David Essex.

Anyway, Armstrong's money was limited after 1984 but they had won a big army contract to make bikes so they decided to rearrange their racing set-up and handed over the team to the owners of the Silverstone racing circuit. The team was then called the Silverstone Armstrong GP Team, and Armstrong supplied the bikes and spares while letting Silverstone run the team and cover costs. The circuit put up about £25,000 which was a lot back then and they also supplied premises for the team so it was a good arrangement. The idea was to contest a full season of 250cc Grands Prix and fit in whatever British championship rounds we could as well on both the 250 and 350cc Armstrongs.

The team's other sponsor, Dalmac, was a Scottish plant hire firm run by Ali McGregor, Willie Dalrymple and Jock Gibb – the Scottish plant hire Mafia, as we used to call them. They were the best sponsors to have because win, lose or draw, they always insisted we let our hair down on a Sunday night and went out for a few drinks. Well, with those boys it was usually more than a few and dancing on tables was normally compulsory too. Suffice to say there wasn't much time for feeling depressed on a Sunday night if I'd had a bad result.

My team-mate was to be Donnie McLeod who had gone well in 250 GPs on a private Yamaha. He was also a fellow Scot so I knew we'd be able to have a few laughs along the way and I couldn't wait to do more GPs as I loved all the travelling.

Everything was a laugh apart from the time I spent on the bike, which I took very seriously. I kept thinking I was going to be 'found out' by someone. I mean, I couldn't believe I was getting paid to play on bikes and have a carry on. I was always waiting for someone to tap me on the shoulder and say 'Right, the game's up mate. Time to go back to a real job. We know what you've been up to.' All the way through my career I thought I was going to be rumbled. Even when I put my serious head on to ride the bike, I was still doing it because I wanted to go faster than everyone else so even that didn't feel like work.

The first Grand Prix in 1985 was the South African at Kyalami and I was twenty-fourth from twenty-eight which wasn't the best start to the season. I thought I was doing all right in the race because I was with some pretty good riders but then Freddie Spencer (who went on to win both the 250 and 500 titles that year) came past me about half way through the race. I thought 'Bloody hell, he must have had a bad start' but then Anton Mang and Mario Rademeyer came past too and it was only then that I realised I was actually being lapped! It really demoralised me. There were no blue flags to let me know I was being lapped and I started getting depressed in the remaining laps but again, it was a really fast circuit so I shouldn't have let it get to me so much.

At Kyalami, the Armstrong was giving away about 15–20mph to the top bikes, which is a hell of a lot over a full race distance.

I was also in a great deal of pain because of my pale Scottish complexion. I had gone from a freezing Scottish winter into thirty-five degrees of sub-tropical heat in South Africa and my pale blue skin just couldn't take it. As Billy Connolly says, it took me a while in the sun to go from blue to white and then I just seemed to go lobster red in a matter of minutes. Come race day, I could hardly get my leathers on because of the pain of the sunburn and I was shedding skin like a snake all over the garage floor. I could probably have had an extra set of leathers made out of my own skin! Real Mackenzie reps!

Again, I was out of my depth racing against the GP stars just as I had been when I started racing in British championships but I still knew it was the only way to really improve my riding. But at the next race in Jarama, it started to pay off because I qualified in tenth place, by far my best performance in a GP to date. Then the bike broke after just fourteen laps in the race itself so it was disappointment time again.

At that stage in my career, neither the team members nor I were technically minded enough to have debriefings after a race so we just accepted our result, whatever it was, and packed up the kit. We'd have a quick bitch and a moan then just go for a beer. I was still too young and happy about life to let it get me down and be miserable. I always tried to keep a smile on my face, even when there wasn't a lot of personal space to be had in the little caravan I shared with my team-mate Donnie McLeod.

I suppose to some people, Donnie could be quite a difficult person to get on with but I tend to get on with most people so we never had any real problems. The pair of us lived in that little caravan for the best part of two years and never had a proper argument so that must say something. He kept his cards fairly close to his chest but he was a level-headed person and very serious at the racetrack although he liked to have a few beers when the racing was over.

But when I first got to know him he would piss me off because he'd finish fifth in a GP and I'd say 'Fantastic result mate' but he'd just moan that it wasn't good enough. I'd have been ecstatic at getting fifth in a GP back then but as I got older, I started thinking like Donnie and was never happy with my results either, always thinking I could have done better so now I know what he meant.

I learnt a lot from Donnie because I was young and daft when we met and I was still treating racing as a bit of a laugh. He was a lot more experienced and serious about his racing and some of that rubbed off on me.

I had to watch my step in the caravan though as Donnie lived life by the clock and he'd have strict routines such as eating lunch at exactly twelve noon and stuff like that. He'd also do things like cut a tomato in half, eat one half, then wrap the other neatly in silver foil and put it back in the fridge. He was very particular about those sorts of things. In the early days, I'd just waltz into the caravan and eat whatever was in the fridge, which used to really annoy him. But I soon realised that I wasn't allowed to eat his half tomato or his quarter egg because he had very specific plans for them and they didn't involve me!

However once I knew what the rules and boundaries were we became best mates. It just meant I had to find another food source. Donnie's now managing a glass fibre company back in Scotland and he lectured at Napier University in Edinburgh for a while too. He's a smart bloke. I respected him as a rider just as I respected Alan Carter who was another Brit doing 250 GPs. But I figured that if I was beating Alan in the Pro-Am series the year before then the only reason he and Donnie were going so well in GPs was because they were more experienced than me. I thought that once I'd gained more experience I'd be able to beat them.

I've never really been one to suffer from negative thoughts; there were a few times when I thought maybe I should have been doing something else but usually I looked at things in a positive manner and worked hard at improving my weaknesses. Some riders are beaten before they get to the start line because their thinking is just so negative.

I didn't know too many people when I first started on the GP circuit. But I hung around with Alan and Donnie and I soon got to know people like Ron Haslam, Wayne Gardner and Rob McElnea who had all raced in the UK at the same time as me so the paddock social scene became quite good.

Before the first GP in South Africa, a group of us went on a safari, which was awesome, not least because my hero Randy Mamola came along too. Just being in the same paddock as Randy was an honour and there I was on safari with him! I must admit I was a bit star-struck with it all.

We had a lot of non-finishes in 1985 and when the bike did keep going, it was pretty slow. Having said that, we did manage to score quite a few top fifteen places which these days would net a rider some decent points. Back then though, points only went down to tenth place so we weren't rewarded for our efforts.

As I said before, the good thing about doing GPs was coming back to race in the UK because I felt so much more confident than before. I was right up there with Donnie and Alan Carter who were the best 250 riders in Britain at the time and I could pretty much beat anyone else on the scene. I put in just as much effort when I raced in the UK because I wanted to be as impressive as possible to get noticed and I tried to break the lap record wherever I went.

It was a two way thing because when you compete in GPs, you're more confident when you get back home, then when you win at home by a distance, you feel more confident about the next GP. One big difference was the time actually spent on a bike at a GP meeting; it was far more than at a domestic event, which really helped bring my riding along. The other thing is that you're pushed to the limit. You see riders doing things that you don't think are possible and you wouldn't attempt if you hadn't seen them being done. That sort of thing really stretches you as a rider.

Consistency is another thing that marks out the top foreign riders from some of the more erratic racers at home. I learned to have markers at every point on the circuit so I was accelerating, braking and cornering at exactly the same points, lap after lap after lap. For me, racing was never a seat-of-the-pants affair like it was for some guys – it was all about being precise. It was like doing a connect-the-dot puzzle and just joining up all the points.

A lot of people over the years have commented on the fact that I seem to ride very smoothly and I suppose I did work at that, even if I didn't quite realise it. I had always admired Eddie Lawson and they don't come much smoother than 'Steady Eddie.' Having said that, he could still hang it out with the best of them when he wanted to. Eddie was the only guy in 500s that I felt I could model myself on since I didn't think I could ride loose and sideways like Mamola or Spencer because I didn't come from a dirt bike background as they did. I had never ridden a Superbike either, which helps to develop a loose style. Just look at Jamie Whitham and Chris Walker when they're riding.

Some riders are happy to stick with 250s and I feel that I could have done well on them if I'd stuck with them. But I always wanted to move to 500s – it was another challenge and another step upwards.

Anyway, at the Austrian GP in June, I finished fourteenth beating both Donnie McLeod and Alan Carter for the first time. It was really nice to finish because we'd had another three non-finishes in the last three GPs in Spain, Germany and Italy. It was also a few more quid in my pocket because there was prize money for all finishers. A win back then was worth about £3000 in the 250 class and about £6000 in the 500s but I was still a long way off that kind of cash. It's a different system now as the team gets the prize money and they do with it what they will. But if a team now has two

500 riders having a good finish, they'll get around £25,000.

In the next four GPs I scored a sixteenth in Yugoslavia, fourteenth in Holland, had another DNF in Belgium and another fourteenth in France, then it was time for the big one – the British Grand Prix at Silverstone. Obviously it was a big race for us, especially since my team was sponsored by the circuit we would be racing on! Talk about pressure. It was really wet for the race and I guess the pressure must have got to me because I only lasted four laps until I crashed out. Alan Carter, was leading the race by miles but then he fell off too at exactly the same spot as I did. It was cruel for both of us because I had been running in the top ten when I fell and Alan looked on for a home win.

At the next round in Sweden however, I managed to score my first ever point in Grand Prix racing with tenth place. It turned out to be my only point of the year, and was scant reward for all the hard work and travelling we had put in. But it was a point at last and meant I featured in the final championship results, even though I was in twenty-eighth and last equal place with none other than Joey Dunlop. Joey had scored his solitary point by finishing tenth in a one-off ride at that wet British GP, showing he wasn't just a pure road specialist.

The 250 GP class had an incredible depth of field so there were some very good riders finishing between tenth place and twentieth places unlike the 500 class which had just a few brilliant riders up front and many lesser ones down the field. I knew I was riding quite well and it was a learning year for me so I couldn't be too disappointed with myself. Of course, I would have liked more points but the bike was outclassed and I was still relatively inexperienced at GP level.

While the bike may have been slow, the Silverstone

Armstrong squad had a pretty civilised set-up in the paddock. We had a new truck for the bikes, spares and tools and the little caravan to stay in when we were at the circuit. No one had big flashy motor homes back then so we didn't look too out of place.

The mechanics would often pick up female hitch-hikers in the truck on the way to circuits and they'd help cook and clean all weekend. At least that's what they said they were all doing when they disappeared into the van for hours on end. The rest of us called those girls skunks because they always had blonde streaks and always smelled. Of course, Donnie and I had no interest in such shameful extra curricular activities. We were too busy with the racing.

I remember there was always a big fight for the power points in the paddock because there were so few. Paddocks were pretty basic up until about 1987 and even water wasn't readily available. We desperately needed a power point because we had no generator so we had lots of fights, pulling other peoples' plugs out and plugging ours in! But the paddock was more friendly back then and everyone socialised and had barbecues unlike now when riders just lock themselves away.

Donnie and I would go to all the European races in the car with Chas Mortimer, the team manager, while the mechanics drove the van to the races. We only flew to the far off, non-European races but I quite liked driving anyway; it was a real adventure for a little lad from Fankerton who hadn't seen much of the world.

I didn't do so well on the food front in the paddock though. After being apprehended nicking Donnie's carefully halved tomatoes, I got a notion in my head that if I didn't eat at all, I'd be much lighter and so the bike would go faster. It was a new version of the Mackenzie fitness regime that had started with the duffel coat sauna technique. This time, I completely stopped eating and just lived on slimming drinks until I lost so much weight that I became really ill and developed pneumonia. It sounds really stupid now but we didn't have any dieticians to advise us back then and all I thought about was the power to weight ratio of myself and the bike. What was the point of fighting to make the bike lighter when I could just lose weight myself? I had developed a dark shadow over my lungs by the time I got to Mugello in Italy so Dr Costa, the GP doctor, X-rayed me, told me I had pneumonia, put me on a course of antibiotics and told me that I would have to start eating again. Pretty sound advice, I suppose.

Still, whenever I returned from the GPs to race in the UK in 1985, I won just about everything I entered. In the Circuit Promoters 350cc Championship, for example, I won every round that I raced in except one when I finished second. That was enough to give me the title for the second year running with one round still to go, even though I had missed some rounds because I was racing abroad.

I must admit it was easy winning at home but, as I said, I still tried one hundred per cent every lap so that I didn't just win, I won by the biggest margin possible and set the fastest laps whenever I could.

I won the 250cc British Championship as well for the first time in 1985 but I had to employ some cunning to make sure I did. The title was between Alan Carter and myself and there were only six points between us when we went to the final round at Oulton Park. There were two races but basically we just had to beat each other and ignore everyone else. In the first leg on the Saturday, it was raining and Carter was leading me when I fell off. I realised immediately that he didn't know I had crashed so I hid my bike and myself behind the hay bales before he came round on the next lap. The theory was that if he didn't know I had crashed, he might still think I was right behind him and be pressured into making a mistake. If he saw me with my crashed bike, he could easily have slackened the pace and cruised round to victory. So he came back round and I hid there watching him and sure enough, within three or four laps he slid off! It worked perfectly. All's fair in love, war and bike racing. I remember after the race, Scottish bike racing journalist Norrie Whyte said to me: 'Aye, ye tried tae gee the championship tae Carter and he gave ye it right back!'

I told Alan Carter what I had done because we were good mates and he just laughed about it. On the Sunday, I needed to finish third in the final race to win the title and I actually finished second to my team-mate Donnie McLeod with Carter third, so I won the championship fair and square-ish.

Racing aside, 1985 was a year that marked another major event in my life as that was when I met my future wife, Jan Burtenshaw (I think she only married me to get rid of her surname!) even though it was under pretty strange circumstances. She was working as secretary to Robert Fearnall at Donington Park and I was a very good friend of his. I first met him in 1982 and ever since then he has helped me as a genuine friend. Every year he did something major to help me whether it was with financial advice or just really useful information about what was going on with racing at the circuits. We'd meet up now and again and exchange info; I'd tell him all about what was happening in racing with teams and sponsors and he'd fill me in with what was happening with the promoters and organisers.

Because we were good friends, Robert always asked me to phone him to let him know how I'd done in every race and when he wasn't in, his new secretary called Jan answered the phone. We were both twenty-four at the time and I remember thinking she sounded really nice on the phone but I'd been caught out with that old trap a few times so I didn't want to pre-judge her. After all, she might have been a bit rough! Anyway, I got chatting to her each time I called and said 'Tell Robert I won again' but I don't know if it impressed her. I suspect not. Then on one occasion Robert said he and Jan were travelling up to the Ingliston circuit near Edinburgh (it's just a small, armco-lined track more like a Go-Kart track) and asked if we wanted to meet up and have a chat. I was very interested to see what this Jan looked like so me and my best mate Wullie McKay decided we'd go along and have a look from a distance without actually introducing ourselves. I watched her walking around and thought she looked all right so we went up and introduced ourselves. I liked what I saw and I met her again at some of the British meetings towards the end of the year and we went out on a date.

I still can't believe what a plonker I was on that date. I was wearing horrible clothes (including a really naff Renault jumper as Jan still reminds me) which I got free from sponsors and I remember actually telling Jan that I had washed my hair especially thinking that would impress her. What a nobber! I may have won the 350cc championship that day but I was still obviously still lacking in the 'What women want to hear' department. The other thing I thought would impress her was having my Rod Stewart tape on in my white Ford Fiesta XR2 but I don't think that quite did the trick either. Sorry Rod. And to make things worse, I took her to a hotel called The Rodney! If only I'd seen Only Fools and Horses . . .

Anyway, it can't have been that bad because we met up again a few times afterwards but it was a bumpy ride for those first few months. I'd never really had a proper girlfriend before and I didn't know how to act so I appeared really selfish. It wasn't intentional, but I'd only make one cup of tea or one sandwich when we were together because I'd been so used to fending for myself and I forgot that I was supposed to make two of everything! I was completely clueless.

Another big mistake was chatting up other girls at parties when Jan was there, which didn't go down too well but again, it was just what I had always done and I didn't know any differently. As a consequence of this, Jan dumped me several times but we always made up and saw each other again which is surprising really because her mum Bet had always told her never to get involved with anyone in the army or with a Scotsman! But Bet and her husband Derek seemed to like me straight away when we met so I think her mum changed her mind.

All in all, 1985 was a pretty good year for me. I'd seen a bit of the world, met my future wife and improved massively as a rider. But my biggest disappointment was not meeting Andrew Ridgeley from Wham!

He was flirting with car racing at the time and Jan knew him through her job at Donington Park. So at the end of 1985, I was invited to a Christmas bash in Ashby de la Zouch (where I now live) and Ridgeley was going to be there too.

Problem was, by the time Andrew showed up, I was completely drunk and everything was just a blur so all I can remember of Andrew Ridgeley was a big sheepskin jacket. I was gutted the next day when I realised I had messed up my chance to meet a real, live pop star.

Incidentally, I messed up again in 2001 when I did a charity Go-Kart race with Neil Primrose, the drummer from Travis. They're my favourite band at the moment and I would love to have spoken with him but no one told me who he was and I didn't recognise him! Still, Simon Le Bon came to the Cadbury's Boost Yamaha team launch in 1996 along with his supermodel wife Yasmin so at least I've met one decent pop star!

The other major mess-up I made at the end of '85 was losing my driving licence for drink driving in Edinburgh. Drink driving wasn't the big social issue back then as it is now so I stupidly decided to drive back home from Edinburgh after attending an awards ceremony. I was stopped by the police and lost my licence for a year – again.

But apart from the Andrew Ridgeley disaster and my run-in with the law, things had gone well in 1985 though what I didn't know back then was that my big break was just around the corner. Well, two big breaks actually. One was to my left leg and the other was the chance to ride a 500 in the British Grand Prix.

CHAPTER FIVE

Watching the
Washing Machine

As a racer, it's always a nice feeling to know what you're going to be doing the following season as there's always a chance in this business that you'll be left without a ride.

Silverstone Armstrong offered me a job for 1986 as far back as August in 1985. They wanted me to ride in the 250 Grands Prix and the 250 British Championship again and they promised me a new bike that would be much faster than the '85 model. I had no other options on the table at that point but it was still very early to be signing contracts and part of me, just out of interest, wanted to look at other possibilities. At the same time I really liked all the guys in the Armstrong team and I knew I could do a lot worse than re-sign so that's what I eventually decided to do.

I think they realised I might receive other options so they tried to sign me up early and sure enough, soon after I had signed, Garry Taylor from the Suzuki 500 Grand Prix team called me and asked if I would be interested in riding for him. His rider from 1985, Rob McElnea, had joined Marlboro Yamaha and Garry wanted a British rider to replace him. I think Alan Carter was in the frame at one point but apparently he made Suzuki a bit nervous because of his slightly off-the-wall reputation.

I had no idea that anyone would be interested in signing me for a 500 ride but Suzuki offered me exactly the same set-up as Rob had the year before which was a pretty good one, certainly for me at that point in my career. Factory engines, two bikes, the whole deal. I couldn't believe it. Here was my ticket into 500 Grand Prix racing where I'd dreamed of being for so many years and I had to pass it up because I'd signed a contract with Armstrong. I was gutted. Usually, chances like that only come along once in a lifetime and it looked like I was going to miss the boat.

I asked Armstrong if they would be prepared to let me out of my contract and they said 'Not really' but looking back, I probably didn't push them hard enough. I suppose if I had said 'I hate you all, I'm going to ride like an old granny all year and not speak to anyone in the team', then it might have been different but riding for Armstrong wasn't the end of the world. It was a good team and they had done a lot for me, so I just accepted the situation.

Garry Taylor was understanding and told me to keep in touch anyway so there was still a chance I could get a ride with Suzuki at some point which was encouraging. Armstrong also said they might let me ride the 500 Suzuki as a one-off at the British Grand Prix if the chance came up.

As it happened, I got to ride the Suzuki in November of 1985 at Oran Park in Australia. I was there riding the Armstrong and was chatting to Suzuki's Mike Sinclair about 500s and he asked me if I'd like a ride on Rob McElnea's bike which I jumped at. I only did a few laps in practice and never really got up to speed because I was under strict instructions not to crash it, but that was the first time I ever rode a 500cc

Grand Prix bike – the ultimate racing motorcycle. Well at least it was before the 990cc, four-stroke GP bikes came along in 2002.

With the start of the 1986 season in the UK, I went to Cadwell Park and ended up suffering the worst injury of my career which, I suppose, compared to some other riders' injuries, wasn't all that bad. I've been very lucky that way in that I survived twenty years of riding bikes at high speeds without any lasting damage to myself. At Cadwell, I was slammed across the track unconscious and broke the tibia and fibula in my left leg (the two bones in the lower leg) and was out of action for the best part of two months. It was a major setback because I effectively missed the whole of the first half of the season.

I also heard some terrible news while I was laid up in bed in Louth hospital. My friend Alan Carter's brother Kenny, who was a brilliant speedway rider, had shot his wife in a rage and then turned the gun on himself leaving two small kids with no mum or dad. It was tragic and I felt so bad for Alan who was abroad at the German GP at the time. I was sure he'd fly straight home but he showed incredible focus by continuing with practice and racing as well. I suppose it was just his way of dealing with the tragedy – it gave him something else to concentrate on.

My first Grand Prix of the year wasn't until June when I went to Assen in Holland and only finished twelfth because I was still a bit rusty from the accident. But by the time the Belgian race came round in July I was feeling almost fully fit again and was as high as sixth place in qualifying at one point and then finished eighth in the race. I liked Spa and I know I could have been in the top five if the bike hadn't been misfiring so badly in the wet conditions.

I had a terrible French Grand Prix at Paul Ricard only managing to finish twenty-first but I still had a laugh in practice. Alan Carter had managed to get some small crabs from a local restaurant and we put them in the crotch of Donnie McLeod's leathers between the leather and the mesh lining. Donnie had a terrible practice session and only qualified twenty-second, saying that he just couldn't get comfortable on the bike for some reason! Alan and I thought the crabs would have fallen out but they didn't and poor Donnie struggled through the whole session with crabs in his crotch. Still, at least they weren't the kind that required medical attention – or liberal dosings of Old Spice.

My poor French GP was quickly forgotten about at the next round which was my home GP at Silverstone. Garry Taylor had been as good as his word and offered me a ride on Suzuki's 500 despite my poor result in France. My only problem was that my employers had had a rethink and weren't keen on me riding for another team as they thought it might detract from my performance on their 250 so they refused me permission. But I was pretty determined and felt I was in a position to force things a bit more than I had done beforehand. I had about a month's notice to try and persuade them and eventually they gave me their blessing to ride for Suzuki. After all, the firms weren't exactly rivals.

The bike I rode was built out of spare parts kept as replacements for Paul Lewis's two bikes – he was the little Australian who had replaced Rob McElnea as Suzuki's full time GP rider. I only qualified in fourteenth place but couldn't believe the power of the 500 especially round such a fast circuit as Silverstone. Going down the straights at a proper speed was brilliant instead of counting the minutes as I seemed to be doing on the 250. The XR70 500 handled really well too; just like a fast

250. It was spinning up a lot in the rain but it still felt like a big, comfy armchair to me after years spent tucked up on a cramped little 250.

I think I took to the 500 fairly quickly because I didn't have any preconceptions about it being a ferocious monster that wanted to spit me off. Some riders are completely overawed at the prospect of riding a 500 and it affects the way they ride them. I just looked at it as a big 250 and didn't get hung up about it and didn't try to change my riding style or anything.

I was hoping for a top ten place in the dry but race day was wet so I didn't know what to expect. I just went into the race with an open mind and tried my best to keep the bike upright and get a decent result. As it turned out, I got seventh place which was the result I wanted but I did ride quite conservatively to make sure I brought the bike home so I feel if I'd pushed it I could probably have done even better.

I got a few pats on the back for my efforts and I was pretty pleased with myself too as it was a good start to my 500 career. Incidentally, I finished tenth in the 250 race so it was quite a productive day for me all in all.

After Silverstone, my confidence was up and I qualified in fourth place on the 250 in the Swedish Grand Prix after being fastest in the second session. It was my best qualifying performance to date by far but I had other things to think about too as I had been given another chance on the 500 Suzuki. Full time rider Paul Lewis had crashed on the first corner at the British GP forcing the race to be re-started. He'd broken some bones in his foot and had to sit out the Swedish race so I now had two full bikes at my disposal. I was actually as high as third place in one qualifying session and finished seventh in the race, one place ahead of my hero, Randy Mamola, which felt pretty awesome.

The last round of the world championships (there was actually one more round for the 80cc, 125cc and Sidecar classes) was held at Misano in Italy and again I was riding both the 250 Armstrong and the 500 Skoal Bandit Suzuki. I went pretty well in practice on the Suzuki and in the first session, I was considerably quicker than Suzuki's other new rider and future world champion, Kevin Schwantz. In fact my time was good enough to set provisional pole position but I eventually ended up third on the grid behind Eddie Lawson, who had just been crowned 1986 world champion, and his arch rival Wayne Gardner.

I was disappointed at just finishing eighth in the race but my tyres shredded pretty early on, which meant I couldn't do the times I had done in practice. The 250 race was even worse as I only lasted one lap before the bike seized and I had to retire.

My tyre problems in the 500 race were indicative of a difference in riding style between people like Mamola and Gardner and myself. I never really learned how to ride a 500 like the Americans, backing it into turns and sliding it out sideways on the exit of the corner and in an era of vicious power delivery and relatively poor tyres that's what it took to win races. There's no question in my mind that the reason I failed to win a GP was because of my European, high corner speed, 250cc riding style. The American and Australian riders just had an edge over me with their dirt track style. That's all changed in recent years with the advent of a smoother power delivery and breakthroughs in tyre technology and that's why Europeans have started winning GPs again.

Back in the '80s, I'd be finishing on the rostrum one weekend and then I'd be sixth or seventh the following week and I couldn't understand why. I felt I was riding just as hard but some weeks I was just getting left behind. I realise now that it was because the Americans and Aussies could adjust their style as the tyres went off. For me, less grip meant I had to slow down but for those guys it just meant they had to spin the tyres up harder and slide the bikes round the corners. That's what won them races – their adaptability.

All I knew was how to ride the front really hard like Max Biaggi does today. That's why he has so many front-end crashes and that's why I had so many too. It's no coincidence that he's another ex-250 rider (a four times 250 world champ in fact) and he seems to be having the same problems I had in that he doesn't seem to be able to change his style to suit the 500. Valentino Rossi, on the other hand, also raced 250s but he's worked hard and realised he needed to adapt to the 500 and he now rides it like it needs to be ridden and that's why he's a world champion.

Anyway, 1986 was a busy year for me riding in the 250 and 350cc British championships, the 250GPs and the occasional 500GP as well as in various other domestic races. However I would have raced every day of the week back then as I just loved racing and I certainly never felt like I had taken on too much.

The year ended on a tragic note when my friend Neil Robinson was killed at Oliver's Mount circuit in Scarborough. It's a very dangerous, narrow and bumpy track that is lined with trees and isn't really fit for racing on. Neil was killed in September in a round of the British championship that should never have been held there and it was a great loss to racing. Our careers had run almost in parallel as he used to club race at Knockhill at the same time as me and he also did some Pro-Am races. He then went on to become British 250cc champion in 1983 as I did later on and he even rode for Skoal Bandit Suzuki in the Formula One World Championship while

I rode for the same team in 500GPs. 'Smutty' was only twenty-four when he died and it was another shocking reminder for me of how dangerous bike racing can be.

Every racing death is a shock but I had this kind of safety valve system that must have developed subconsciously. When I was first told of a death I'd think 'Shit, no, no, no' just like everyone else but then after about five minutes I wouldn't think about it again. It's not that I didn't accept that it had happened but I refused to let it bother me, or at least tried to. That sounds very cold and I don't mean it to be but every racer has to have a way of dealing with the dangers of the sport and their own mortality. If a really close friend or team-mate had been killed I might have stopped racing but it's hard to say now what I would have done. Who can tell? Ron Haslam lost two brothers racing but he carried on and Robert Dunlop still raced after his brother Joey was killed. It's strange and sounds heartless, perhaps even selfish to others but it's just a defence mechanism. After all, you don't stop driving a car when you hear that someone's been killed in a car crash, do you?

I didn't make a habit of going to funerals either and that's not out of disrespect, it's just all part of the same defence mechanism that allowed me to shut the dangers of what I did out of my mind as much as possible.

Most of the time you believe you're in control when you're racing but then when you have a crash you realise that you've just been fooling yourself and that a serious accident could happen to anyone at any time. Many times I sat on the grid after the warm up lap and wondered if I would make it back alive, but as soon as I started the race, all my attention was focused on just going as fast as I could.

I don't know if bike racers should be considered brave or stupid but there are certainly some riders who are braver than others are, or more stupid than others, but I think the two go hand in hand really. Speaking for myself, I consider that I was as safe as I could have been given the nature of my profession. Many people outside racing think it's just the guy with the biggest balls that wins but it's really not like that. The thing is that everyone starts racing when they're young and daft and it's just a laugh. You don't have as much fear then but by the time you do start to have some fear you've also got some experience and a feel for when things are likely to go wrong. It may look like you're still mad but you're actually in control. Honda's technical guru Erv Kanemoto, who became my team boss in 1987, once said to me that as a rider gets older he starts to weigh up the percentages and that's when it's all over. When you're twenty, you might do something really risky to win a race that you wouldn't be prepared to do as a thirty year old – at that age you'd be more likely to back off and accept second place.

You could almost draw a chart with a line for bravery/ stupidity and a line for experience and where those two meet a rider should be at his peak. Before that point the rider's too gung-ho and after it he becomes too cautious. That's the best way I can explain it and if you understand all that I'll be impressed! It's not an easy thing to explain.

My performances on the 500 Suzuki had been good enough to attract a lot of attention and for the 1987 season I had lots of offers on the table. Armstrong offered me a ride again but I wasn't going to be caught out as I had been the year before by signing a contract before I'd even spoken to other teams so I declined to sign there and then. They had been really good about letting me ride for Suzuki in three GPs so I was very grateful to the team for all they had done for me.

Suzuki offered me a contract worth £50,000 after the

Swedish Grand Prix to ride their new V4 and that was a lot of money compared to what I had been on so I signed a letter of intent to ride for them. But I was still open to other offers if anything better came along. I tested the Cagiva just after the final GP in Misano and the firm seemed impressed that I was as quick as Kenny Roberts Senior had been when he tested it.

Anyway, my times were good enough for me to be offered a ride on the Cagiva as well but I still wanted the Suzuki more than the relatively underdeveloped Italian bike, which handled nicely, but the engine just wasn't strong enough so I didn't commit. We never really got round to discussing money and I suppose if they had offered me a mental sum of cash I might have been tempted but things never got that far. At that time I had no idea of how much I should be paid – all I knew was what Suzuki had offered and that sounded pretty good to me!

Erv Kanemoto, who had steered Freddie Spencer to three world titles, had expressed some interest in me at the Swedish GP. After the last practice session on Saturday at the Italian GP, when I had qualified third, he summoned some Honda Racing Corporation (HRC) top brass and myself for a meeting. Erv said he wanted a two-man team in 1987 and Freddie Spencer would be the number one rider. Did I want to be the other rider? Does the Pope wear a mitred hat? Freddie Spencer was my hero and Honda was the biggest motorcycle company in the world so it sounded like a dream job and the best offer that I was likely to receive.

I had one other chat, however, which I now wish I had pursued further because it may have been better for my career in the long term. Kenny Roberts, the three times world champion and manager of the Lucky Strike Yamaha team, asked me what my plans were for 1987. I told him I would probably sign for Honda but he asked me to keep him posted. He may have been an ideal mentor for me at that stage of my career but things never developed any further between the two of us. Instead, Honda asked me to go to Japan for talks after I had competed in the Castrol Six Hour race in Australia. I thought I was just going to be offered a contract but apparently some of the Japanese weren't convinced about signing me so they asked me to do some laps round Suzuka on Spencer's 1986 bike.

I had never been to the track before but even before lunchtime I was getting round it at lap record pace. I knew this was my big chance and I had to do something special so I gave it everything. I don't know how many times I nearly crashed (somewhere in the region of six I think) but somehow I kept the bike upright and posted one really good lap that equalled the lap record. The bike had been built around Spencer and I hadn't a clue where I was going but somehow I did it. That's when I started thinking I was just going to breeze the world championship. It was enough to convince HRC too.

When I came back into the pits Mr Oguma, who was the main man at HRC, just said 'So, you've got a problem with Suzuki contract?' and I told him that, yes, I had signed a letter of intent. Mr Oguma phoned the head of Suzuki's racing division, Mr Itoh, there and then and said he had Niall Mackenzie with him and he wanted to sign him. All the Japanese manufacturers talk to each other regularly, which is not what most people imagine, and after a few words in Japanese he put the phone down and said something like 'Suzuki think you are very dishonourable. But you are now free from your contract if you want to sign for Honda.'

That's the way the Japanese work and I actually rode for Suzuki again in 1990 because the whole thing had been sorted out properly man to man. I think that's where Chris Walker went wrong when he left Suzuki for Honda in 2001 and it all got a bit messy and ended up causing a lot of bad feeling.

Spencer's bike was amazing. The power band was so narrow and ferocious; there would be nothing then all of a sudden I'd be catapulted forward like a rocket from a launcher. The Suzuki had felt like a big 250 but the NSR Honda was the real deal. It really felt like a 500 and I couldn't wait to get my hands on one for my first proper crack at a 500 Grand Prix season.

After signing for Honda, I bought a little semi-detached house in Denny and Jan moved in with me. I'd given up telling her when I had washed my hair and didn't take her to any more hotels called 'The Rodney' and that seemed to do the trick as we'd became a pretty serious item. It was the right time for me to get into a serious relationship because I had been spending too much time in the pub with my mates and you can't really do that as a works 500 rider so the timing of meeting Jan worked out well. I might have gone off the rails by now if we hadn't got together when we did. As it was, Jan settled me down and helped me get focused for the season ahead which was obviously the most important so far in my career.

In 1985 and 1986, I was pretty much just travelling all the time and had no real fixed abode. Jan was still living with her parents in Wolverhampton when I met her so it was really nice to have our own place for the first time. Having said that, the first time I ever took her to the house in Fankerton there was frost on the *inside* of my bedroom windows because it was so cold and we didn't have any double glazing or central heating. Back then, they were luxuries that only real snobs could afford. Speaking of household luxuries, I remember when my mum got her first washing machine back in 1976 when I was fourteen and we thought it was the ultimate in technology. This may sound daft but it's true; we pulled out two chairs, put the washing on and sat in front of the machine watching a whole wash cycle as if it was a terrific movie we were glued to. We simply couldn't believe it could do all those things itself. It was fascinating.

By the time Jan and I got a washing machine though, the novelty had worn off somewhat. Our little house wasn't exactly a palace but it was our first home together and we were proud of it, even if we didn't see much of it once the 1987 season had begun.

CHAPTER SIX

I'm Not Really a Welder

Even though I had signed a six figure contract with Honda and along with Kevin Schwantz, was being touted as 'the man most likely to in Grand Prix racing', I didn't feel under pressure at the start of the 1987 season.

My Honda deal was for one year with an option on a second year and I felt really happy with my whole set-up, which was by far and away the best I'd ever had. The early days of club racing from the back of a van at Knockhill seemed a long way off but I still approached my racing without the scowl of a man under pressure. However that was all to change after the first GP at Suzuka in Japan.

By the time I got to Japan, I knew most of the other riders in the paddock and it was good to catch up with some people that I hadn't seen since the year before as well as meeting some new faces.

My team-mate and erstwhile hero Freddie Spencer was always a decent guy to be around when he showed up, which wasn't that often due to a catalogue of injuries, and I had become good friends with Honda's other rider Wayne Gardner who won the world championship that year. He used to ride hard and party hard in the typical Australian manner and we had a lot in common as we both came from working class backgrounds, called a spade a spade and liked a few beers. Having said that, Wayne was really ruthless when it came to racing and when I became a Honda rider as well I could tell he was starting to put his guard up a bit when it came to sharing information on the bikes. We remained friends but he definitely changed a little when I signed for Honda. But although he was less amiable at the racetracks we still had some good laughs away from that environment.

One time in Japan Wayne and I were being driven to a press conference by a Japanese bloke from HRC and Wayne wanted to know what kind of car we were in. We knew it was a Honda but he asked the driver if it was a Honda Accord. 'No, bigger' replied the driver. 'Is it a Honda Legend then?' asked Wayne. 'No bigger' said the driver. Wayne pointed out that Honda didn't have a bigger car than the Legend in its range so we gave up asking. When we got out and the driver pointed to the name of the car we just cracked up. It was a Honda Vigor! The Japanese don't discriminate between Bs and Vs and the poor man was sure he was saying 'Vigor' and couldn't understand why we didn't get it!

Wayne's girlfriend, Donna, became friends with Jan and they used to have a laugh round the paddock together. On one occasion, again in Japan, they were watching practice with a Japanese guy from HRC and Donna, looking up at the sky, mentioned it was very cloudy to which the Japanese guy replied 'Yes, there are many, many people today. Very crowdie.' I think Jan almost fell off the pit wall and onto the track with tears of laughter!

With regard to the other riders, I remember feeling quite awkward when I spoke to people such as Randy Mamola because just a few years before I'd been sitting at home in

Fankerton watching him winning the British Grand Prix and he was quite a hero to me – someone you only ever saw on TV.

Spencer had also been a mythical figure in my eyes and yet there I was racing and hanging round with him and Randy, the biggest names in bike racing. After a while though, I realised they had two arms and two legs like everyone else and they were just pretty normal blokes. Even so, I couldn't believe that I was there with them because they seemed as if they were put on this planet just to be GP racing and I didn't think I was.

I'm sure a lot of that is to do with being brought up in small town Scotland. Americans and Australians develop a different psyche when they're growing up; they're encouraged to be open and to achieve things from a very early age whereas the Scottish mentality is more focused around getting a job, keeping your head down and getting on with life by being normal. Even huge international Scottish stars like Billy Connolly have admitted they don't feel qualified to be doing what they're doing. It's daft really, but in Fankerton where I came from you're not supposed to go any further than the local papermill. That's no disrespect to anyone who wants to do that, but I didn't, yet I still couldn't seem to shake off that mentality.

However, with my first full-time factory 500 ride I was really thrown in at the deep end. If Freddie Spencer had been around as the number one rider the pressure would have been taken off me and I could also have learned a lot from him. But as it turned out, he injured some tendons in testing then broke his collarbone at Daytona before the GP season kicked off so he struggled with injury all year.

As I mentioned before, Freddie was a strange fish but

massively talented on a motorcycle. For example, we were supposed to do three days' testing at Surfers Paradise in Australia pre-season and he didn't even turn up until lunchtime of the third day but he still went faster than everyone else including Wayne Gardner, myself, and all the top Japanese riders!

On top of Spencer's continued absence, the NSR Honda was a completely new bike for 1987 so I had to try to develop that as well. The chassis was different, the engine was different; it was effectively a totally new bike so all the data from the years before was of limited use and I really didn't need that additional pressure when I was so new to 500 racing.

To make things worse, the bike had been developed around Wayne Gardner and, with all due respect, he was more of a racer than a development rider though it's pretty much unheard of for any two riders to want the same things from a bike anyway. I didn't even know what I wanted from the NSR because I wasn't experienced enough so I just let Erv Kanemoto make all the decisions. The Honda was always fast but Erv was used to people like Spencer who knew exactly what they wanted or at least he was used to riders who could ride round any problems, which I couldn't really do at that stage.

Just before the Japanese GP I raced in a one-off event in Japan called the Two Plus Four International and won it on the NSR, which I suppose put even more pressure on me to do well in the GP itself. Things were looking pretty good at the first practice session though, as I was on the pace straight away and apparently surprised the other GP riders with the angles of lean I was achieving. It was nothing special, I just used to lean the 250 over a long way so I did the same with the 500. In fact I remember asking Donnie McLeod why I used to crash so much on the 250 Armstrong and with a deadpan expression he just said 'Because you lean over too far. When you do that, you fall off.'

I thought the more you leaned a bike over, the faster you would go round a corner and, as it turned out, that worked well at Suzuka with all its long, hanging corners but not always at other tracks. In fact it got to the point where Erv told me to stop leaning the bike so much because he wanted me to pick it up and use the rear wheel instead of pushing the front so hard. But I didn't know how to rear wheel steer so instead I just didn't lean it over as much and went slower thinking I'd fool Erv that I'd changed my style!

I fell in practice in Japan trying to get used to radial tyres instead of the cross-plys I'd been accustomed to. The radials had less feel when the bike was cranked over a long way; they felt hard and rigid and I suppose that's one of the reasons why I shouldn't have been leaning over so far.

But to my amazement I ended up getting pole position for my first GP with Honda at the track which the firm actually owns and I really felt I could win the race because it didn't even feel like I was pushing too hard in practice. Whenever anyone got close to my time I just went out and did a faster lap quite comfortably and my best lap was actually two seconds under the existing lap record.

So there I was on pole and I had to attend my first press conference before the race itself. When the microphone was passed to me in front of all these very serious Japanese people, I hadn't a clue what to talk about so I just said 'I've got nothing much to say so I'm going to sing' and launched into a few verses of 'Amazing Grace'. The Japanese didn't think it was too amazing although they did have the grace not to say anything but I think it was a good example of my Fankerton humour not going down too well amidst another culture on the other side of the world. Oh well . . .

I later discovered I was a bigger star in Japan than I thought as there was a famous Japanese pop singer called Nema (pronounced Neema) Kenji. Said together in a Japanese accent, it sounds uncannily like my name and the Japanese thought that was great. I was even presented with one of Nema's albums amidst much giggling athough I must confess I've never listened to it.

The Suzuka race itself was wet and I'd never ridden the Honda in those conditions so I just had to feel my way round until I got used to it. I was in the top seven for most of the race but as I progressively got a feel for the bike I moved up into third and was chasing Randy Mamola and Wayne Gardner. I knew Ron Haslam was on my tail going into the last lap but I didn't look round to see how close he was. I wish I had now because he fell off and if I'd known that I could have cruised round for third place. Instead, I fell off at Spoon Curve on the last lap trying to go too fast to protect my position. That was when I started to feel the pressure of a factory 500 ride and I was gutted because I had been in pole position and looked set for a podium finish but ended up with nothing except egg on my miserable face.

Honda was less than pleased that I had fallen off, to say the least. They didn't say anything directly to me but at the post-race HRC party one of the top brass said it had been a fantastic weekend and there had been only one mistake – Niall Mackenzie falling off when he didn't need to. I thought 'Ohhh you bas . . .' but when you start getting paid a lot of money to race a bike, you realise that you're expected to deliver which I hadn't done so I suppose I started to understand why they were so mad and then I really started feeling the pressure.

Left: Me aged three in Stirling with my mum, Amelia, in 1964. The picture was taken outside the local bank, as you do.

Below: With my dad, Neil, in 1971 when I was 10. He died when I was 13. Note our Hillman Avenger 1.5 GL in the background!

Left: Me in the foreground practicing with the Denny & Dunipace Boys Brigade pipe band at the Cowal Highland games in 1973. My haircut has since come back into fashion.

Right: Mum's gloves, a fake leather jacket, my overalls, a free helmet and my first bike – a Honda C90! In the background are the hedges I jumped when playing 'The Grand National.'

Left: Sporting a Bay City Rollers-style jumper by the Argyll House in Glasgow when I was 15. All my mates had them too with the same tartan patches – it was a tribal thing. I've still got mine.

Below: Duffus Dip, Knockhill, 1981. My first year of racing and my first crash. There were just over 400 more to come.

Bottom: Cadwell Park 1982, on my beloved Yamaha RD350LC: the bike I learned my trade on.

Above: On the Silverstone Armstrong during practice for the Spanish Grand Prix at Jarama in 1985. I qualified tenth but the bike seized in the race.

Right: 'No, take another plug lead off, it's still too fast.' Getting used to the Suzuki during my first 500 GP ride at Silverstone in 1986.

Below: Chasing my friend, the late Kenny Irons, in the same 500 GP at Silverstone. Ron Haslam is on my tail but I went on to beat them both for seventh place.

Above: 'Excuse me, is this where I put the bike for pole position?' My first GP with Honda at Suzuka in 1987 after breaking the lap record in practice and qualifying on pole.

Left: Chasing Christian Sarron, Ron Haslam and Kevin Magee at Suzuka in 1987. I passed them all then fell off on the last lap! Not clever.

Honda's technical guru and my team boss in 1987 and 1988, Erv Kanemoto, asking me if I've seen my team-mate Freddie Spencer.

Kickin' ass in the USA. Leading Wayne Gardner, Eddie Lawson, Wayne Rainey, Kevin Schwantz and the rest of the pack at Laguna Seca in 1988. I finished third.

Donnie McLeod (in front) and I failed to see the 'Stop' sign on the road until the last moment at Spa, Belgium, 1988.

Left: By the time I mounted the podium at Laguna Seca in 1988, I'd moved on from Pomagne to champagne. The effects were much the same.

Below: The British Grand Prix, 1989. I battled through to lead the race from Kevin Schwantz but my front tyre went off and I had to settle for fourth.

Bottom: My wife Jan with 15 times world champion Giacomo Agostini. He was my team boss at Marlboro Yamaha in 1989.

Preparing for pain at Hockenheim, Germany in 1989. The result was a broken and dislocated kneecap and a broken wrist. And yes, it did hurt.

'Then the rear spun up man, drifted sideways and it got all kinda squirrelly …' I wonder what the hell Kevin Schwantz is talking about as Mick Doohan laughs knowingly.

With my best friend Rob McElnea who also used to be my sparring partner in Grands Prix and my team boss in British Superbikes.

Above: On the RGV500 Suzuki at Assen in 1990 where I finished fifth. There's lots of grass in Holland as this picture shows.

Below: Kerb crawling at the North West 200 in Northern Ireland on a Honda RVF750 in 1991. Unfortunately, the bike was crawling more than I wanted it to.

But I wasn't the only one upsetting HRC; Freddie made so many no-shows that season it became a bit of an on-going comedy. Apparently, word went out at Honda that no members of his crew were to fly to a GP until Freddie had actually shown up, but then even that system backfired. When word got back to Japan that Freddie had been spotted in the paddock at Hockenheim in Germany, his Japanese crew jumped on the first flight they could get. But when Freddie realised he had no crew, he got on the first plane back to Louisiana so when the Japanese guys arrived he was gone!

He kept showing up and then retiring all season and apart from upsetting Honda and HRC, it upset our team because Erv needed a winner and I just wasn't ready to be winning GPs at that stage. If Erv had been winning races with Freddie then there would have been more information for me and Erv would have been happier because that's what he was used to. He was too proud to ask Wayne Gardner's crew for any info because he felt he should be able to find out for himself. HRC would have insisted that Gardner shared his information but Erv just wouldn't have it, which may have been admirable but it certainly wasn't any help to me in my rookie year.

The next race was at Jerez in Spain and I qualified third and finished fourth but again, I felt I should have got at least third place in the race but I made some mistakes near the end and was very annoyed with myself.

One thing I didn't have a problem with in my first full season in 500s was passing other riders when I had the chance. Many racers have a psychological problem with passing their heroes because they think that if they're faster than they are, then they must be going too fast and they're headed for a crash. On the contrary, I always thought it was a good thing; it was such a buzz but I still had too much respect for them and I always thought they were a lot more special than I was. I shouldn't have thought like that but I guess it was the American versus Scottish psyche thing again. But on the other hand, when I came back to race in the UK from GPs, I'd look at other riders on the grid and think 'I can beat you easily' which is exactly what the top GP boys were probably thinking about me. So it was swings and roundabouts.

As the 1987 season unfolded, I eventually got to know my team-mate Spencer. We never became best mates but he was always very polite and amusing though I never really knew what was going on in his head and I don't know if anybody – or even Freddie himself for that matter – did.

He started coming up with the most bizarre excuses for missing races like saying his contact lenses were misting up or they kept falling out or whatever. At first I believed anything he said because he was such a god to me, but I eventually started having my doubts and wondered if maybe he was just signing fat contracts on the strength of his name and had no intention of racing at all. I even tried to stop swearing and drinking because Freddie didn't swear or drink and I almost started reading the Bible too thinking it would make me faster, but I soon came to my senses – it wasn't the life for me!

There's no doubt that in his day he was a genius on a motorcycle but like many a genius he had his flaws and ended up making more comebacks than Frank Sinatra. However, he was always pleasant enough to me and a brilliant rider, so I still have lots of respect for him.

Freddie missed the second round of the championships in Spain where as I said before, I got fourth, but only after crashing on those damned radials again in practice.

Worse was to come in Germany though when I could only manage seventh place and I actually felt embarrassed to be on a works bike after that race. I felt so bad because Honda was paying me so much money and I could only reward them with seventh place even though I was trying my hardest.

Things went from bad to worse at Monza in Italy when I finished tenth and by that time I was dying inside, I was so upset for myself, the team and Honda. What was happening? I started the year on pole position and was on the pace up front in the first two races, then I was finishing in tenth place. It just didn't make any sense because I knew I was still riding as hard as ever. I would have been quite happy if the team had sacked me on the spot after Monza – I certainly felt like I deserved it. It was hell.

Erv Kanemoto showed no emotion at all through all of this so it was really difficult to figure out what he was thinking. He looked the same whether I finished third or tenth so I never really knew how disappointed he was in me.

After I'd had a bad result as I did in Germany, I wasn't very approachable. Usually, I was more than happy to chat to people or sign autographs but for about an hour after a bad race I was always very snappy and not nice to be around – I didn't even speak to Jan. Some riders are like that all the time though whether they've had a bad race or not so I don't think I did too badly when it came to being stroppy.

Straight after Germany we went testing in Yugoslavia where Erv sorted me out and turned my season around. It sounds stupid but it was obvious things like holding on with both hands which made a difference! Before you laugh too much, let me explain. Two-stroke motorcycles are prone to engine seizures and the only way to save yourself getting high-sided off the bike is to whip the clutch in when the engine seizes. When I was racing the Armstrongs I always covered the clutch with my left hand for such an eventuality. That was fine on a light 250 but with the 500, both hands were needed to muscle the thing around and get it to steer more quickly. Erv told me not to worry about seizures and said that he would take care of the engines so they would never seize. He told me just to concentrate on hauling the bike around and it really did help once I got my head round it. Pulling up on the left hand bar to flip from a left-hander into a right hand corner made such a difference and the extra speed I discovered really boosted my confidence.

Erv analysed everything and asked me endless questions about the bike and my riding. All the same, he was always very wary of actually *telling* me what to do in case it had the wrong effect. He was very good that way. We also found that a narrower front rim on the NSR helped me to turn the bike more quickly and with those pretty simple changes, we were back on the pace. So much so that I stood on the podium for the first time in the next race in Austria at the super fast Salzburgring.

I was actually challenging Randy Mamola and Wayne Gardner for the lead during most of the race but destroyed my front tyre again and had to settle for third. You may hear racers making excuses on TV all the time after a race and I can only speak for myself but believe me, I never gave up in a race or blamed a mechanical problem if there wasn't one. I'd ride the bike until it couldn't go any farther because that's what I was being paid to do. On top of that, there's always the fact that five riders could fall off in front of you and you could still win the race even if your bike or tyres weren't performing as well as they might.

Having said that, there are many times I wished I could have crashed just so that I didn't have to finish eighth but I forced myself to keep trying. It's just that it's really demoralising for a racer to finish down the field.

My third place in Austria was very, very special to me and one of the best of my seven career podiums. It was a proper fast, dry race at the front of the pack with Gardner and Mamola alongside me and to cap it all off, my mum had flown out to Austria to watch me! It was her first GP and there I was on the podium, feeling really proud. In fact, it was her first time abroad which made it even more special. Jan's mum and dad were there too so it was good to put on a decent performance in front of them all.

My confidence was up after that third place and I knew I was on for a good result in the next round at Yugoslavia especially as we had tested extensively there. But GP racing is full of lows as well as highs and I broke my ankle in practice just as my season was getting back on track. Again, I had been as high as third in qualifying without trying too hard but I fell in the second session and was ruled out of the race. I actually ran back to the pits to get my second bike without realising I had broken my ankle but then it started swelling so badly that I knew it was bust. Freddie had flown back to the States too with his collarbone giving him grief so poor old Erv had no riders left. Still, I suppose it was a weekend off.

I spent a week at the famous Austrian clinic called Willi Dungl's trying to get healed up and the singer Falco was there at the same time. He had a big hit single that year with 'Rock me Amadeus' inspired by the film *Amadeus* and he was being treated for alcoholism – the standard rock star illness! But he seemed like a decent guy and we had a few laughs. In fact, one night he sneaked out with Rob McElnea and myself for a few beers saying that he needed a break from his treatment for alcoholism because it was too intense! As far as I remember there was nothing wrong with Rob but he stayed in the clinic car park for a week to give me moral support.

I raced at the next round in Holland but was in too much pain to be competitive and as I didn't want to risk hurting my ankle further, I pulled in. I got seventh place in France as I started to heal and then it was back to Britain for my home GP.

There was a joke around at the time of the British GP about a little boy playing in the street with a welder's mask and it came to have huge relevance for me. The boy is asked by a man in a passing car if he wants to go and see some puppies but he refuses, then the man asks if he wants a sweetie which he also refuses. This goes on for some time until the boy, in his innocence, admits that he's not really a welder! The boy obviously thinks he's been mistaken for a real welder and that's why he's being asked these strange questions. As I sat on the front row of the grid for the British GP and looked at the racing legends on either side of me, the huge partisan crowd all cheering and all the TV cameras and razzamatazz, this joke came into my head. I didn't belong there. I was a fake. How could a little guy from Fankerton be sitting there at the pinnacle of motorcycle sport when he should be at home working in the papermill? The whole thing got me giggling, and when a TV reporter shoved a microphone in my face and asked me for my thoughts before the race I simply replied 'I'm not really a welder.' He didn't have a clue what I was talking about but it was the most accurate thing I could think of to say that would express my true feelings at the time. I was wearing the costume of a GP racer but it felt like I'd stolen the bike and sneaked onto the grid! That feeling never really went away and sometimes even now I look back on my career and think 'What the hell was that all about? Was that really me?' I always felt that I was just getting away with it like a naughty schoolboy when I should really have had a normal job like everybody else. Anyway, whether I was a welder or not, expectations of me were high for my home Grand Prix and I was keen not to disappoint. It was the first time the race had been held at Donington after spending ten years at Silverstone (previous to Silverstone in 1977, the Isle of Man TT had been the British round of the world championships) and the hype and organisation was mega. Freddie Spencer turned up again and did his usual disappearing trick both from the front of the pack and from the circuit shortly afterwards. He just blasted away from the line at a pace no one could believe, let alone hope to match, but after four laps he retired blaming a rear wheel lock-up problem which his mechanics later couldn't trace. It was typical Freddie – fast as ever and just as mystical. He had a brilliant ability to know how hard he could push cold tyres from the start of a race and that's a skill I never really learned. I suppose I was always just too cautious and preferred to get some heat into them and then start pushing instead of risking falling off on the first lap.

I lost the front a lot in 1987 with the Honda and I think that dented my confidence for the rest of my career. Even tyre warmers never really warmed the extreme sides of the tyres enough and my style depended on having good grip at maximum lean. To get round this, people like Freddie would pick the bike up mid-corner and open the throttle whereas I liked to go round the corner fast and then pick the bike up.

I had a pretty good race at Donington though, finishing in fourth place which was agonisingly close to the podium in front of my home supporters but not quite there.

One thing that had improved for me in GPs was my lifestyle when I wasn't on the bike, as racing for Honda was a far cry from my old Armstrong days. We flew business class everywhere and we always stayed in the best five star hotels. It was also the first year I bought a proper motorhome and me and the other British riders like Rob McElnea and Roger Burnett lived on the continent between races and came home for the British round. It was great fun, just our girlfriends and us cruising round Europe, and Jan had even left her job so she could be with me.

I had a good, new, reliable motorhome so I never had any nightmare breakdown scenarios but Rob Mac's was a bit of a troublesome shed. It was always breaking down and being botched up again. There were welding marks all over it and the alternator was usually held on with mole grips. You'd get a shock when you opened the door because the thing was never earthed and there were even mushrooms growing under the passenger seat at one point! But we'd cover about 14,000 miles a year in the motorhomes and it was all good fun.

When Rob was riding for Marlboro Yamaha in 1986, they gave him some money to paint his motorhome like a big packet of fags so he was happy to oblige. But when the Marlboro people saw it they decided they didn't like it and gave him some more money to paint it beige!

When we weren't patching up his motorhome, Rob Mac and I had some good on-track battles and at the Swedish GP he pointed out that my Honda was as slow as his Yamaha which shouldn't have been the case. All the other works Hondas were way faster than the Yams but we must have got the set-up wrong on mine for some reason and it never really performed as well as it should have. Anyway, I finished fifth and headed off to Brno for the Czechoslovakian GP where I was fifth again.

Seventh at Misano in Italy was nothing to write home about and then, bizarrely, it was off to Spain for the Portuguese GP. The Portuguese had sold the rights to the Spanish to run the race because they didn't have the infrastructure to run it themselves at that point.

In the race I was enjoying riding with Rob Mac again and having good fun but at one point we made contact and I thought 'I'm down here' because there's no way you can bash into Rob Mac and get away with it – he's built like a brick shit house. But as it happened, I stayed on and it was Rob who got all crossed up and crashed, unbeknown to me at the time. On the next lap he didn't come past me and I started thinking maybe he'd gone down so I was dreading passing the point where we had touched because I didn't want to see how angry he was! As I've already said, he was much bigger than me and I wanted the race to last all day so I didn't have to face him in the paddock but he was cool about it all and I hung on to finish sixth.

An eighth in Brazil and seventh in Argentina finished off my first full season in 500s and that was enough to give me fifth place overall in the final world championship standings. I must admit I was disappointed with that. Before the season started, I would have been delighted with fifth but after setting pole in the first race, my expectations were raised and I really thought I could have been challenging for the world title.

The man who took that honour in 1987 was Wayne Gardner and I was genuinely pleased for him. He really rode with his heart and fully deserved to win but I'll always wonder if Eddie Lawson would have won that year had he been on a Honda. Wayne had done it the hard way and came from nothing to be on top of the world so it was fitting to see him win.

Away from the track, I got on okay with both men even if they hated each other. Eddie had a very dry sense of humour and didn't like the media very much but he was a bit of a party animal when the shutters were down. He used to say to me with a deadpan face 'Niall, let's go get drunk and be some-body.' Or he'd quip about Gardner 'Wayne's really brilliant you know and if you don't believe me just ask him.' He was a very funny bloke and he loved to race bikes but he just hated all the media attention that went along with racing.

Wayne and me had our share of daft moments like the time we raced kiddie's pedal cars through the kitchen in a posh Japanese restaurant. We sent pots and pans flying everywhere and caused a total upheaval amongst all that glorious, exotic Japanese food during our 'kitchen GP'. No one even said anything to us because the Japanese just didn't know what to do in situations like that as their own people are always well behaved.

Another time in Austria we were having some beers after the race when I decided I wanted to swap clothes with an Austrian bloke who was all dressed up in his national cos-tume. He thought it was a laugh at first but then refused to wear my clothes because they were all manky and covered in beer and food from my post-race partying. It didn't bother me too much – I just ran round the paddock half-naked for a while instead!

My clothes-exchanging tendency stems from a daft game my mates and I used to play in the pubs of Denny. I can't remember how it all started but we'd just nod at each other, strip off there and then and swap clothes. It used to amuse the hell out of us that we were all wearing things that didn't fit properly, but I suppose you had to be there. I never got any of my own clothes back either so my wardrobe was full of old tat that didn't fit me and Jan used to get really mad at me for losing all my decent clothes.

As far as the paddock went, I don't think there was anyone who I disliked to any great extent. I mean everyone had their turns bitching and moaning about everyone else but that's only natural when you see the same faces every weekend in the same small paddock, especially when everyone's trying to beat each other out on the track.

One thing I was disappointed about in 1987 was the Suzuka 8 Hour race. It's the biggest single bike race event in the world and means as much to the Japanese as winning the 500cc world championship. As its name suggests, it's an eight hour endurance race and back in the '80s all the top GP riders were expected to compete in it even though the race was for four-stroke Formula One machines and not two-stroke GP bikes.

The money was a big attraction for many riders as the Japanese would pay whatever they had to in order to get the right riders. Eddie Lawson was determined not to go one year until Yamaha upped their offer to $100,000 just for that one race. It was an offer Eddie couldn't, and didn't, refuse.

Anyway, in 1987 I was teamed up with Australian racer Mal Campbell and I had been fastest in every session in practice with Wayne Gardner just behind me. He pipped me towards the end of practice and I was ready to go out and put in a faster lap but Mr Oguma from HRC stopped me. Gardner had the nickname 'Mr One Hundred Per Cent' in Japan because he had won everything he'd entered there so Mr Oguma didn't want me to break his record and as we were both Honda riders, I had to play along. I was really annoyed though because I knew I could have gone faster but I suppose that's part and parcel of fulfilling a contract.

Anyway it didn't matter too much in the end because Mal and I were lying second in the race when he crashed and that was the end of it for us.

I may have been disappointed with my GP performances in 1987 but Honda seemed happy enough and they signed me again for 1988 when I attended the Fuji International in Japan at the end of the season. It was a great feeling to be all sorted out for the following season and to know I was going to get another bite at the cherry. But one of the nicest feelings in 1987 was being able to buy a house for my mum with the money I got from Honda. I bought her a little bungalow just a few miles from our old council house in Fankerton so she was still close to all her friends and knew where everything was. It was the least I could do for her after all the support she'd given me over the years.

CHAPTER SEVEN

Thanks for the Watch

I spent most of the winter of 1987–88 in America learning how to ride a dirt track bike and also learning about getting fit the proper way. Apparently, living off slimming drinks and sweating my nuts off in a duffel coat wasn't the answer.

Kenny Roberts was kind enough to invite me to his ranch to train and ride dirt bikes even though I was a Honda rider and he ran a factory Yamaha team. But Erv Kanemoto reckoned there would be too much of a chance of getting hurt at Kenny's place because they were all very fast guys there and rode really hard and were a bit mental so I went to train with Doug Chandler instead.

Doug became a successful Grand Prix rider himself in the 1990s but at the time he was racing in the States and he was a really good dirt track rider. I spent all of December and January learning how to ride on loose surfaces, working out in the gym and running. I even had access to Dean Miller's clinic while I was there and Dean has worked with lots of riders over the years including Kenny Roberts (Senior and Junior), Wayne Rainey and Eddie Lawson, so he knew his stuff. He taught me a great deal about proper diets and nutrition and I soon realised that pasta was in and haggis suppers from the chip shop were out.

As much as I have respect for Dean, I couldn't help laughing some years later at a quip Mick Doohan made about him. Dean made a variety of energy drinks for riders and they would have different mixtures to drink before and after a race. Mick wasn't too impressed by all this fuss and once said to me: 'I can make my own milk shakes.'

That was a real measure of Mick's talent. He didn't need to rely on external aids to win races – he just went out there and rode harder than anyone else.

While I was in the States, Randy Mamola insisted that Jan and I lived in one of his houses and used his 4X4 Jeep. He had two homes but all the time I was in America, he lived with his mum because he had recently split up with his fiancé so we had our pick of houses. It was really good of him and just one indication of the decent guy he is. He's done loads of sterling work for Riders for Health over the years, which is a charity that buys bikes for medics in Africa to reach remote villages with essential health supplies and treatment. I've tried to help over the years for Riders for Health (which is a branch of Save the Children) too and one bonus was getting to meet Princess Anne a few times as she's the head of the charity. It's run, incidentally, by Andrea Coleman (who was married to top Irish rider, the late Tom Herron) and her husband Barry.

I learned a lot during my stay in the States and ended up being able to ride a dirt track bike quite well lapping as fast as Doug and Freddie Spencer, but I still couldn't translate those skills to a GP bike as well as the Americans.

Despite all his problems with injuries and no-shows in the last couple of seasons, Freddie Spencer was to be my team-mate again at Honda in 1988.

He looked overweight and not in the best of shape when he turned up to train with me and I could tell that he hadn't been doing much training as he sometimes threw up in the gym with the effort. Sometimes he'd just disappear and I wouldn't see him again for ages. We even checked out his hotel room a couple of times and found he'd just left all his belongings and clothes and flown back to Louisiana. I didn't know what was going on in his head.

Our first test was at Oran Park in Australia and, true to form, Freddie didn't show until the second day of testing, but for him that was quite good because at least he showed up. I was fastest in the tests, which pleased me because Wayne Gardner was there too and as he was the reigning world champion, that was not a bad yardstick.

Freddie and I were supposed to be a two-man team both running in HB colours for the year and Fred said he was going to be back bigger, badder and fitter than ever. So you can imagine my surprise at the first Grand Prix of the year at Suzuka in Japan when he announced his retirement from racing before he'd even lined up on the grid!

Freddie had decided that the tendon damage to his wrist that had troubled him since 1986 was just not healing properly despite several operations to mend it and he formally announced his retirement from racing despite the fact that he had signed to compete for Honda in 1988. I don't know what happened contract-wise but I was left in a one-man team for the season ahead as Honda didn't sign anyone to replace Freddie.

By 1988 there was a definite change for the better in the look and professionalism of the paddock and it was not before time. The International Race Teams Association (IRTA) had been formed in 1987 and brought about a lot of sensible changes. They issued every rider with season passes, which hadn't been available before; there were more power points and water supplies fitted in the paddocks and the races were actually run in the same order and at the same time for every round. The motorhomes were getting flashier too. Most of the Americans had always had decent ones but now everyone was getting into them. It became a bit of a competition to see who could get the biggest one with the most accessories. Freddie Spencer had always had the flashiest vehicle before he retired but Eddie Lawson used to make me laugh with his old shed, which he kept throughout his whole GP career. He pushed it, pulled it or did whatever he had to do to get it round Europe year after year and it became a paddock legend. I remember having a party in that motorhome after my first 500cc podium in Austria in 1987; I was completely drunk and running around half-naked throwing food around and making a right old mess but Eddie didn't care. The day after, you couldn't see a square inch of carpet for stains and squashed food and there was salami stuck to all the walls. Ed had never seen anything like it but he thought it was top fun. Jan wasn't so amused though and at one point she slapped me for acting like a fool. But hey, I'd gotten on the podium so I was going to party. Incidentally, Eddie had to have his motorhome totally refurbished after that party because it was in such a mess, mostly created by me.

It used to amuse me that everyone else in the paddock had a big 'Welcome' mat outside their motorhomes but Eddie had one saying 'Go Away.' Mega. That was him all over.

Randy Mamola was the very opposite to Ed; he spent about $400,000 on a motorhome and had the ceilings decked out with small fibre optic lights to make it look like the stars were out! I just opened the roof skylight – it was cheaper.

I had a pretty decent motorhome myself and it was the source of much hilarity when I stopped at filling stations in the middle of the night. When I went to pay for fuel, people always asked me what famous person I was driving for so I used to tell them it was Rod Stewart but he was sleeping so, no, they couldn't have his autograph.

My earnings went up considerably for the 1988 season and I suppose I've got my friends back home to thank for that. They asked me what I was getting and said I should try to ask for another £100,000 just for the hell of it! I felt it was a bit cheeky but I tried it anyway and it worked. Result! If you don't ask you don't get and I had no idea what I was worth so picking a figure out of thin air seemed as good a plan as any.

Riders didn't really talk about what they were earning with each other but they all wanted to be on more than the next guy so lots of rumours flew around about who was on what. I never made a secret of what I was getting.

I spoke to HRC about a pay rise in Japan then when I got home to Scotland there was a contract ready to sign. They were obviously still keen to have me as they happily added another £100,000 to my contract which made me think I should have asked for even more! Honda also gave me one of their gorgeous RC30 road bikes as part of my contract and I still have it in mint condition today.

I was starting to get a bit more streetwise with personal sponsorship deals too by this point. In 1987 Dainese paid me $40,000 US dollars (which is about £25,000) to wear their leathers and AGV paid me the same to wear their helmets. But when I asked Arai helmets if they would pay me the same, they told me to come back and talk to them when I had woken up!

Anyway, I sat down with another leather company, RS

Taichi, and decided to ask for $10,000 US dollars more than Dainese had paid me but didn't really think I'd get it. After all, that was another £6250 in UK money. At the meeting I said to them 'I need fifty . . .' and before I could say anything else, they said 'Ah, fifty thousand UK pounds, no problem. But you must sign a two year deal.' I thought 'Brilliant. That's about double what I had hoped for and for two years as well and all because they didn't hear me out!'

I got all the kit delivered to my house: six leather suits, six helmets, twelve pairs of boots, in fact everything to keep me going for the year. It made me think back to the days when I was begging for a helmet at a discounted rate and wore whatever old leathers I could afford even if they offered very limited protection. It's weird that when you don't need freebies you get them thrown at you (and paid silly money for wearing them) and when you really need them because you're skint, no one wants to give them to you but that's just the way it works.

Even when I was a factory Armstrong rider I only got two sets of leathers and I had to make them last all year. With the amount of crashing I was doing back then, there's no way I could have survived without the regular services of Gillespie's cobblers back home in Denny! I was in and out of there all the time getting my leathers patched up.

I didn't even have to do any promotional work for the big leather firms when I rode for Honda; all they paid for was the rights to use photographs of me wearing their kit in order to promote it. It was money for nothing really but I wasn't complaining.

Race-wise, I was more confident at the start of 1988 than I had been in my entire career. I was definitely expecting to finish in the top three, if not higher and I had no reason not to think like that. HRC had shown confidence in me by sign-ing me again and I'd finished fifth in my rookie year in 1987. Surely I could only improve now that I had more experience?

I got off to a good start by qualifying on pole in the Two Plus Four International in Japan and then went on to win the race as well. I was under the lap record again and all set for the GP at the same circuit, Suzuka. I was on fire and ready to go.

Practice didn't go too well and my fire was soon put out as I ended up eighteenth on the grid because my time was set in a wet session and I never managed to get a good dry time to improve my position. But the race was dry and I finished fourth after clawing my way through the field from that lowly start. I was still disappointed because I was going a second a lap slower than I had at the Two Plus Four meeting and couldn't figure out why. But it was a memorable day for Kevin Schwantz as he won his first GP of many that day. Later in the year Kevin and his parents, Jim and Shirley, joined our little convoy in their motorhome and we travelled round Europe together stopping at campsites for big Texas cook-outs. Jim and Shirley do the best.

The American GP was up next and I'd seen the Laguna circuit when I was staying in the States during the winter so I knew what to expect. It reminded me of Knockhill back home in Scotland – except the sun was always out! In particular the downhill Corkscrew section looked like Duffus Dip, which is the first corner at Knockhill.

I just lost out on pole in the final moments of practice because I couldn't get my tyres changed in time but I liked the track whereas most of the other riders seemed to hate it. I qualified third and it felt good to be as fast as the Americans on their home turf.

I loved going to America and I still do because the people seem so genuine. Sure, they're loud and over the top compared to us Scots but they're really open and what you see is what you get with them. At first I was suspicious because I thought they were phoney and just being nice to my face but they're not, they're really helpful. I like their positive attitude too.

I really thought I was going to win that GP as I led from the end of the first lap and stayed in front until lap eighteen when Eddie Lawson came past me. My front brake discs were warping and the same thing was happening on Wayne Gardner's bike which meant we couldn't brake as hard as we needed to going into turns like the Corkscrew and I actually overshot that corner and ran up the kerb on one lap.

Lawson said later that the only place he could gain on me was under braking and that's what really ruined my race. It turned out that we were running thinner and larger discs than the year before and that was the first time we had used them in a dry, hot race and they just warped. Gardner eventually got past me too, despite having the same problem, and I finished third but I felt I should have won it.

The good thing was that my riding style had changed after my dirt track training and it was obviously working well. Lawson and Mamola had commented on my lean angles before and that was a result of my 250cc racing days, but after Laguna they both noticed that I was getting on the power earlier too when the bike was still cranked over. I positioned myself on the bike differently and had started to slide the tyres a bit and it felt quite comfortable.

It was no problem in slower corners but because I had learned to slide on a quarter mile track while the other guys had learned on very fast one mile ovals, I just didn't have the experience to slide the bike through fast corners which was where I lost out.

I was really confident after Laguna Seca and actually said at the post-race press conference that I should be winning races soon which I really believed. I still didn't know exactly what I wanted from the bike as far as set-up went but I was certainly a lot more experienced than in '87 and Erv and me got it working pretty well at most circuits. Wayne Gardner moaned that the Honda was unrideable before he got a new frame at the Italian GP but as Eddie Lawson pointed out, all the changes that had been made to Gardner's bike were ones he'd requested so if there was a problem it was actually his own fault.

I found the Honda okay but Yamaha had improved their own bike for 1988 and Eddie liked it so he was on a charge that year.

Bike problems aside, I had rider problems to worry about in the shape of Frenchman Christian Sarron. Don't get me wrong, he was a great friend off the track but a liability on it! I hated riding alongside him because I was always waiting for him to fall off and take me out. I felt that way for good reason too as he knocked me off or held me up about three or four times that season.

The first time was in the third GP of the season at Jarama in Spain. I was right up with the leaders going into the first corner when Christian came underneath me and forced me to run off the track and I ended up down in fifth place as a result.

There was a bit of tension before that race as well because when I walked into the garage ten minutes before the start, as was my usual routine, both of my bikes were up on benches and still being worked on. They should have been ready long before then so I panicked and asked what the hell was going on. Apparently one of the mechanics Glyn Redmile had been warming one bike up by gently blipping the throttle while the other Jim Woods was trying to push start my spare bike to get it ready too. He had his head down to push it and rammed it straight into my number one bike damaging both machines! Not the best thing for pre-race nerves.

The Portuguese GP was again held in Spain but it was a forgettable race for me. I almost stalled the bike on the line, lost touch with the leaders and could only manage seventh place.

After that it was off to Imola for the Italian Grand Prix where I met Formula One car racing legend and my fellow countryman Jackie Stewart. He dropped by the garage to say hello and I even got to try on his favourite flat cap. What an honour!

Anyway, Italy was where Christian Sarron really messed things up for me. I was lining up to pass him at the Acqua Minerale chicane when he highsided right in front of me and I had to crash to avoid hitting him. I managed to get back on the bike but the fairing was scraping along the track and the handlebars were bent so eleventh place was the best I could do.

As a friend, Christian would have done anything for me (except retire) but as he crashed in Italy I seriously considered running him over so that he'd be too sore to ride for a while! He always invited me and some other riders down to stay with him in France for a holiday when we had a break in the racing calendar though it usually turned out to be anything but a holiday. We'd be sitting happily chilling out watching the telly or something and see Christian's head bobbing past the window, screeching a ping-pong table across the yard. Then we'd hear 'Okay let us play ze peeng-pong now' or 'Let us 'ave ze swimming race.' He'd never let us sit still for five minutes; he was always arranging activities for us so we had to avoid going there if we actually wanted a proper break.

When you've crashed as much as Christian, you should learn where the limits are but he never did. He'd push and push till he fell off again then look at me all bewildered and say 'I 'aven't a clue what 'appened' in his best *'Allo, 'Allo* accent. Bless. I'm just glad he retired in one piece and can spend his retirement coaxing people into playing ping-pong!

1988 was Wayne Rainey's first season in 500 GPs although he had done a season of 250 GPs in 1984. I clicked with Wayne immediately and didn't have to spend any time getting to know him like I'd had to with Eddie Lawson and Randy Mamola. Jan also became friends with Wayne's wife, Shae, and they were a cool, sociable couple.

It was just little things he did for me that showed what kind of a guy he was. He'd come back from the States to a race and say 'Niall, I was down the RV store (recreational vehicle shop to you and me) and thought I'd buy you this.' It may just have been a little tool for cleaning the toilet but those things were hard for me to get in the UK. Little gestures like that impressed me and showed he was always thinking about other people.

Wayne and I had a lot of drunken Sunday nights as he did like a beer or ten. He'd have fitted in at The Pines back in Denny no problem. It was a bit harder for me to chat to Wayne's mentor, Kenny Roberts Senior. He had been such a hero to me that I always felt awkward talking to him. He was like the biking version of Muhammad Ali and, like Ali, he had a razor sharp tongue when he wanted to, but he always offered advice freely and it was always worth listening to. If he was watching his riders at one point on the circuit and saw that I wasn't picking the bike up early enough in the corner he'd tell me and also tell me how to correct my faults. And considering we worked for rival teams, that was a really cool thing to do.

Anyway, to get back to the racing, I finished a lowly ninth in Germany because it was wet and I didn't feel confident riding in the rain that year. My crash at Suzuka the year before had dented my wet weather confidence and I don't think I ever recovered fully from that throughout my career. I got better in the wet but never as good as I should have done.

Austria was dry but I crashed pushing a front tyre that was too hard and which had never really worked properly.

At Assen in Holland, I had a decent finish in fifth place but it meant nothing when I heard about the death of my long time friend and racing colleague, Kenny Irons. I had already had one terrible shock when Neil Robinson was killed in 1986 and now Kenny was gone too. I was in the Argentinian embassy in Brussels getting a visa for the GP there when I was told. It was very tough coming to terms with Kenny's death and I remember thinking a rider of his talent should never have been racing at Cadwell Park in England where he was killed. Kenny had some good rides with Suzuki in 500 GPs in 1987 and deserved a factory bike but instead he was forced to go back and race in the UK at dangerous tracks because he didn't get any GP offers.

My only consolation was remembering how Kenny had lived. I was always very careful with money but Kenny spent it before he even had it. He bought a Porsche and was always mortgaged to the hilt so he lived life to the full despite me warning him to take it easy and now I'm so glad he didn't take my advice – at least he enjoyed his pleasures while he was alive.

The next round of the series was at Spa in Belgium and that's where Eddie Lawson sprang a surprise on me. He came round for a drink in my motorhome and started quizzing me what it was like working for Honda then asked if I could set up a meeting between Erv Kanemoto and him. Eddie knew the Honda was faster than his Yamaha, he didn't like his team manager Giacomo Agostini and he had just had enough so he wanted to switch teams. I told him I would set up a meeting and I did without realising that in doing so I was not doing myself any favours. If Honda signed Eddie Lawson *and* Wayne Gardner, would there still be room in the team for me? And would there be enough budget to pay for us all? Unlikely.

But as I said, I didn't think of that at the time and I was just excited about the prospect of Eddie riding for Honda – I thought it was a great idea. So Eddie spoke to Erv and somewhere along the line he must have agreed terms with HRC because Ed was on a Honda the following year.

The race in Belgium was wet again and I only finished eleventh but that was better than my non-finish in Yugoslavia when the bike seized on the fourth lap. It was the first of several retirements caused by the crankshaft breaking which was caused by the bike revving too high; it was revving to over 14,000rpm. In the middle of 1987, HRC had asked me what I wanted for the following year and I said 'more revs please' but the bike just couldn't cope with it. Wayne Gardner had similar problems in the GPs and when we went to Suzuka as teammates for the big 8 Hour race, we had the same problem again on the RVF 750 Honda. But that didn't wind me up as much as Wayne did on that trip. I had always been just behind him with my practice times and he kept taking the piss about me always being second. Even after the race, when we were taken by separate helicopters to the airport, he wound me up because mine landed after his and I was second again! I was ready to nut him by that point.

My bike broke again in the French GP after I'd been first away off the line which meant it was the third time that year and always at tracks where I had expected to go well. I was starting to get really annoyed with Honda because I was losing so many points through no fault of my own.

At least the NSR held together for the British GP, which was obviously my most important race of the year. I always liked racing at the British GP even though the demands on me from the press and spectators were huge. Getting out on track felt like having a break after being hauled from pillar to post from seven in the morning until ten at night. Being on the bike feels quite quiet and peaceful after all that!

I never felt any more pressure racing at home than I did elsewhere and in the 1988 race I realised that even huge sums of money couldn't make me go any faster. A firm called Howitt Printing had put up £50,000 for any British rider who could win the British GP and I was battling for third with Christian Sarron thinking 'Faster, faster, there's fifty grand in this' but I just couldn't go any faster.

You know when you can't possibly go any quicker because the bike is telling you it's on the limit for the way it's set up. You're sideways into corners, it's moving through the corners, the back wheel's skipping under braking and if you try to ride it harder, you'll just fall off. The only way to go faster when you reach those limits is to change the set-up and/or change your riding style. But during a race you can't change your set-up and it's not easy changing your style either so you have to do the best you can with what you've got.

In my case at the British GP, I got fourth place and had to be content with that and I got the same result in the next round in Sweden before dropping to sixth in Czechoslovakia.

It was another fourth place at the final round in Brazil where I really enjoyed sliding the bike as I'd been taught to in America. The Goiania circuit had a fairly slippery surface and

I was getting more used to sliding as the race went on. I felt really happy after that race because I'd been catching the guys who finished on the rostrum and I felt that I'd moved up from being a top five finisher to being a top three finisher, certainly for the 1989 season.

I finished sixth overall in the 1988 500cc World Championship which was one place lower than the year before. That may not look so good on paper but I knew, and thought everyone else knew, that I had ridden a lot better and was a lot more experienced than I had been in '87. It was just breakdowns and some bad luck that prevented me from finishing any higher.

Incidentally, after the last GP I raced a Honda Britain RC30 at Donington Park in the final round of the Formula One World Championship. I won the race ahead of Roger Burnett while Carl Fogarty finished fifth and took the title. Just for the record, that was the only world championship race I ever won.

Eddie Lawson won the 500cc world title for the third time in 1988 and I was pleased for him. We had a great night out after the last GP in Brazil and all the riders were plastered. Rob McElnea came up with another daft idea to keep things swinging. At midnight he decided he would collect as many pockets from other people's shirts as possible. I don't know why, he just thought it was a good idea at the time. So sure enough, as soon as the clock struck midnight, Rob went waltzing round the room ripping the chest pockets off every shirt he could spot while he stood talking to the wearers. Strange bloke, Rob Mac.

I went to Japan for an end of season race at Fuji (where the crank broke again) but after the race I noticed that everyone in the team had gone a bit quiet. It was hard to put a finger on it but something had changed and I knew it couldn't be my fault because the bike broke and there was nothing I could have done about it. I felt Erv was a close enough friend to tell me what was happening and he told me things were not looking good for next year. When the Japanese say that it means you're out of a job. Simple.

It's a horrible feeling when that happens, make no mistake. But every racer goes through it and you just have to become hardened to it. There's other rides out there. Anyway, Honda didn't even need to tell me I was sacked because I knew from that moment. It almost felt like the day I left school; all my security was gone but I was also excited at the new possibilities that were open to me. It certainly didn't dent my confidence as a rider.

I remember that same night I was still staying at a hotel at Honda's expense and I told fellow rider Roger Burnett what had happened as we had dinner. He suggested the only option was to order the most expensive steak and the most expensive bottle of wine in the house. I can't remember how much the steak cost but the bottle of wine cost £350!

The next day I was driven to the airport by HRC's Japanese co-ordinator Mr O'Hara and it was obviously his job to tell me officially that my services were no longer required. I could see he was nervous and he offered me a cheap watch as a present, which seemed a bit of a pathetic way to end two years of riding my heart out for Honda. Mr O'Hara didn't really explain why I had been sacked but just muttered something about it being a difficult time for HRC. The Japanese aren't very good at being confrontational.

What he did offer me was the chance to ride in a satellite Honda team for Serge Rosset (whom I later rode for in the Yamaha France team) of Honda France using 1988 spec bikes.

Honda was even prepared to forgo the $1 million lease fee – which satellite teams normally had to pay – if I rode for Serge which I suppose shows that they did want to keep me one way or another. I wasn't keen about racing one-year old bikes but at least it was some kind of offer. Mr O'Hara dropped me at the airport hotel and I thanked him for the watch and said I'd think about riding for Serge but when I got into the hotel I had a phone call from Giacomo Agostini, the fifteen times world champion who was running the Marlboro Yamaha team. Yamaha had just lost Eddie Lawson who had signed for Honda (much to Wayne Gardner's fury because he only found out about it in the newspapers and he wasn't too fond of Lawson) and Giacomo asked me if I wanted to ride for Yamaha. As one door closes, another door opens.

I had spoken to Giacomo before and thought he was a good guy but I was too young to be in awe of him because he won most of his world titles in the 1960s and even I'm not old enough to remember that. Respect is due though; Ago won fifteen world titles which is more world championships than anyone else in the history of the sport managed to win. The man knew how to ride a motorbike.

I was invited to Switzerland for a meeting with Ago and the sponsors from Phillip Morris tobacco and I felt like I had won the lottery. Yamaha was the next biggest team to Honda and I really wanted to know what the bike was like because Eddie had won on it in 1988 and it had a reputation for being a good handler.

So I signed a contract in Switzerland in November, did some press photos and that was it; I was an official Yamaha rider and didn't have to go down to the dole office after all. But as I walked into the photo studio I got such a shock at the huge picture on the wall of my new team-mate at Yamaha – it was

Freddie Spencer again, back from retirement and dressed from head to toe in Marlboro red! As we left the room Ago said to me 'You didn't see what you saw in there okay?' It was still a big secret that Freddie was back and riding for Yamaha after so many years with Honda and the photos we had taken weren't due to be released for some time. But at least I knew and liked Freddie so that wasn't going to be a problem. I just wasn't sure what his riding was going to be like though or if he'd turn up for the races on any regular basis.

Back home in Scotland in December, I decided to chance my luck at making an honest woman out of Jan whom I'd then been seeing for three years. I asked her to marry me and thankfully she agreed so the year ended on a high note for me. It was no quickie engagement period though because we didn't actually get married until November 1991.

I didn't really need any Christmas presents that year as I already had all I wanted: a pay rise, a factory Yamaha ride and a happy home life. Mind you, a 500cc world title in 1989 would be nice Santa . . .

CHAPTER EIGHT

Stoney's Return

I sometimes think I should have taken up smoking just because of all the free cigarettes I could have blagged in my Grand Prix years.

My Suzuki was sponsored by Skoal Bandit, which was a tobacco-filled teabag sort of product which you stuck between your teeth and gums, then I was sponsored by HB cigarettes on the Honda and in 1989 I was a Marlboro man! I could have smoked myself to death by that point if I'd chosen to!

The first time I rode the Marlboro YZR500 Yamaha was at Phillip Island in Australia at the end of January 1989. Kel Carruthers was the chief engineer in the team and was over-seeing the whole technical side of things but Freddie Spencer and I had two mechanics each for the real hands-on stuff. My two crew members were Trevor Morris and Colin Davies and funnily enough, Colin now lives about five minutes away from my house in Ashby de la Zouch in Leicestershire.

Kel was brilliant at putting things in perspective and I remember him telling me more than once that year to calm down and not be so depressed when I wasn't getting the results I wanted. He used to remind me that racing was just a game and we were all just playing it. It wasn't World War Three. Wise words.

That test was the first time I had been to Phillip Island because it was a new circuit and there had never been a Grand Prix there before but it was going to host one in '89 so it was a good chance to learn the layout of the place.

I liked the Yamaha straight away, particularly the steering which was more neutral than the Hondas, which tended to understeer. Even so, I still didn't go as fast as I had hoped to although my times were pretty similar to Freddie's – once he'd shown up of course.

Spencer was a day and a half late as usual and the team was getting stressed thinking that he wasn't going to show at all. I couldn't believe that he was up to his old tricks again even with a new team. I could almost understand Honda putting up with him because he'd won three world titles for them but he had no history with Yamaha and I really thought he would have made a bigger effort with a new team, at least at the start of the year.

Freddie looked overweight again but he still put in a couple of fast laps and showed sparks of the genius that had made him a triple world champion in the first place. Right to the end of his racing career, Fred was blindingly fast when he wanted to be.

I liked my new team straight away and Giacomo Agostini, the team manager, was the nicest person you could ever wish to meet. Anytime I was in Italy Ago always asked Jan and I round to his house for dinner and he would cook with his wife Maria and they both really looked after us; they were good hosts. As I said before, I knew who Agostini was but he was a bit before my time so the only real memory I had of him was that I used to own an AGV Agostini replica crash helmet! A lot of people have accused him of being a bit of a dodgy dealer but I never found him that way. With Ago you got exactly what your contract said you'd get. If that meant you were to be allocated three team shirts then you were allocated three team shirts, not four and not two. Some people involved with Ago expected more than they were entitled to and he just didn't work that way. Everything was detailed and laid out and if you accepted that then everything was fine but some riders tried to take liberties and Giacomo wouldn't have any of it, which was fair enough in my book.

It was very different working for Yamaha than it was with Honda. When I was riding for HRC, I was riding for the factory and whenever I was in Japan I'd be expected to go to HRC's headquarters and toe the company line. With Yamaha, it was more like a privateer set-up in that it was a small, independent team even though it was the official factory effort. It was more like a family and much better for that. The bikes were shipped to Bergamo in Italy where Ago's workshops were and Kel Carruthers was allowed to do pretty much anything he wanted to them. Honda, on the other hand, was very strict about what could be changed on their bikes so it was all very different.

Yamaha's race effort was a much smaller outfit than Honda's too. HRC, for example, had around two hundred staff dedicated solely to winning the world championship whereas Yamaha only had about fifty people or maybe even fewer devoted to their GP effort.

The other major difference was the more relaxed mentality that was apparent at Yamaha. In my first year with Honda in 1987, I got into some serious trouble with the top brass for baring my backside in the press. Rob McElnea had the mother of all bruises on his bum from a crash and he was quite happy to show the damage to a photographer. I just wanted to show the world how big and purple Rob's butt was compared to mine so I did a 'moonie' too and the picture appeared in *Motor Cycle News*, which Honda staff always read, so they had seen mine and Rob's bums in all their glory. They were not at all amused. Apparently, I was bringing the company into disrepute or some nonsense like that but I don't understand why.

The people at Yamaha were a bit more realistic about the culture differences between Japan and the West so the atmosphere was more comfortable and relaxed.

Rob Mac and I had some great laughs that year because he'd just bought a home video camera and they were pretty rare back then so we filmed everything we saw. Our speciality was filming inside other riders' motorhomes when they weren't there. We called them the Messy Motorhome Videos. Because the paddock wasn't open to the public, everyone left their vehicles unlocked so we sneaked in and I did the Lloyd Grossman 'Through the Keyhole' bit while Rob did all the camerawork. Some of the things we found were hilarious. We now know which porno magazines each rider prefers, what food they had in their fridge that they shouldn't have been eating and even whether they flushed their toilets properly. Believe me, some of them didn't and it was not a pretty sight!

But the very best bit was when we uncovered the underwear collection of the girlfriends of the riders which we naturally had to do. That was always a treat.

On one occasion I remember an old German guy thought we were mental because we were filming his dog walking down the street and talking to it at the same time. 'Vot are you doing viz mein dog? You are feelming heem? Vy do you feelm mein dog?' It was hilarious and I've still got all those daft videos. Offers of money on a postcard please.

Anyway, after some more testing, we were off to Japan again for the traditional first Grand Prix of the year at Suzuka where I finished sixth in my first race on the Yam. The bike felt okay but for some reason I preferred the way the Honda worked at Suzuka as it just felt more suited to me at that particular circuit. I was annoyed at Wayne Gardner forcibly barging his way past me at one stage but it was probably just a bit of needle because he was still on a Honda and I was riding a Yamaha.

Gardner was probably annoyed about his new team-mate for that year too – his fellow Australian Mick Doohan. Wayne liked all the glory back home in Oz and he saw Mick as a threat to that adulation so the two of them never really got on but I liked Mick straight away. I had met him briefly the year before in Japan when he was racing a Superbike but 1989 was the year that I really got to know him.

I went round to say hello at the first race because he was new to the scene and I remembered what that felt like when everything was unfamiliar so I tried to make him feel welcome because he seemed quite wary of everyone in the paddock at first. Obviously at that point I had no idea that he would go on to become a five times world champion and one of the greatest riders ever. I know he admired Eddie Lawson and of course they were now team-mates, so they became friends as Eddie and Wayne Gardner were obviously never going to get on just as Wayne and Mick weren't for the reasons I've already stated.

Mick had a lot of crashes in '89 but I didn't know how good or bad the Honda was that year. I wasn't sure if it was him or the bike to blame, though I suspect the updated NSR was a bit of an animal to ride. He was quoted at the time as saying he didn't have a clue what he was doing so he thought he'd just keep falling off until he found the limits! Mick picked up a huge number of injuries in his first year because of that but it never fazed him a bit.

It was off to Mick's home race in Australia next and I had my first race crash of the year when the bike highsided me and left me feeling a bit sorry for myself. But Freddie crashed as well a couple of laps later so I didn't feel so bad. You feel a bit of a plonker when you're the only one in the team to crash!

However the Australian GP was more memorable for another reason – the return of Stoney and Beggar! I was lying in bed with Jan in the hotel on the morning of the race when there was an almighty racket outside the door of my room. It was about 7am and someone was hammering on the door and making a hell of a noise. When I opened it, I couldn't believe what I saw. My old childhood mates Stoney (who was in the stolen car with me when the cops caught us) and Beggar were totally drunk and looking for some free T-shirts! Jan didn't know where to look as they stormed into the room so she just pulled the sheets up over her head. I hadn't seen either of those guys since I was a kid and didn't even know where they had ended up after I left Fankerton. It turned out that they headed over to Australia to travel around and get a tan. They'd seen the pre-race publicity for the GP and noticed my name so thought they'd come and surprise me. They certainly did that. I gave them as many Marlboro freebies as I had and a couple of tickets for the paddock and off they went. It was great to see them but perhaps 7am on the morning of a race wasn't the best time for a reunion.

I had a good ride to fifth at Laguna Seca in America where I always seemed to go well but it could have been better if my bike hadn't suffered a partial seizure on the first lap. It just cut out at one point and I was ready to retire when it chimed in again so I got my head down and worked my way back up to fifth which I was reasonably satisfied with.

Spain was good for me too because I rode to third place and mounted the podium with Eddie Lawson and Wayne Rainey so I was in good company.

Although Spain has generally been successful for me as far as results go and I know that some riders have favourite circuits and seem to go well at them every year, it doesn't always work out like that. Changes to the bike or to the track surface or varying weather conditions can really affect how well you ride at any track so it's impossible to say for certain that you'll get a good result, even at your favourite circuit.

But I qualified third and finished third in Spain in front of a hundred and fifty thousand-strong crowd, which was mega. I was getting used to the Yamaha and feeling good about the rest of the season.

What was really annoying in 1989 was that Freddie Spencer was the number one rider in the team and he got all the new parts and all the latest stuff even though I was regularly beating him in the races. I suppose that was written into his contract but it was so frustrating for me as he got new carbon fibre brakes and all sorts of things for which I had to wait much longer. Sometimes Freddie just wouldn't show up at all at races. For example, he never turned up for his home GP in America, (claiming he woke up on race day morning with an ear infection) and his 'A' list tyres (I was on the 'B' list and didn't get first choice of the best rubber) were sitting there doing nothing but I still wasn't allowed to use them! How daft was that? I should've just sneaked them on.

People like Mick Doohan and myself were 'B' list riders and sometimes at the end of qualifying we'd get bunged an 'A' set if we were going well. That could be great at some races but at others, the different tyres threw the suspension set-ups out and the bike felt awful so it was very much a hit or miss situation. Good tyres are only good if you have enough time to set your bike up around them. Thankfully, that system is gone now and most factory riders get decent rubber which levels things out a bit.

The Italian GP was a total shambles. I was chasing the top three in the first few laps but then it started to rain and the race was stopped. It was restarted in the rain but it was too dangerous so most of the top riders refused to continue racing. Pier Francesco Chili was the only big name to compete and he ended up winning the race but he wasn't too popular back in the paddock afterwards – riders are meant to stick together on decisions like that. But at the same time, I understood why he did it for the sake of his sponsors and team and Frankie was well liked anyway so he sort of got away with it.

Disaster awaited me in Germany when the GP circus moved to Hockenheim. I was trying too hard to make up for a new engine which felt slow and I crashed, breaking and dislocating my kneecap and also breaking my scaphoid which is a bone in the wrist. Breaking the scaphoid is a nightmare for a bike racer because it takes so long to heal and it's crucial for riding. It helps with sideways movement in the wrist and you don't need that much in day to day life but when you're hanging off a bike and trying to steer it, you use the scaphoid a lot. It's weird because any other activity feels fine and you think the wrist has healed then you get on a bike and it's murder. Still, I'd had a pretty good injury record up until then so I suppose it had to happen sooner or later.

I missed the Austrian GP then rode again in Yugoslavia but was in too much pain and could only manage twelfth place. I went slightly better in Holland, finishing eighth, but I was still far from fully fit and was grimacing under my helmet a few times. That reminded me of earlier in my career when I used to do a lot of shouting under my lid. Whenever I passed someone I'd start shouting at myself like I was on a horse: 'Come on Niall, come on man, you can beat this guy!' I used to give it big shouts but when I became a better rider and started to concentrate more, I stopped all that and precision became everything. I just went as clinically as possible from braking point to apex and from apex to braking point in total silence. No more shouting, at least for me anyway. I don't know what some of the hotheaded Italian riders were like though!

I may have stopped talking out loud but in long races when it was wet my mind did tend to wander a bit and I'd start thinking about what to have for dinner or what I would do after the race! But then I'd snap back into it and focus again. Most of the time on the bike I was unemotional about things; if someone passed me I wouldn't get angry, I'd just try to pass them back again. If I almost crashed, I would put it out of my mind and just keep going. But towards the end of a race, especially if I was on for a good result, I'd start to get excited and a bit more human and nervous about the whole thing – it was a good buzz. There was nothing better than gaining a few places at the end of a race but then again, there was nothing worse than losing a place in the last couple of laps when I was so close to the finish.

The French GP at Le Mans was a good example of me having to change my style during a race. As I said before, it's not an easy thing to do especially if you're talking about making fundamental changes but there are some things you can do to adapt to a changing race situation. At one point at Le Mans, my front wheel slid in a corner and I ran off the track. I started clawing back positions but kept having slides so I had to change my lines through the corners and not lean over as far so that the rear tyre did more of the work and I wasn't relying on pushing the front all the time. My efforts were rewarded with seventh place.

I was hoping for a better result at Donington Park in the next round, the British Grand Prix. The weekend got off to a pretty sensational start when it was announced that Freddie and Yamaha were to part company. His behaviour had been erratic all year with his usual no-shows and this time his performances on track hadn't been enough to make up for his unpredictable timekeeping.

As far as I was aware, the team did all they could to accommodate him that year, right down to the flight arrangements. Freddie's contract stated he would fly first class on all long haul flights while mine said I would fly business class which is one down from that. To try and save some cash, Giacomo Agostini flew in economy class even though he was such a huge star in motorcycling and one of the most famous racers ever!

I really felt for Ago over the whole Spencer deal because he tried so hard and put his neck on the line to give Freddie another chance. As it turned out, his faith in Freddie indirectly led to Ago losing his Marlboro sponsorship and his 500 team folded at the end of the year.

Anyway, I had my own weekend to think about at Donington and I didn't take much notice of the furore surrounding the Freddie situation.

I usually raced in the Suzuka 8 Hour race before the British GP but I didn't get an offer to ride in '89 so it was one less long haul flight and one less case of jet lag. I was fast all through practice at Donington but got a bit narked when Spencer's replacement, Luca Cadalora, pipped me in the dying moments of the final session and knocked me down onto the second row of the grid. It was a horrible feeling being beaten by someone having their first ride on the same bike as myself but I suppose that's the sort of thing I did when I was riding for Suzuki and Honda so I couldn't really moan too much about it! Still, it got me fired up for the race and I really wanted to beat Cadalora (which I did) so it was probably a good thing.

The race itself turned out to be one of the highlights of my career. No British rider has ever won a 500cc British GP since the event moved to the mainland from the Isle of Man TT course in 1977. Barry Sheene came closest in 1979 but was beaten by Kenny Roberts by half a bike's length. I would love to have been the first to do it and at one stage it looked like I might, but in the end it wasn't to be.

I got away in sixth place and lost some time trying to get past Wayne Gardner, which meant the leaders were well ahead of me. But I kept my head down and on lap five I overtook Christian Sarron at the end of the main straight. At the start of lap six I passed Eddie Lawson at Redgate Corner and then got past Wayne Rainey as well. Things were looking good. Watching that race on TV now I can see the crowd was going mental but I wasn't really aware of that at the time because I was concentrating so much. I was just going from point to point thinking 'Here I come Kevin, here I come, I'm catching you.' Schwantz noticed the crowd and said later that he knew I was on his tail because they were going mental. Don't get me wrong, I was always aware of programmes being waved and of a general movement in the crowd at races but I certainly couldn't ever hear anything because all my senses were fully employed in riding the bike as fast as possible.

Anyway, I dived inside Schwantz at Redgate and there I was

– leading my home Grand Prix! The bike was handling well and working well and I didn't feel I had to try too hard to get past everyone so there seemed no reason why I couldn't clear off and win it. But there was a reason; that damned front tyre again. It was working brilliantly early on but started to slide once I was in the lead and I just couldn't flick the bike around like before. Kevin came back past me as did Lawson and Rainey before the race was over and in the end I finished fourth. It was still a good result at home but a podium would have been nice – and a win even better!

Wayne Rainey has compared the levels of concentration reached on a race bike to an out-of-body experience and that British GP ride actually felt like that to me. I felt as if I was above and behind myself looking down on me riding the bike. I think when you concentrate so hard, the body sort of takes over and it feels like it's doing it all for you and you're just left as a casual observer.

The Michelin technicians blamed themselves for my result but it wasn't their fault. If I'd chosen a harder tyre I might not have got away so quickly and then lost too much ground waiting for it to heat up. If I'd gone for a softer tyre, it would have gone off even earlier. That's just racing – it's always about compromise.

It was a great weekend all the same and I was dragged up onto the winner's rostrum to celebrate with Wayne, Eddie and Kevin anyway. Even now I get people coming up to me saying they're still hoarse from cheering me on that day! I really appreciated that support and I'm sorry I didn't deliver a win for all those people but I tried my best and couldn't do any more than that.

I ended the year with another fourth in Sweden, sixth in Czechoslovakia and ninth in Brazil to take seventh overall in the championship, two places ahead of Mick Doohan and three ahead of Gardner, although to be fair, they had been injured quite a lot that season. I felt I should have been in the top five but I gave away a lot of points through injury and it just didn't work out. It was also more difficult re-learning the circuits on a new bike after two years on a Honda.

Unfortunately, at the end of the year Agostini's Marlboro Yamaha team folded and I collected my P45 again just like the year before. Freddie Spencer's failure to deliver was one factor and the fact that I only finished seventh was another; a team like that expects to be winning GPs and in 1989 we weren't doing that. Out of desperation at the end of that year, Ago tried to sign Wayne Rainey who was riding for Kenny Robert's Lucky Strike Yamaha team and that caused a lot of friction between Ago and Roberts. Roberts then went to Marlboro and said he could offer them better value for their big bucks by running Rainey and Eddie Lawson and actually convinced them to back his team so Ago lost his sponsor and the team folded.

Ago got things together and ran a 250 team in 1990 but I had no options on the table. I was knocking on several doors but they weren't opening for me. It's vitally important to have a good last race in any season as you're remembered for that one result even if you've not done well the rest of the year. Look at Regis Laconi on the Aprilia RSV in World Superbikes in 2001. He had a dreadful year and most people thought he'd be sacked but he won at the final round and ended up signing a deal to race the firm's new GP bike! I had a poor finish to the season with ninth in Brazil and I'm sure that didn't help my case. If the British GP had been the last race of the season things might have been very different.

For a week I thought 'Right, no one's going to give me a job so I'm going to quit racing.' I got really huffy because I felt I was one of the world's top five riders and I had been left out in the cold without a ride. But after my little strop I came to my senses and realised that I still wanted to ride and I would find a way of doing it even if it meant paying for it myself again, just like when I started. And that's how it ended up. I decided to start my own team and fund it myself if I couldn't find enough sponsors.

So I started ringing people in the winter of 1989 to put a one-man team together with the aim of competing in 250 Grands Prix. I bought two bog standard production TZ250s from Yamaha with my own money but famous bike sponsor George Beale later agreed to pay for them and Castrol came up with some cash too. Chas Mortimer, my old team boss from the Silverstone Armstrong days came on board as team manager and supplied a truck so we were ready to go racing.

My change in heart had been incredible as I slowly realised how much I wanted to race. Initially I thought 'Why should I waste all my own money on racing when someone else should be paying me?' but then the passion returned and I remembered just how much I liked racing motorcycles. I had come full circle. I really feel that if it had come to selling my house to raise money I'd probably have done it just to keep racing!

The only place I wanted to be was in Grands Prix. In 1989, the World Superbike series was only two years old and not nearly as prestigious as it is now and the British championships were a bit of a shambles so GPs were the only option as far as I was concerned.

I spoke to Yamaha UK and they agreed to build me an OWO1 Superbike for Daytona and other selected races so at least I would have some racing practice in before the first GP – or so I thought. When I got to Daytona, I qualified on the front row but then got wiped out in the first corner of the race by American rider Jamie James so that was my meeting over.

Back home in Scotland, Jan and I had moved to Dunblane and bought our first detached house so I'm fairly sure she was hoping we wouldn't have to sell it to pay for my racing but she never once complained. Jan knew that racing was what I did and she always accepted that even when things weren't looking too good. In fact, she positively encouraged me, which was great.

The mechanic in my merry little team was none other than Anthony 'Slick' Bass who later went on to help Carl Fogarty to four World Superbike titles and achieved a bit of fame for himself by always sticking his ugly mug in front of the cameras at races!

It was back to basics again as far as travelling arrangements were concerned. We all just piled into the back of our van and drove to the races. One bonus was that I had finished in the top ten in 500 GPs in 1989 so I qualified for some travel allowances to get to the races. That meant we would get some flights and freight costs covered for the far-off rounds or I could cash in the tickets for some ready money if I didn't need them.

I knew I wasn't going to make any money out of the team but I made sure Chas got a wage and we sorted out Slick on a sort of race-by-race basis.

One thing I didn't have a problem with was my ego. Of course, I knew I had taken a step down the ladder and I knew that many factory 500 riders would never dream of doing what I was doing but it really didn't bother me – I just wanted to race again. Anyway, I had roughed it before so it was easier for me to go back to that than it would be for a rider like Freddie Spencer who had the factory treatment from an early age.

We even drove all over Europe during the winter of 1989–90 sorting out product endorsements like helmets, brakes, sprockets and chains and I really didn't mind. I just got on with it and hoped I'd still have a house in a year's time!

After three years of living the high life and five years as a factory rider, I was now a complete privateer again. But I was every bit as excited about 1990 as I had been about any season beforehand. I never went racing so that I could stay in five star hotels – I went racing because I loved it.

On a funnier note, I took part in the one and only truck race of my career at the tail end of 1989. Ron Haslam and Steve Parrish were entered too and it looked like being a bit of fun. It was organised by my pal Robert Fearnall and my mechanic Colin Davies was watching from the pit wall before he was asked to move because no one was allowed to watch from there during a truck race. It was a good job he moved too because on my second lap of practice I spun out and smashed right through the pit lane wall where Colin had been standing!

I don't know how much that cost Robert Fearnall but it was the last time he invited me to race a truck. As a matter of fact, it was the last time anyone ever invited me to a truck race. Strange that.

CHAPTER NINE

A Lucky Strike

When I lined up on the grid in twenty-fourth place for the Japanese 250 Grand Prix at Suzuka in 1990, I was in a very different position from the year before. No 500 to ride, no big team hanging on my every word and no flashy 'brolly dollies' on the grid!

But I didn't give a monkey's; all I wanted to do was race and I had a pretty good race too considering I had never sat on the bike until the first day of practice. In fact I'd never even seen the bike before I got to the race. We had arranged for it to be delivered straight to Suzuka instead of the UK so we could cash in our freight allowance.

I finished the race thirteenth from thirty-eight starters and because there was a new points scoring system which went down to fifteenth place instead of just tenth, I scored three world championship points. Not bad for a bog standard bike and a small private team especially since there were loads of fast Japanese riders having one-off rides alongside the GP regulars.

I begged some information from my old team boss Giacomo Agostini who was running his new 250 Yamaha team and he helped all he could even though there was no resemblance between my standard bikes and his factory ones, but I appreciated everything he told me.

The bike felt really slow compared to the factory 500s that I'd been used to but it was good fun to ride because I could thrash it everywhere. Speaking of 500s, I was still hanging around with all the 500 riders in the paddock because I didn't know the 250 riders so well. But they probably thought I was mad racing a 250, and a private one at that.

The next round was at Laguna Seca in America and I scored some more points by finishing in fourteenth place. But something else happened at that meeting which was of far more significance and was destined to re-launch my 500 GP career but, sadly, it would be at the expense of another rider's 500 career.

Young Australian Kevin Magee was emerging as a hot new talent on the GP scene and had been signed up by Lucky Strike Suzuki for 1990. He finished fourth in Japan and was running in fifth place at Laguna when he crashed on the second lap of the race and was taken to hospital where he underwent an operation to have a blood clot removed from his brain. It was a very serious accident.

When the rest of us finished the race and realised how bad Kevin was, we just sat around hoping that he would pull through. Fortunately, Kevin eventually recovered and went racing again in the Japanese championship but he never regained the form that he'd shown before the crash.

It was ironic that Kevin was so badly injured at Laguna Seca because the year before he was involved in a crash which ended the career of Bubba Schobert, another talented rider. Magee was doing a burnout on the slowing down lap and Bubba ran right into the back of him sustaining serious head injuries.

Even though I was sorry for Kevin, I must admit to thinking

there was now a factory Suzuki available. However, I was pretty sure I wouldn't be the first choice to ride it as I'd already had some chances and there were always younger kids coming along who deserved a shot.

I went to the World Superbike round at Donington Park after Laguna Seca and rode the Loctite Yamaha OWO1 to fourth place in one of the legs. Then, after the races, Garry Taylor from Suzuki's GP team called me and asked if I'd go and see him. This was one week after Laguna and I was pretty sure what the meeting would be about so I was quite excited. At the meeting he told me that I'd been in the running for the Suzuki ride initially but just lost out to Magee and then he asked me if I would like to ride the bike for the rest of the season. When he said there was also $200,000 (about £125,000) in the kitty to pay my wages and a really good bonus contract ready to be signed I didn't take much persuading. After all, my only other option was going back to paying for my own 250 racing. It was a done deal.

I was obviously very excited and happy to be getting back into a factory 500 team but I was dreading telling my own little team who had done so much work over winter to make things happen. I hoped they would be happy for me getting such a good offer but what were they going to do for the rest of the season? We had no contracts but so many people had put themselves out to contribute to the team and I ended up only doing two races with them. I felt bad.

In the end, Chas Mortimer signed Kevin Mitchell to ride for him so the team kept going all year, which was good even though they had a pretty tough season. After breaking the news, I had about a week to get some Suzuki leathers made up then I was off to Jerez for the Spanish Grand Prix to swing my leg back over a 500.

Back in 1986, I'd turned my back on Suzuki to go and ride for Honda but it just goes to show that the Japanese don't hold any grudges about things like that as long as they're done properly. Because Honda and Suzuki had spoken openly about my 'defection' there were no problems and I slotted in quite happily at Suzuki again.

I had gone from being a 250 privateer to being Kevin Schwantz's team-mate in a factory 500 squad in just over a week. It was a big relief.

Time being tight, I had no chance to test the bike so my first outing on it was during practice for the Spanish GP and I crashed in the first official qualifying session, finding the front end too light just as Schwantz and Magee had said. The Suzuki was very fast and topped the top speed charts at most of the circuits that year. But it vibrated more than anything I'd ridden before and it was very fickle in that it would work brilliantly at some circuits and then be absolutely awful at others. It worked the other way round too sometimes as I'd be dreading going to a particular circuit thinking the bike wouldn't suit the place and it would turn out to be great.

I had known Kevin Schwantz for a couple of years and we got on fine but, just like the situation with Wayne Gardner some years before, Kev seemed to be a slightly different person when he was my team-mate. I don't think he ever saw me as a threat but I definitely had to keep my head down in the garage to avoid flying missiles! He was fond of throwing things around when his racing wasn't going too well and most of the time I just sat with my helmet on, glad that I had it. It was quite funny to watch from my side of the pit garage.

Sometimes Schwantz would totally ignore me and I took it really personally for a while until I realised that he just had his 'race face' on. When he was concentrating really hard he was in a world of his own and didn't acknowledge anyone. It's not that he was being rude, it's just that he genuinely wasn't aware of anyone else's presence such were his levels of concentration and focus.

The Suzuki team was the smallest outfit I had ever worked for in 500 GPs and I knew most of the guys because I'd worked with them before at one time or another. My mechanic, for example, was Geoff Crust with whom I had worked back in the Armstrong days. Incidentally, just to give Geoff some credit, he used to beat me when he raced at East Fortune in Scotland in 1981 on a beaten up old Yamaha RD400 so he was pretty tasty riding a bike as well as looking after one. Geoff's now the team manager for the Marlboro Yamaha 500 GP team.

We were a tightly knit little bunch at Suzuki and there was a good atmosphere in the camp. Suzuki didn't have the resources to change things on the bikes like Honda and Yamaha did but there was still a good budget and the bikes were certainly capable of winning races as Schwantz had shown.

I got on with team manager Garry Taylor really well, after all, he was the guy who gave me my break in 500 GPs back in 1986. I was pleased he accepted me back so readily because I thought I might have really annoyed him when I went to Honda. Racers should learn never to upset anyone in the business because you never know when you're going to rely on them in future. Garry Taylor had now given me a second chance in 500s and I was grateful to him for that.

The Lucky Strike Suzuki was a very different animal to the old Skoal Bandit bike I'd ridden years before. That had seemed like a big, tame, dopey pet whereas the new bike was a vicious beast with a power delivery like a kick in the teeth – from a steel toe-capped boot. Someone had obviously been doing their homework at Suzuki over the last three years and the new V-Four RGV had a hell of a lot more power than the old square four XR70.

The grids were very small in 1990 for several different reasons. One was that some of the top riders like Wayne Gardner and Eddie Lawson missed some rounds due to injury and another was the sheer expense of going racing. If you didn't have a factory contract it cost a fortune to compete and it was hardly worth it because you couldn't hope for any decent results. This was before teams could lease decent bikes from the manufacturers so it was a pretty barren period as far as depth of field went. Fortunately, the organisers and manufacturers realised this and came up with rent-a-racers and better financial packages over the next few years and grids began to fill out again.

Anyway, I finished eighth in Spain on my debut on the Suzuki which I wasn't too disappointed with considering I had never even practised on the bike before the weekend. A fifth in Italy was a bit of an improvement and my confidence started to build up a bit for the rest of the year. I could feel that I was making progress and we had a test at Assen before the next GP in Germany so the more times I got on the bike, the better I felt. I was also confident of a good result in Germany because we had tested there just after the Spanish GP so we had a basic set-up to work with.

The German GP at the Nürburgring was brilliant for me and the team as Kevin won the race and I finished in third place. The race is probably remembered even more for the famous and almost unbelievable synchronised crashes involving Pier Francesco Chili and Mick Doohan. In two separate incidents they were highsided at the same corner and in exactly the same manner. It was spooky how similar they looked and those crashes turn up on all the crash videos that flood the market so most race fans have probably seen them at some point.

On the grid in Germany Geoff Crust for some reason said to me 'I'll see you on the podium' and I thought 'Yeah, that would be nice' and that's the way it turned out. But not before I'd had some problems with my boot. I had actually worn a hole right through the sole on my gear change foot and the footrest kept getting stuck in the hole when I tried to move my foot back on top of the rest. It was annoying and unsettling but I managed to stay on and got my best result of the year so maybe I should have kept that boot.

It was also Suzuki's best result since 1982, which was the last time they had two bikes on the podium so we had a few beers that night. It was great fun partying with the Suzuki team because they were so tightly knit. They always ate and drank together and the guys from Lucky Strike were really cool too. If there was no big party in the riders' motorhomes we'd all head off to a local pub or restaurant because there was usually something near the circuit or a short taxi ride away.

My bike never really felt stable at the Austrian Grand Prix, which was next on the calendar, but I managed to secure fifth place by pulling away from Sito Pons in the last few laps. Yugoslavia was next and it will always be a very sad memory for me because Reinhold Roth, the 250cc rider, was left terribly disabled after a crash there. He hit a backmarker towards the end of the race and suffered serious brain damage that left him paralysed and he's practically helpless to this day. He's conscious but that's about it; he needs twenty-four hour care and that really upsets me because he's a lovely bloke.

None of us knew the extent of his injuries as we lined up for the 500 race and, as far as the race went, it was good for me and one of the closest battles I ever had with Kevin Schwantz.

We were scrapping for second place for most of the race as Wayne Rainey led and I found it no problem staying with Kevin. I knew I could have passed him at a couple of places but he was chasing Rainey for the championship and I didn't want to get in the way. There were no team orders as such but I just figured it was the decent thing to do. Looking back, I realise I was too decent for my own good on a lot of occasions but it's too late for regrets. Anyway, I ended up with third place and another podium celebration so once again, both Suzukis were in the top three which was great for the team and my championship points tally as I moved up from eighth place to fourth overall, despite missing the first two rounds.

I had a terrible start at Assen in the Dutch GP and finished fifth but that was still much better than my dismal twelfth place in Belgium after a poor tyre choice in the wet conditions. A sixth place in France was a bit more like it but I was ready for a win in the next round at home in the UK.

Before that, I made a return to the Suzuka 8 Hour race in Japan on a Suzuki GSX-R750 with British rider Roger Burnett as my team-mate. The bike wasn't competitive though and I was quite pleased when Roger fell off (unhurt) so we could pack up and go home. Just like any other racer I don't like riding uncompetitive bikes.

Riding at Suzuka meant I missed some practice for the British GP and I couldn't get the Suzuki to do anything I wanted to when I got to Donington so the extra practice would have been valuable. I had Japanese Suzuki guys standing on every corner watching me to try to spot what was going wrong but even that didn't help. I was desperate because I really thought I was going to win that year after coming so close in 1989. The weird thing was that Schwantz had his bike working great, or at least he was very fast on it even if it wasn't working great. But I remember almost crying under my helmet during the race because it was so frustrating seeing people coming past me that I didn't think should be able to come past me. I didn't even think Mick Doohan at that stage in his career should have been passing me at Donington Park and I got really annoyed.

Part of the problem in the race was the old 'A' and 'B' tyre system again. I was given an 'A' tyre after practice and Kevin said it was the best one for the race so I went with it but it gave so much grip that it threw out all my settings. The rear tyre was digging in so hard that the front end was all over the place.

Knowing you can't go any faster because of a machine or tyre problem is very frustrating because the crowd don't know you're having problems; they just think you're not trying hard enough and you know yourself you're giving it everything you've got, even if you're down in tenth place.

I ended up with fifth place which was a far cry from what I'd hoped and dreamed for but I was just glad when it was all over. I hated every minute of that race.

The 1990 British GP also marked the 500cc Grand Prix debut of a certain Carl Fogarty who would go on to win four World Superbike championships but never had a proper crack at GPs apart from the occasional one-off outing. In this instance, it was on a Honda NSR500 but Carl crashed out of seventh place after just three laps so it wasn't a great day for him either.

I had a top laugh after the race with Wayne Rainey and Jamie Whitham. Wayne took his hire car and Jamie took his Honda Prelude out onto the track at night-time and were thundering round in the pitch black. I piled as many straw bales as I could find across the road at Goddard's which is the last corner on the track so when they came back round they crashed right into them and sent them flying everywhere. Whitham came round first and after crashing through the bales, he tried to drive into the paddock not seeing the massive, thick chain barring the way. It caught under his front wings and the bonnet and practically ripped the front of the car off. It was a terrible mess.

I had a good race with Foggy at the Swedish GP (or Swedish TT as it was known, just like Assen was called the Dutch TT for historical reasons) where he finished in sixth place, one behind me. I never worried about Carl becoming 'best Brit' – I was just concentrating on trying to finish third in the world championship and he was just another rider to me who turned up at some GPs and wasn't a threat in the overall standings. In fact, I was pleased to see another Brit doing the GPs because there weren't many of us around at that time, although things are even worse now. I spoke to Foggy in the paddock and we passed the time of day but we never became best buddies.

From really early on he looked like a very aggressive rider and he always seemed to have pretty good teams around him and the raw talent to go somewhere. But it's always hard to tell how far a rider will go. Many show promise early on and come to nothing, others burn out too young while others come good late in their career. But Carl always looked aggressive, I'll give him that.

Carl opted to follow the four-stroke route in racing and WSB became more prestigious every year in the 1990s. But in 1990, it was still a new and little known series that the GP paddock took little notice of.

Over the years, Foggy has had a running battle with just about everyone in the WSB paddock and I suppose that's just the way he is but I couldn't be like that. Because the paddock is so small it's much easier just to get on with people because if you do fall out with them, it's impossible to avoid them and that just creates even more embarrassing situations. There were some momentous bust-ups in the GP paddocks such as when Kenny Roberts and Giacomo Agostini were fighting over riders and sponsors and Roberts (again) argued bitterly with Randy Mamola which probably led to Randy's contract not being renewed. Agostini (there seems to be a recurring pattern here!) and Eddie Lawson didn't see eye to eye either and Eddie used to completely blank people he didn't like so he didn't talk to Ago for ages. But the arguments always seemed to blow over and, as far as I know, all those guys are friends again.

There's a lot of aggression and tension in a GP paddock and sometimes even a lot of hatred but, like I said, everyone bumps into each other every day so it's very hard to maintain any animosity. I still love to annoy people who are trying to blank me, by being overly cheerful with them and I'll go out of my way to talk and give them big smiles if they're ignoring me. It's like when shopkeepers who are happy to take your money won't look at you when they're serving you; that really winds me up so I make sure I wish them a merry Christmas or whatever just to try and show that at least I'm willing to be pleasant. It doesn't hurt after all.

But I digress; back to the racing. Riding for Suzuki in 1990 was effectively my first season with a team-mate as Freddie Spencer had never shown up on a regular enough basis to be considered a team-mate. And it was good working with Kevin because he was quite happy to share information but because our styles were so different it was usually of no use to me! At some tracks Kevin seemed to have the bike working fant- astically and I would try his settings and was all over the place.

Donington Park was a good example of that. So I pretty much had to find my own settings in the end and for the Czechoslovakian GP at Brno, it worked well and I finished fourth behind Rainey, Lawson and Gardner.

With Schwantz crashing out and Rainey winning the race, it meant Rainey was the new champion while I was still fourth in the points table, twenty-two points behind Mick Doohan and just fifteen ahead of Wayne Gardner going into the Hungarian Grand Prix.

My right arm pumped up badly in Brno with the bumpy circuit and heavy braking involved so I could only finish seventh, with Foggy again one place behind me. I knew I couldn't catch Doohan in third place in the points table but Gardner was only eleven points behind me going into the final race in Australia and that was his home GP so I thought he would go well there. I needed a good finish to secure fourth overall and I was determined to get one. The race was a blinder with Gardner winning despite damaging his bike (his fairing was hanging off for most of the race) and hurting his wrist in a huge slide and nearly falling off. Schwantz did crash, broke some bones and was coughing up blood but still made it to the end of season party later that night. Top man!

I finished fifth which meant I ended the season just two points clear of Gardner in fourth place in the final standings. It had been my best season ever and I hadn't even competed in the full series. The reason I finished fourth was because I had scored points in every race and kept my crashing for qualifying and practice sessions. It's consistency which is rewarded in season-long championships and that was something I had lacked in the past because I simply wasn't experienced enough. Most riders are the same until they mature and to cite just one example, I'm sure Kevin Schwantz would have been world champion more than once if he hadn't been a 'crash or win' type of rider in his earlier years.

It felt very satisfying because at the start of the year I had no job. Yet there I was, fourth in the world championship behind Wayne Rainey, Kevin Schwantz and Mick Doohan, and ahead of Wayne Gardner, Eddie Lawson and Randy Mamola in the toughest road racing championship in the world.

Bike racing doesn't get any harder than Grands Prix. It's the very top level of the sport and it's mentally and physically tougher than any other series. Part of that is because the races are so much longer than national races and everyone is so good that one small slip can leave you nowhere. Mentally, there's a lot of pressure too because you're being paid a lot of money to deliver and you just have to get results or you won't get another job. There are sponsors to keep happy and even if you're in pain, you have to keep going or someone else will soon take your place.

I felt I had done a good job for Suzuki and Lucky Strike in 1990 and thought I would automatically be offered a job for the following season, so when we flew out to Sugo in Japan for the end of season race, I was confident of signing on for 1991.

Schwantz and I both fell off in practice and qualified quite badly but we finished first and second in the race, which I thought was the perfect way for the team to end the season. Wrong. For some reason, the Japanese Suzuki bosses thought Kevin and I didn't take the race seriously enough despite us finishing first and second – that's Japanese logic for you. Maybe it was some daft excuse for getting rid of me but that's what Mr Itoh said and he was the boss so that was that.

Anyway, nothing more was said and I actually did an international race in Malaysia before going home and won that for

Suzuki as further proof they should sign me again. I even tested with the team at Donington Park in November but after that everything went quiet. No one would take my phone calls, no one answered my faxes, either in Japan or at the racing team's UK headquarters, so I knew something was going on. Eventually, I just kept my finger on the 'send' button on my fax and got a reply after about fifteen attempts. I was told that Suzuki had changed their plans for the following season and that Belgian rider Didier de Radigues would be riding as Schwantz's team-mate in 1991. I was gutted. The fourth best rider in the world that year and I was bloody sacked again! This was becoming a habit.

Rumours went round that Didier was bringing a lot of sponsorship money to the team and that's what the press reported at the time but I never knew for sure. The official line from Suzuki was that Lucky Strike had a huge market in Belgium and they wanted a Belgian rider, but who knows? The result for me was the same; it was December and I was jobless once more.

Yet again, I had the burning desire to race a motorcycle but had no motorcycle to race.

CHAPTER TEN

A Baboon on the Lawn

In 1991, we moved to a lovely little village called Deanston near Stirling and lived there happily for the next ten years.

However I wondered what I had gotten myself into as I stood at the kitchen window admiring my new garden not long after Jan and I had moved in. Without putting too fine a point on it, there was a baboon strolling across the lawn. Now I'm not a renowned naturalist but I've seen enough documentaries on television to know what a baboon looks like and to know they're not a species native to Central Scotland.

I shouted to my father-in-law that there was a baboon on the lawn and at first got the expected response. But when he actually looked, my sanity was confirmed and just as we were rushing to the telephone to report it, a safari jeep came rattling round the drive and a bunch of *Jurassic Park*-style wardens jumped out and started giving chase to the creature.

As it turned out, Deanston was close to Blair Drummond Safari Park and the baboon had escaped from there sometime before. It was eventually caught and I'm pleased to say it was the last run-in I had with the local wildlife.

As far as racing went, I had no plans for the coming season at the beginning of 1991. Santa didn't bring me a works factory ride for Christmas but I still wasn't panicking. These things have a way of working themselves out.

I went to a bike show at Earls Court in London and bumped into Neil Tuxworth, the former racer, who was at that time managing the Silkolene Honda team with Carl Fogarty as his rider. He asked me what I was up to and when I said I didn't have a ride he asked if I'd be interested in joining Foggy at Honda to race in the World Superbike Championship and the British championship. I said I'd think about it but told him I was still hoping to get back into Grands Prix.

But by mid-January I had no other decent offers on the table so I came to an agreement with Neil to race for £25,000 including perks like a motocross bike and even a lawnmower. It was a bit of a step down from what I was used to but it was better than nothing.

Deep down, I still felt as though I had some unfinished business in Grands Prix and thought I still had a lot to offer, but riding in WSB was better than not riding at all. Neil really sold the idea to me when he said it was a factory-supported team and that I'd be getting a really good bike, just the same as Foggy's. It didn't quite work out that way but it wasn't all Neil's fault.

Later that day I asked Foggy what he was up to and he said he was in a one-man Honda team built exclusively around him which I found quite amusing after my little chat with Neil Tuxworth.

The World Superbike Championship was becoming more prestigious but it still didn't impress me much. I'd been to some of the races and while they were quite well attended in the UK because British riders were doing well in the series, in other countries the crowd attendance was very poor and the series got very little coverage. I had a lot of respect for riders

144

like Doug Polen and Raymond Roche who were riding in WSB at the time but I still saw the championship as a poor relation to GPs.

I quite liked the idea of working for Honda again though and there were some good perks lined up like a full factory bike for the Suzuka 8 Hour race in Japan midway through the year. I also thought it might provide a route back into GPs with Honda so I signed a deal to race an RC30 for the 1991 season. Big mistake!

I was promised two factory-supported bikes would be turning up for me and Carl before the start of the season and they were supposed to be 1991 WSB spec, just like the one Fred Merkel was using in that championship. One turned up for Carl but my bike didn't appear so I was given a machine cobbled together from two of the bikes Jamie Whitham had ridden the previous season. Jamie had an awful season in 1990 so I knew the bikes must have been below par because he's no slouch.

I got on pretty well with Carl and there was certainly never any friction between us in the team. He's quite easy to deal with if you accept that he's just the way he is. He says what he thinks and that's not always diplomatic but that's part of the reason he's so popular.

Carl would never admit to having any respect for a team-mate no matter who it was. He always had to think he was the best and if that's what motivated him to win then fair enough. I knew exactly where I stood with him and he certainly didn't faze me so we just got on with our own things and it worked out all right.

Our first race of the year was at Daytona in America and both Carl and I used one-year old bikes which was the best we could get for the event. In practice, my bike spewed oil all over

Daytona's famous banking which is taken at something like 180mph so that didn't do much for my confidence. I didn't want to imitate Barry Sheene's notorious 178mph crash on the banking, thank you very much.

Incidentally, I remember the first time I saw that banking and thought that the quickest line around it would be to hug the very bottom! It was only when bikes came past about twenty feet above me and going about 50mph quicker, that I realised I was wrong.

I finished seventh in the race but knew I could have gone much better on a decent bike as I had been in with a chance of winning the year before on a Yamaha before I was punted off. But I loved the meeting and the whole experience was so different to any other race I'd taken part in – especially the incident with Kevin Schwantz and Rob McElnea in the hotel foyer.

Kevin and Rob had been team-mates at Pepsi Suzuki in 1988 and they had always got on well but that night Kevin was really winding Rob up. All night he was mouthing off, twisting Rob's nipples and just generally getting on his nerves. Kevin's full-on with everything he does and the more he realised he was getting to Rob, the more he wound him up. Rob eventually cracked and started laying into Schwantz who curled up in a ball on the floor. Now Rob's a big lad and he wasn't holding back but Kev was just giggling like a school-girl as Rob put the boot in. It must have hurt and I could hear the 'oofs' and 'ooyahs' as Rob was kicking Kevin but he just curled up tighter and giggled more! Anyway, there were no grudges held and Kev soon healed up, but that's an example of the extreme kind of bloke Schwantz is and that's why the crowds loved him so much when he was on a bike – he was just full-on every step of the way. Incidentally, Schwantz won the next GP and said it was down to Rob giving him a good hoofing!

But if Daytona was different, so too was the North West 200 which we did that year. The contrast between the two events couldn't have been greater. Gone were the bikini-clad babes, the Florida sunshine and the multi-million pound raceway, to be replaced by old men in flat caps, Irish coastal weather and a makeshift public roads circuit. But the North West's got a fantastic atmosphere and the enthusiasm of the supporters and organisers was brilliant.

I was offered a fair amount of money to race there because I was known as a Grand Prix racer and the organisers gave me the number one plate to wear as I was expected to do really well.

But I must admit that I was very hesitant about going to the North West on a Superbike. I had great memories of the event from the mid-1980s but that was on a 250cc bike that was much slower to ride. The prospect of racing a 190mph machine (well, in theory the Honda should have been capable of that) round the streets was a bit daunting especially since I had no faith in the bikes after my Daytona experience. Having a mechanical failure while flat out at the North West doesn't bear thinking about.

I got a sixth place in one race and broke down in the other race and in the end I felt really embarrassed about my performances especially because of all the pre-race attention I had received. Either the bike was really, really bad or the mechanics were doing a poor job because every time I got on the Honda I ended up with a belly pan full of oil and obviously that shouldn't be happening.

I didn't fare any better in the World Superbike rounds the team entered with the Honda. At Jarama in Spain I was wiped out in the first corner by a guy called Russel Wood, who was from South Africa. He had a flying start from the back row and just smacked right into me. I woke up in the medical centre wondering what the hell had happened and simply wasn't fit enough to race in the second leg. But I wasn't bothered because the bike had been useless in practice anyway.

We did Donington World Superbikes too and I got two seventh places which was about as good as I could have hoped for. Then my proper factory bike arrived in time for the British Supercup championship round at the same circuit in May. Just as well because I was thinking about quitting the team as the old bike was so slow.

Anyway, I was delighted when the new bike arrived and thought I could turn my season round from that point onwards but I was soon to be disappointed. Neil Tuxworth told me I couldn't ride the bike before Nick Jefferies had ridden it at the Isle of Man TT. It wasn't Neil's decision, the order came straight from Japan, but my face hit the floor at the news as I realised I had to ride the old bike again.

As it happened, both of my old bikes blew up in practice (and no, I didn't sabotage them) so Honda reluctantly gave me permission to race the new machine. I was under strict orders not to break it because it was needed for the TT. But I qualified second, won the race, and set the fastest lap, which hopefully proved to any doubters that it had been the bike and not me that had been preventing me from winning races.

The new bike was taken off me again after that meeting and we flew to America for the WSB round at Brainerd in Minnesota with the old plodder again. That was when I was given a visual demonstration of how bad the bike really was, not that I needed any reminding. As I was racing down the main straight in unofficial practice, all tucked in and with the throttle pinned to the stop, French-Canadian rider Miguel du Hamel came screaming past me on a Honda CBR600. For anyone who doesn't know the difference, I was on a (supposedly) factory-supported 750cc Superbike and was being passed by a 600cc production bike which should have been about 30mph slower than my machine. Something was very obviously wrong.

I told the mechanics there must be something amiss and asked them to strip the engine, check everything and put it back together before the race but they refused to do it which I wasn't too happy about. The bike lasted the race but it was painfully slow and I finished fourteenth and fifteenth in races where I should have been running near the front quite easily. I made the decision on the long flight home to quit the team.

I knew I was fighting a losing battle and it was really embarrassing finishing so far down in races so leaving the team was the only realistic option as far as I was concerned, although I hadn't told anyone at that point. The factory bike did come back from the TT in one piece and it would have been mine from then on but any bike which comes back from the TT is always very second hand because they are put under so much strain during practice and race week.

I raced the bike at Brands Hatch and came third but it was as loose and knackered as I thought it would be, so after that race I told Neil Tuxworth I was leaving the team. He was really good about it and knew I wasn't happy so he allowed me out of my contract without any fuss. The head of HRC in Japan, Mr Oguma, wasn't too chuffed though and I got a bit of a nasty letter from him about my 'defection!' Apparently, I was being dishonourable again as Honda had put such a good team together for the Suzuka 8 Hour and I was deserting them! Mr

Oguma would probably have been even more upset if he had known that the first people I called after leaving the team was Yamaha – Honda's arch rivals.

While I was at the North West 200 earlier in the year I had received a phone call from a Mr Maekawa at Yamaha who had somehow heard that I wasn't happy at Honda. I don't know how he knew but he did and he asked me if I wanted to ride for the Hayashi factory Yamaha team based at Mount Fuji in Japan starting with a ride at the Suzuka 8 Hour race. I told him at the time that I had a contract with Honda and I intended to honour it but thanked him for the offer. It was good to know my services were still being sought.

I had nothing set up when I left Honda so Mr Maekawa was the first man I phoned. He offered me the same deal again, racing in the 8 Hour and the Japanese F1 Championship and I accepted on one condition – that he got a 500 for me to race in the British Grand Prix. He came good and arranged for me to ride one of Kenny Robert's spare 'B Team' bikes alongside my old mate Doug Chandler with whom I had trained in America back in the winter of 1987–88. Doug had two bikes but one hadn't been used so that the team could avoid paying its lease cost. Mr Maekawa had obviously arranged to have that cost scrapped and I was given the bike for a one-off race. I was back in GPs again – at least for a weekend!

But first of all, I had to honour my side of the bargain and ride at Suzuka in the 8 Hours. I was teamed up with Peter Goddard who crashed twice in the race and I crashed once so we ended up finishing a lowly twenty-second after having been as high as third at one stage. But it was the British GP I was looking forward to and a chance to ride the YZR Yamaha again.

Motor Cycle News and Castrol sponsored my efforts and the

bike was very rideable but not the fastest thing out there. Still, I'd been quite used to that scenario with the Honda. I had no practice before official qualifying started but I qualified in tenth and finished seventh in the race, just one place behind Eddie Lawson, which I was really happy with.

Eddie was riding for Cagiva in '91 and I really admired him for that. He never felt that he had to stick with the same manufacturer every year like some riders and he enjoyed a new challenge instead of always going for the comfortable option. Eddie could have ridden for any team he wanted but he chose to go with Cagiva. I know he was paid a huge amount of money to ride for them but he loved trying to bring the bike along all the same and he wasn't just cruising around on it – he actually turned it into a race winner which was probably beyond anyone's expectations.

But while people like Eddie could have their pick of teams, it was obvious that there were no new British names coming through and getting factory rides. It's been very difficult for British riders over the last twenty years to become established in GPs because they never seem to get more than one year in the same team. You need at least two years, preferably three, with the same team and bike to perform at your best. If I'd known in 1987 that Honda would be signing me again in 1988, it would have taken the pressure off me a bit and I could have treated it more like a learning year instead of trying too hard as I did. Then I would have been in a better position in my second year to challenge for wins.

Nottingham rider Chris Walker was booted out of his Honda team in 2001 after just a few months, while Spaniard Alex Criville had a factory NSR for years just because he was Spanish and the sport is huge in Spain. This means there's lots of interest and lots of cash available to support riders. Bike racing in Britain just isn't that big and there's no infrastructure such as Spain and Italy have to bring on young riders.

Of all the British riders who were in GPs at the same time as me, I rate Rob McElnea as the best. Few people knew just how talented he was as he was giving away at least two stone to every other rider because of his size. That was a terrible handicap and if it hadn't been for that, I'm sure he could have been a rostrum regular. Rob was very determined and had an incredible amount of natural talent. He knew instinctively just what was needed on a bike and could slide it or spin it up or do whatever was required at will. I know Eddie Lawson rated him and that's about as much praise as a rider can get.

I had felt so relieved when I left Honda because I'd got to the point with them where I was almost expecting to be last in every race. I remember some friends came to see me at Mallory Park and they asked me how they would recognise me out on the track. I told them I'd be the guy at the back! I was dicing with people I'd never even heard of and I knew I was worth much more than that so to get a good result at the British Grand Prix again was a great boost for my confidence.

I felt it was a pretty strong performance under the circumstances and fortunately for me, so did my old sparring partner Christian Sarron who had moved on to manage the Sonauto Yamaha France team. He called me the week after the British GP and asked me if I wanted to race one of his factory bikes at Mugello in the San Marino GP. But there was another reason for that offer other than my British GP result.

Christian's two riders Jean-Philippe Ruggia and Adrien Morillas were having a bad year and Christian wondered whether it was down to the riders or the bikes. Ruggia had tested a new engine in practice at Mugello and said he hated it even though it had shown good figures on the dyno. Christian pulled me aside and asked if I would ride that bike so that he could find out what it was really like. I accepted and qualified eighth overall, ahead of Ruggia and Morillas so obviously the bike was good enough.

The YZR went well in the race and I finished fifth ahead of John Kocinski and the Yamaha France riders and the man who Suzuki had hired to replace me, Didier de Radigues, so it was a doubly satisfying result for me. Ruggia wasn't too happy at being beaten by me though. His dad followed him to all the races and the two of them had a massive row after that race, shouting and flailing their arms at the rest of the team. I couldn't make out much of it but I knew what it was about. They accused Yamaha France of giving me a really fast engine when in actual fact I rode the one that Ruggia had rejected. I just kept my head down in the garage but I found the whole thing quite amusing. It probably didn't help matters when someone had the bright idea of calling me Jean-Pierre Mac-kenzie at that race and the name stuck for the next few races!

I had been thrown into GPs at the deep end because I was racing against people who had been doing it all year but I still really enjoyed myself which I hadn't been able to do on the uncompetitive Honda. I had even started doubting my own ability when I was with Honda so it was great to know that it wasn't a problem with my riding.

The Mugello ride was another one-race deal and I didn't get paid for it apart from collecting my expenses and some prize money, but I was happy to ride for nothing just to prove myself again. After that it was off to Japan for a couple of national F1 races and a round of the World Superbike Championship where I finished sixth in one leg and had a non-finish in the second race.

Christian Sarron offered me another ride on the Sonauto

500 bike at Le Mans for the French Grand Prix where I lost the front in practice and cracked a bone in my foot but still managed to race, even though I fell off, remounted and struggled to twelfth place.

The YZR felt like a totally different bike to the one I had ridden in Mugello and it may well have been for all I know. As the team's number one rider, Ruggia had first choice of all the bikes and maybe he opted to ride the one I had used in Mugello.

I always got the feeling that I was a bit of a guinea pig at Yamaha France for any developmental work they were carrying out. It was the same at the next round at Shah Alam in Malaysia: the bike just didn't feel the same despite Christian's assurances that it was. My feelings seemed to be justified when Ruggia started going better after I joined the team. I suppose I'll never know for sure but my bet is that after Mugello, I was given a different bike.

I still finished sixth in Shah Alam after a battle with Didier de Radigues in which we made a lot of contact. It wasn't intentional but I must admit that I didn't mind barging into him because I felt he was on a bike that I had earned the right to be on after finishing fourth in the world on it the year before. Besides, it was the last race of the season so everyone was riding hard to try and get a job for the following year and I was no exception.

After the last GP, there was an international race at Cataluña in Spain and Yamaha France had announced that Ruggia and Morillas were being dropped from the team so they wanted to test me, Kevin Magee and Miguel du Hamel as possible replacements for 1992. They definitely wanted du Hamel because he was French-Canadian, which was the closest thing they could get to a good French rider so it was really a toss-up between Magee and myself. I had beaten both of those riders in all three races so I thought I would definitely have a job for 1992 but the team still couldn't make their minds up so things dragged on for a bit. Jan was upset by this, because even on our wedding day, I was still wondering if I'd get a job for the following season!

We were married on 15 November in Dunblane in Scotland and stayed at the Gleneagles Hotel on our wedding night and I was still phoning Christian for any news, much to Jan's annoyance. It was such a load on my mind and I couldn't relax until I knew what was happening. Even so, our wedding was a great day with brilliant sunshine and some of my best friends from racing came up to Scotland with their wives, including Rob and Sharon McElnea, Paul and 'Weed' Iddon, sidecar world champion Steve Webster and his wife Karen, Colin (my former GP mechanic) and Sally Davies, and 250cc rider Nigel Bosworth.

When I rang Christian the morning after the wedding, he told me that it was all off and that Kevin Magee had got the job. I was gutted and it definitely took the edge off our honeymoon, which would otherwise have been perfect, as we toured the Scottish Highlands for five days and I love it up there. I have vowed to take Jan on a second honeymoon because I think my behaviour spoiled our first one a bit and I still feel bad about that.

But one week later, just as I was beginning to get really depressed, the phone rang again and it was Christian telling me that Yamaha Japan had reversed Yamaha France's decision and decided to have Magee race in Japan and I had the ride after all. I didn't question why and just signed the contract quite happily and accepted the £125,000 pay cheque that came with it. Thank you very much.

CHAPTER ELEVEN

A Horse at the Traffic Lights

The Yamaha France bike I rode in 1992 was supposedly a bang up-to-date factory model, the same as Kenny Roberts was running with Wayne Rainey and John Kocinski that year.

But it's quite difficult to know exactly what you're riding since favoured riders can sometimes be supplied with trick, new, one-off parts at the factory's discretion. It's also difficult to tell how well your own bike stacks up against someone else's out on the track. You may see that they can get on the power earlier than you in a corner, for example, but that could be as much to do with their suspension set-up, their tyres or just their riding style as it could be to do with a more powerful engine. It could even be a mix of all four so the only way you really know if someone else has a faster bike is if they blow you away on the straights every lap when your bike is flat out. But top speed isn't everything either so if you've got a bike which is handling well, you could still beat someone on a faster bike which is handling badly. It's all swings and roundabouts.

Riders who repeatedly moan about other bikes being better than their own are usually just suffering from the 'grass is always greener' syndrome. Either that or they're just trying to find excuses for being beaten. I like to think I was pretty honest about the performances of the bikes I rode and I don't think I moaned unduly.

I certainly thought the Sonauto Yamaha France bike was good enough to challenge for top three places and maybe even capable of winning races, but in the end it wasn't the bike that let me down, it was more likely the people who were supposed to be looking after it.

The first Grand Prix of the year was again in Japan and it was very wet and very cold. I finished seventh, just determined to bring the bike home in one piece and get some points, but I was so cold I didn't stop shaking for ages after I got off the bike. You don't notice how cold you are when you're riding because you're so focused on the race but it soon becomes apparent afterwards when the adrenaline has subsided.

Christian Sarron, the team manager, was quite happy with that first result but as the season wore on he proved to be really difficult to work for, as did the rest of the team. At the beginning of the season I was usually faster than my team-mate Miguel du Hamel in qualifying, so the whole team gathered round me when I came in to the garage and practically ignored him. It's difficult to notice that when you're the one being crowded but occasionally, as Miguel got faster, the situation changed and the team gave him all the attention. That's not the way to run a team.

Miguel incidentally was quite a decent bloke but he did have a bit of a tendency to talk about himself. He used to send me videos of him racing and magazines with features about himself. He would ask me about them afterwards and I always said I was impressed but what would I want with those?

Anyway, both riders in a team need to be looked after, no matter how well or how poorly they're riding – that's what a team's for. But it didn't work like that with Yamaha France. It sometimes got to the point later in the season when I'd pull into the garage and almost had to find a stand myself to put the bike on because the French were all huddled together and ignoring me.

Christian Sarron was the exact opposite of Erv Kanemoto with whom I worked at Honda. Erv always had the same temperament – level headed and apparently devoid of emotion – but Christian swung from one extreme to the other and it's very difficult to work with people like that. One week he'd ask me what I needed for the following year as if I was guaranteed a job, then the next week he'd totally ignore me if I'd had a bad race. I realise now that he just had a strong Latin temperament but it was difficult to deal with at the time.

I did a year of French at school so I knew a few words but the language barrier was another problem. I asked for an English mechanic and eventually had Nick Davis allocated to me in time for the start of the season. He'd worked with Kevin Schwantz and was a great mechanic and a real lifeline for me. But Serge Rosset, (who owned the Roc engineering firm that managed the team) always overruled anything that Nick and I wanted to do. I think he wanted to have the glory for any decent results we got and was always changing things on the bike, even if I didn't want to make any changes. It was extremely frustrating and actually became quite dangerous at some tracks. I'm sure there was no malice intended, maybe he's just a control freak, but it made for some hairy moments.

It's absolutely paramount to have a good working relationship with your chief engineer or mechanic and you need to be able to discuss very subtle changes to the bike and understand each other perfectly. Technical jargon does not translate very well from one language to another so it's a great help to have a mechanic who speaks the same first language as you.

You've also got to have very competent mechanics looking after your bike and I got a harsh reminder of the importance of that in the Australian GP when the main carburettor jets fell out of the bike during the race! One of the French mechanics had forgotten to tighten them properly which is just unforgivable and I was not at all happy about it. Breakdowns are one thing but something like that is totally avoidable with a bit of care and professionalism. I didn't fly to the other side of the world to risk life and limb in a race just to retire because of someone else's negligence. What a waste of time!

The only saving grace about Australia was going to stay with Mick Doohan for a few days. I love the Gold Coast where he lives – it just seems to have everything going for it. Great weather, great beaches, great restaurants, all those waterways like Venice but without the foul smells – it's awesome.

We spent days simply cruising around on Mick's boat, which was less than reliable back then. I've not seen his new boat, which apparently needs a proper crew just to keep it going, but in those days he had a boat called an Eliminator and he was only interested in speed. If a boat didn't do about 100mph Mick wasn't interested. He kept massive amounts of fuel on board so he could go for really long trips but Jan and I always felt as if we were sitting on a floating bomb. At one point it broke down and we were surrounded with what looked like deadly jellyfish, which wasn't too pleasant, but Mick got it going again.

The other funny thing about Australia are the mad place names, presumably all taken from Aboriginal names. There were places like Mooloolaba and Tangalooma and Wollongong. But I think Mick was winding me up when he told me there were towns called 'Wheelabarrowback' and 'Kickatinalong!' They were good days chilling out in Oz, away from all the misery of the Yamaha France pit.

As far as racing went, my mechanic Nick Davis had all the right ideas about setting the bike up and I just wanted to work with him but Serge Rosset wouldn't have it. After Australia, Serge decided on a strange compromise that meant Nick would have one bike to work on and Serge would look after another bike via his French mechanics. He tried all his bizarre ideas on 'his' bike while Nick and I concentrated on finding a good set-up that would actually work in a race. After all, that's what racing's all about.

Incidentally, I recently bought the bike that Nick worked on, as it had been lying in parts in a garage in France for ten years. You don't get the chance to buy a proper factory 500 every day, so when one of the guys from Yamaha France asked me if I wanted to buy it I jumped at the chance. I'm not quite sure what I'm going to do with it but I might take it on a few track days and let my mates live out their dreams of being a factory 500 rider!

Anyway, I crashed in the rain in Malaysia after running in fourth and bruised my ankle but was fit enough to race in the next round at Jerez in Spain where I finished third, using Nick's bike of course. It was a great race, in fact *Motocourse* (the Grand Prix racing annual) called it the race of my life because I got off to my usual bad start and had to work my way through the field again to get up with the leaders. I was battling with Kevin Schwantz and Alex Criville but I was confident I could take them both before the end of the race. I overtook Schwantz and made it stick then took Criville on the last lap but he was riding in front of his home crowd and was obviously on a 'rostrum or hospital' mission. He came back past me at such a speed that I thought 'fair enough mate, you can have it if you're that desperate' but he was going way too fast and couldn't make the corner so he landed in a heap in the dust.

I must admit I smiled under my helmet then because I knew I was home and dry. Or at least, once I had dodged all the missiles the Spanish crowd threw at me after Criville crashed! They're patriotic to extremes in Spain and seemed to blame me for his crash. But it was great to be on the podium again, especially with riders like Mick Doohan and Wayne Rainey.

In the Italian GP I realised quite early on that I had made a bad tyre choice, but in those situations you just have to keep plugging away because any points you manage to get could make a vital difference in the overall championship. There are on-board lap timers on GP bikes so every time I passed the pits my last lap time would flash up before me. That's really useful because it allows you to try different lines or styles and see how they compare. Obviously if you're going slower with a new line you drop it and revert to your old one or try another one. By that method, you can chip away for the next twenty laps or whatever and keep trying to improve your lap times by keeping a close eye on your timer.

I ended up in ninth place in Italy but that meeting proved far more memorable for another reason as my first son Taylor was conceived in the paddock. I was washing the roof of the motorhome when I heard Jan banging on the ceiling from inside. I went down to see what she wanted and found out she'd just done an ovulation test and the time was right to try for a baby. She said we had a half hour window to try so I had to prove my manhood on the spot before I could get back to washing the motorhome and as it turned out the test proved right and we had little Taylor nine months later. And no, his middle name isn't Paddock but that was one result from the Italian Grand Prix that I never expected.

I followed up my Mugello 'result' with a seventh place in Cataluña but by then, the team was really starting to fall apart.

I was actually forced to race Serge Rosset's bike instead of using the bike I had set up to my liking with Nick. Rosset was accusing Nick and I of having an 'English alliance' and not co-operating with the rest of the team, which was a load of nonsense.

At Hockenheim for the German Grand Prix, I was again made to ride Rosset's bike and after morning practice he decided it needed some oil drained from the forks. He didn't tell me he was going to do it (it was only when Nick told me afterwards that I found out) and I still have no idea why he wanted to do it but he went ahead all the same. The only thing that adjustment could perhaps help with is to offer better mid-corner grip but I wasn't having a problem with grip and anyway, you don't start changing things on the bike after morning warm-up as there's no time to assess the changes before the race itself. It was absolute madness. Rosset was even known to change all the settings on my bike overnight to ones he thought were better – as if I wouldn't notice!

Of course, Rosset denied all this but Nick and I checked out the settings any time I suspected they were different and they had definitely been tampered with on more than one occasion.

He messed about with carburation settings, suspension settings, steering geometry, rear shocks, anything he could possibly change when all Nick and I wanted was a decent race set-up so I could go out there and race.

In the German race the forks bottomed out because Rosset had removed too much oil from them and I crashed. I broke my ankle badly and was taken to hospital by helicopter where I had an epidural – an injection into the spine that causes temporary paralysis of the lower body – in order for them to put my ankle back together and wire it up. Those injections are quite risky and it was weird being paralysed so the whole experience was pretty scary, not least because I couldn't feel when I needed to go to the toilet. I remember lying alone in bed and thinking that the drains were smelling really bad until I lifted the bed sheets and realised I'd crapped myself! I couldn't move so all I could do was ring for the nurse to come and clean me up.

Speaking of injuries, I've not done too badly compared to some riders but I've still had my fair share of breaks and pains. In twenty years of racing, I've had eight broken ankles, six broken wrists, three broken legs, two broken scaphoids, a smashed and dislocated kneecap, a broken shoulder and I've also broken most of my fingers and toes at some point. Oh, and I've been knocked out nine times! I reckon I've had more than four hundred crashes over the years so I've been pretty lucky in getting away with it really.

It's compulsory to have medical insurance to get an international racing licence but the amount you need under that law is minimal. Most riders opt for as good a package as they can get and it's up to them as individuals to pay for it. People like Mick Doohan and Wayne Rainey must have racked up hundreds of thousands of pounds' worth of medical treatment with the injuries they suffered so it's well worth having a good insurance policy. I always over-insured myself and found that when I paid for it I didn't need it, so it was almost like a good luck thing for me as well. I always tried to project what I was going to earn at the start of every season and covered myself with disability insurance so that if I got injured badly and couldn't ride all year, I'd still get paid roughly the same as I would have earned.

After my crash in Germany, the doctors told me I'd be out of action for six weeks but I was back racing in two weeks. The figure doctors give is the time it will take for the injury to heal properly but most riders race again as soon as they can. This isn't through stupidity, it's just that bike racers (or any other athletes for that matter) are usually very fit and tend to heal more quickly than most other people. They're also highly motivated and it's incredible how much your attitude can affect the healing process. It's almost as if you tell your body 'the next race is in three weeks so that's how long you've got to recover' and usually it works out that way.

The Grand Prix doctor who takes his mobile clinic to all the races is Dr Costa and he's an incredible man with a huge passion for racing. He knows exactly what movement you need to ride a bike and has some ingenious ways of strapping you up while still allowing enough movement to ride.

Dr Costa never disputed what other doctors said but he always asked if you wanted to race sooner and if you said yes, he'd fix you up. He's been criticised for that sometimes and I think it's been unfair criticism because I've got no aches or pains from twenty years of injuries and for many of those years I was under his care. He knows how much racers want to race and he helps them do that. There's no point trying to stop them or they would just go to some dodgy, back-street doctor for treatment and still race anyway.

I spent a week at Costa's house in Italy recovering after my German crash and he looked after me really well. His mum cooked huge Italian meals for me and I had physiotherapy treatment every day. That's the way to recover.

It's always amazed me how I've been able to 'think' an injury away. I see normal people with a simple break and they're hobbling about useless for weeks. I hated sitting around so I really tried to move about and get on with things even if I was in pain. You have to keep going and get the body working.

I only ever missed one Grand Prix through injury in nine years of 500 racing and that was only because my leg was in a cast up to my hip so I couldn't get my leathers on!

However, I got another shock after the Dutch round where I finished seventh because the team sacked Nick Davis without telling me. I didn't know until Nick called me on his way home and broke the news. I knew it was going to be downhill after that but all I could do was carry on as best as I could with a team that I had really learned to dislike.

I finished fourteenth in Hungary and sixth in France but couldn't help thinking that I'd have been a regular top five finisher if Nick and I had been allowed to work away ourselves. After all, I'd finished third at Jerez when I had the bike set the way I wanted it but as soon as Serge Rosset forced his settings on me, my results dropped away. In my opinion, that's why Yamaha France never achieved much in all their years as a factory team; there was too much messing about within the team so the riders didn't know what was going on.

I had my best ever result at the Suzuka 8 Hour race in Japan in 1992 finishing second with Kevin Magee as my team-mate. Wayne Gardner and Daryl Beattie won the race so we did pretty well on our Nescafé Yamaha against competition like that.

After Suzuka it was back to Donington Park again for the British Grand Prix where I had a big-bang engine for the first time. It was a new engine design pioneered by Honda where the firing order of the cylinders was closer together, which led to fewer power pulses which in turn gave the rear tyre more time to find grip. After Honda had success with their engine at the beginning of 1992, all the other teams developed their own versions and my team gave me one for Donington so I had quite high hopes for the race and was pretty confident of a rostrum position.

I had my usual bad start but eventually passed John Kocinski and was chasing the leaders when a primary gear blew. I was gutted because the bike had been going like a dream before that and I knew I was on for a result. When I pulled in, Christian Sarron was acting as if it was my fault that the bike broke! I couldn't believe it. Did he really think I'd intentionally destroy my bike at my home GP? I don't think so.

That's when I started thinking that I didn't even want to get a good result for my team because I was so annoyed with them. A good team manager will help you when you're down but Christian only wanted to know you if you were doing well. It was totally demoralising.

The Brazilian GP at Interlagos was the penultimate round of the championship and it was a complete disaster. Safety was a joke: there were concrete walls everywhere, the medical and paddock facilities were pathetic and no one wanted to race there except Wayne Rainey. I suppose I can understand why, because he knew he could win the championship if the event went ahead, but there's no way he would have raced there normally. Even Mick Doohan, who still had an outside chance of winning the title if he raced, didn't want to ride. I've got massive respect for Rainey but on that occasion I think he was wrong to want to ride.

It was a really horrible weekend altogether. São Paulo was a terrible place with animals running around on the streets everywhere and horses pulling up alongside you at the traffic lights – sometimes with no riders on! It was totally bizarre and unpleasant and I just wanted to go home.

I ended up riding as safely as I could to ninth place then

finished the season with an uneventful ride to eighth at the South African GP at Kyalami and that was my duty fulfilled as far as the Yamaha France team was concerned. As a matter of fact, I became the first rider ever to test the benefits of the now-common air fence. It was being used for the first time in practice at Kyalami and I went down in the first session. I was knocked out but suffered no injuries so it seemed to work.

I certainly didn't want to ride for the team again and I suppose they were equally glad to be shot of me. It had been a miserable year even though it was financially profitable, so when Christian Sarron said after the last race that I was free to do what I wanted I was delighted. I was delighted that night too with the scale of the end-of-season party held in downtown Johannesburg. It got totally out of control and the venue was wrecked by the end of it but the owners still thought it was hilarious! I think they were amazed that GP riders could let their hair down as much – either that or they were used to having the place trashed.

Looking back, I'm quite sad about how things went in 1992 because if Nick and I had been left alone to set the bike up I really believe I could have been as strong as any other rider on the grid and it could have been my best year ever. As it was, I finished the championship down in eleventh place, one ahead of my team-mate, Miguel du Hamel.

Wayne Rainey won his third and last 500 world championship that year from Mick Doohan with John Kocinski third on his Marlboro Yamaha.

I remember John Kocinski was talked about a lot in 1992 and not just for finishing third in the championship either! Most people have got a Kocinski tale to tell and it's hard to separate the truth from the rumours but with John, the truth is strange enough. What myself and the other riders didn't know back then was that John had an obsessive compulsive disorder about cleanliness which is a genuine, if mystifying, medical problem. It meant that John spent the best part of every day cleaning his motorhome and everything else he came into contact with. He refused to go into the motorhome until he was stripped out of his leathers and down to his underpants because he couldn't bear to bring any dirt into it. Rob McElnea used to video him doing that through the curtains in his motorhome because he thought it was so funny.

John also insisted on binding up his luggage in plastic wrapping so only the handles showed, the idea being to keep the bags immaculate. But he always used his free Marlboro bags which were not worth much anyway so he could have thrown them away every time if he'd wanted to but he chose to wrap them up instead. Strange boy.

John reminded me very much of Alan Carter from the old days. Both were very fast, very mouthy about how fast they were and a bit weird to boot! But John was a huge talent and an absolute joy to watch when he was on the bike – so smooth and precise. What annoyed me about him though, was that he had no respect for anyone he didn't think was important such as journalists or other 'normal' people in the paddock.

Any time I spoke to John, our conversations always ended up in a bit of a mess because neither of us know where the other was coming from. He once asked me what I was doing after a race and I told him I was going to drive my motorhome until I found a campsite and then park up for the night. He found that incredible. He couldn't believe that I could drive my own motorhome – and all alone too! John always had someone pick him up at the airport to take him to the track and someone else to drive his motorhome for him. But I could never make up my mind if that conversation was a subtle put-down to me because I didn't have a driver or if he was genuinely amazed by my independence. He definitely lived on Planet Kocinski did little John.

Once again, at the end of the season, I had no ride lined up for the following year but my old mate Rob McElnea called me with a proposition of a different kind. He was running a rider called Paul Brown in the 250cc British Championship and wondered if I'd mind riding another 250 in the last round of the series to try and help Paul win the title at Brands Hatch. I thought it might be a bit of a laugh so I agreed. The idea was that I just followed Paul and kept his rival Nigel Bosworth behind me. In the race, Bosworth crashed, which meant Paul was automatically champion and even during the race our team was celebrating on the pit wall. But then Paul decided he had to prove a point by trying to pull away from me and he fell off, giving the title to Steve Sawford. I was quite happy sitting behind Paul so there was no need for him to do that. Anyway, after Paul went down, I ended up racing my old rival and friend from the Pro-Am days, Alan Carter, but he just pipped me to the line after a really good dice. It was great fun and it took me back to the old days riding with him again.

I rode the same bike at Kirkistown in Northern Ireland just for fun and had a good battle with Jeremy McWilliams (who became the first Brit to win a 250 GP since Alan Carter in 1983, when he won at Assen in 2001), broke the lap record and won the race.

I had one more race at Brands in the rain at the very end of the season but the bike broke down and that was the end of racing for 1992. And apart from those 250 races that were enjoyable, I was very glad to see the back of that year. It doesn't hold the best memories for me.

CHAPTER TWELVE

Steak Instead of Spam

By the end of 1992, I felt I had pretty much exhausted all my Grand Prix options over the previous seven years and didn't know what my next move was going to be.

I was thirty-one years old and couldn't really see me getting another ride in a factory 500 team, but I knew I still wanted to race so I just hoped the phone would ring with some sort of offer and eventually, it did.

Former racer and bike journalist, Peter Clifford, called and made me an offer that sounded intriguing. Peter and I had been friends since 1985 and he had run a 500 GP team in 1992 with wealthy American businessman Bob McLean as the backer, and Australian Peter Goddard as the rider. Valvoline had provided some cash and it was a small, but very efficient private team. He told me they were going to buy a brand new Roc Yamaha, which was a bike bought from the Yamaha factory with a chassis made by French engineering firm Roc that, incidentally, was owned by Serge Rosset, my old nemesis from the Yamaha France team.

Peter wanted me to ride for the team with increased sponsorship from Valvoline for 1993 and he offered me a £50,000 deal. It wasn't the kind of cash I'd been making as a factory rider but it was a good offer for a private team and I was very tempted.

More importantly, I knew the mechanics were good and I was told I'd be allowed to do my own thing set-up wise so it sounded like a good arrangement and within a week I agreed to ride for the team. Bob and Peter asked me what I thought I could achieve in the championship and I told him a top ten position was possible which he seemed happy with, and in fact we actually achieved that by the end of the year.

Peter and Bob were very genuine people and great racing enthusiasts and that's what appealed to me most about the whole set up. Peter in particular was a workaholic: he acted as team manager, commentated on every race for TV and worked as a journalist at every round as well. He even acted as team cook most of the time and I must say he did a great job in all his roles and it was a pleasure working with him, Bob and the rest of the crew, which consisted of two mechanics and a helper. The happy family atmosphere was especially noticeable after my miserable experience with Yamaha France in 1992.

It was my first year as a privateer in Grands Prix and I was really looking forward to the challenge of trying to harass the factory bikes and making sure I finished in front of all the other privateers. At least I knew what I could realistically aim for so I wasn't going to be disappointed at not getting on the rostrum.

The biggest drawback was that I only had one bike so I had to be very careful not to crash it. That obviously meant I couldn't afford to go quite as fast as I was capable of going, but Peter did tell me that part of the reason I was hired was because I didn't have a reputation as a crasher! As it turned out, I only had one race crash all year so I kept my end of the bargain.

When you consider that one bike alone cost £90,000, it's easy to understand why there was no chance of getting a spare. Bob may have been wealthy but he wasn't mad. Our total budget, including the cost of the bike was probably about £200,000, whereas a firm like Honda would spend around £2 million a year on their GP team so that's a measure of what we were up against. But it was going to be fun trying to steal a few points off the big factories.

I still felt I could finish in the top ten in GPs, which is why I never returned to racing in the UK at that stage. Anyway, I still liked all the travelling and enjoyed the lifestyle in Europe and Jan was keen to come along too so it seemed like the best option.

Our son Taylor was born on 24 February that year and I was lucky enough to be there for the birth. I had been testing abroad and just made it back to Scotland in time so I was grateful that Jan managed to keep her legs crossed and waited for me! Incidentally, Bob McLean has still got the Roc bike from that year at home in Wyoming and says he might one day present it to Taylor as a memento.

Taylor was pretty much just bundled into the motorhome at a few weeks old and taken round Europe for his first season of GPs so he really was born to the paddock – after having been conceived in it.

The Valvoline bike was fairly fast after we had the engine doctored by Austrian tuning specialist Harald Bartol and most weekends during the season I was dicing with at least one or two of the lowlier factory riders like Shinichi Itoh, Luca Cadalora or Alex Criville. The only disappointment was that we didn't get enough support from Dunlop tyres because we were a private team and tyres make such a difference to the performance of a bike so that was a big disadvantage for us.

Even though I could only afford to ride at ninety-five per cent because of the one-bike deal, I was still confident of getting some good top six finishes. I suppose I could have pushed a bit harder and finished slightly higher up the leader board but Bob McLean was always very open about our budget limitations and I didn't want to let him down or cost him too much money.

It turned out to be a really enjoyable year in a sort of David and Goliath fashion and when we did get a decent result everyone in the team really appreciated it so we had a lot of fun. At one point in the championship I was lying seventh so we were right on target for a good overall position but it was hard to sustain those kind of results and eventually we finished ninth which was still pretty good for a small private team.

I started the season with a tenth in Australia and was the top privateer so I couldn't grumble but I remember that GP more because of an incident in the hotel. There was a reception held in the foyer for all the riders and we were having a few quiet drinks when a car smashed straight through the glass windows of the foyer. The windows were about fifteen feet high and ran the whole length of the room and this car just shattered glass and shrapnel everywhere. At first everyone thought it was a bomb but I thought it was my old mates Stoney and Beggar coming to see me again! Turns out it was a sacked staff member trying to get his revenge but he didn't look like he'd achieved much as the police frogmarched him away.

At the next round in Malaysia I beat two factory bikes to eighth place which was even better than my performance in Oz and I was pretty happy with that. Then a bad start saw me finish thirteenth in Japan but that was after a local rider shot past me and cut across the chicane to his advantage. I protested but it was slung out so there was nothing more I could do and it wasn't really worth crying over so we moved on to Jerez in Spain for the first European round.

The entire meeting was overshadowed by the tragic death of popular Japanese rider Noboyuki Wakai who was killed when a spectator ran in front of him in pit lane. It was a senseless accident and should never have happened: there's enough danger inherent in motorcycle racing without having to worry about spectators running out in front of you.

However, the racing went ahead as always and I finished seventh which was my best result to date on the private bike although I hardly felt like celebrating after what had happened. I followed that up with a disastrous qualifying session in Austria because my bike kept jumping out of gear so I ended up starting the race from twenty-sixth place on the grid. I worked my way up to eleventh place in the race but it was another example of me having to fight my way through the field, which was really frustrating.

Obviously, you lose a lot of time doing that and the farther up the field you get, the longer it takes to get past other riders as they're obviously progressively faster. It also ruins tyres because you're on the limit trying to make up for lost time. If you get away in the leading bunch, the pace usually settles and tyres can be conserved so they're still in good shape for the last few crucial laps. However, by the time I caught the front runners from the back row in Austria, my tyres were well past their best.

Anyway, Hockenheim was up next and it was the fastest track on the GP calendar. Japanese rider Shinichi Itoh was clocked at over 200mph in practice that year and although that may sound mind-numbing, it really doesn't feel that fast when you're used to it. Once you get over 100mph, your actual speed becomes academic because it all seems the same when you're on the bike. It's only when you start braking that you realise how quick you've been going because no matter how hard you pull the lever, you don't seem to be scrubbing off enough speed and it's easy to overshoot corners.

Speed isn't the real kick in racing anyway, despite what many people might think. It soon feels normal because, as a racer, you spend so much time going fast. In reality you're concentrating much more on reference points like braking markers, peeling off points and apexes than you are on how fast you're going. At pure road races like the North West 200 in Northern Ireland you're more aware of the speed because houses and walls are rushing past really close by but on purpose built tracks with lots of run-off space it's hardly noticeable.

When you're racing and testing so much, the need for speed is taken care of and there's no need to try to race down to the supermarket for a kick, so you can leave the lunacy behind at the track . . . mostly. I mean, I still enjoy riding road bikes but I don't feel the need to go fast on them any more because I can get my kicks on track days or in my role as a tester for Suzuki now that I've retired from racing.

Speaking of retirement, Wayne Gardner stopped racing at the end of 1992 but I think he stopped too early because in 1993 it was obvious that he hadn't completely switched off from the whole racing trip. When I speak to people like Mick Doohan and Kevin Schwantz today, it's obvious to see that they've left racing behind and got it completely out of their systems and they're very comfortable with that. In '93, Wayne wasn't like that. He looked like he was missing the whole thing too much and he was disappointed that Honda hadn't involved him more in their plans after his retirement. He'd been with them for a while and I think he expected Honda to give him a role of some sorts but they just seemed to cut all ties with him when he stopped racing. He freely admitted that he missed the buzz, the attention and the cash that he got from racing.

But there was no shortage of fast young Aussies to replace Wayne and one of the best, Daryl Beattie, became a good friend of mine. I first got to know him in 1991 when we both raced in Japan and we became best of mates pretty quickly. The Japanese don't know what to do when people break the rules and Daryl and I took advantage of that quite a lot. We'd drive the wrong way up one-way streets, chase each other through hotel kitchens or do whatever we thought would get a reaction just to watch the complete bewilderment and help-lessness on the faces of the Japanese. I know it was always very childish but it was bloody amusing all the same we had to amuse ourselves somehow when we weren't racing.

Daryl Beattie was a good friend of Mick Doohan's and they just happened to be team-mates too, so the three of us hung out together in 1993. Daryl joined our motorhome convoy as we travelled from campsite to campsite but Mick had his place in Monaco and usually went back there between races. Eventually, Daryl got a place there too and I considered moving at one point but I wasn't prepared to sacrifice my freedom in the UK. To live in Monaco, you need to give up all your interests in the UK and I didn't want to give up my house in sunny Scotland so it was a no-no for me.

But back to the racing and Assen was the next round on the calendar. I had a good battle with Luca Cadalora on his factory Yamaha but he just pipped me with superior speed at the end of the race to steal seventh place by two-tenths of a second.

I had a great race with the Brazilian Alex Barros at the Grand Prix of Europe at Cataluña and just missed out on beating him for fifth spot. I actually thought I had got fifth place because that's what the digital readout said as I crossed the line but a few seconds later it changed to sixth. Shame really, but it was another decent ride and we were lying eighth overall in the championship ahead of three factory riders.

Once again, it was time for my biggest race of the year, the British Grand Prix at Donington Park, and it turned out to be the surprise of the year for me.

Everyone remembers the massive crash near the end of the first lap when Mick Doohan, Kevin Schwantz and Alex Barros got all tangled up and landed in a heap but at that point, I couldn't see who had gone down because I was so far back down the field.

It's hard to know who was to blame for that incident even watching a replay of it on video today. Doohan thought Barros braked too early while Barros thought Doohan braked too late and poor old Schwantz just got caught up in the middle of the whole thing. It looked to me like a racing accident and they do happen from time to time – there's nothing anyone can do about it.

Still, I kept my head down and rode as hard as I could, keeping my eyes on my pit board. Some riders like lots of data to be displayed on their pit boards but I only ever asked the team to show a plus or minus to the next rider, either in front or behind, depending on where I was in the race. A good crew will know instinctively who they should be watching and telling me about so they usually have every answer I need before I've even thought of the question.

People often wonder how a rider can read a pit board when he's travelling at 160mph but it's quite easy really. I checked where my board was at the start of the warm-up lap and then just scanned the pit wall on the way past each time. In fact, there was even time to check out what was on other riders' boards which was quite interesting! If I saw another riders' board coming out at the same time as mine, for example, then I knew they were right behind me. There's other information to be gleaned too, like how many laps there are to go. If my board was too busy with info I could look at the other boards and sometimes see how many laps were left because some riders always have that info relayed to them. Everyone played the same game . . . I think.

Before the race at Donington, I was hoping for a top six position because practice had gone really well. The only problem was that my tyres were going off after fourteen laps and the race was over thirty laps. But then Lars from Ohlins – who supplied our bike's suspension parts – gave me a new shock after morning warm-up and said 'Put that on your bike and your tyres will last longer.'

I didn't ask any questions and just told the mechanics to fit it and it worked like a dream and doubled the lifespan of the tyres, which meant they lasted well for the entire race.

By the time I'd worked my way up to fourth place, only Carl Fogarty stood between me and a podium finish at my home GP and I was determined not to let him stop me. Carl was having a one-off ride on the factory Cagiva and I suppose it must have been good for British fans to have two riders to cheer in a GP for a change.

It didn't matter to me that it was Carl who was in front of me – it could have been anybody because all I wanted was that third place. My lap times were faster than his and I caught and passed him so I felt I deserved to get the result but he barged past me at one point and pushed me wide costing me time. I didn't really think it was a dirty move though; Carl was just trying as hard as I was and I just kept on pushing him as hard as I could, hoping to coax him into making a mistake in the final few laps. It was the one time in the year that I was prepared to risk the team's budget so I rode harder in that race than I did all year knowing it was my big chance for a top result and I was in no mood to be beaten.

After Carl came past me, I could tell that he was in a bit of a flap. I'd ridden with him a lot over the years and I could read his body language, which at that point was reading aggression and panic because of all his really exaggerated movements. As a result, he was actually going quite slowly because he was defending his lines everywhere and just looked very flustered while I still felt relaxed. Carl knew Goddard's (the last corner on the track) would be my last chance to get past him on the final lap and I think he panicked on the entry to that corner. To the spectators, it looked like Carl had run out of fuel and that's what he told the press after the race. Usually, you have to believe what a rider says, and I'm not doubting that Foggy thought he'd ran out of fuel but at the time I remember thinking that he actually selected the wrong gear going into Goddard's, which is a tight, second gear left-hander. I saw his foot slipping off the foot peg as he was trying to change gear and my feeling at the time was that he engaged third gear by mistake instead of second gear. That meant his bike wasn't in the power band coming out of the corner and he had no drive so I out-dragged him to the line. Carl's team boss Giacomo Agostini said to the press after the race that he didn't know how Carl could have made the slowing down lap if he'd run out of fuel.

I suppose I'll never know what happened and I don't really care because, either way, I got third place and achieved a lifetime's ambition by standing on the podium at my home Grand Prix. I'd been dragged up onto the podium after finishing fourth in 1989 but this was the real thing. It was the first time a Roc bike had ever finished in the top three and the first time for years that a privateer had gotten on to the rostrum so I was well chuffed for my team and myself.

The team had sacrificed a lot for me that year and often went beyond what my contract specified, such as flying Jan out to races, so it was great to get a result for them after all their efforts.

Considering the circumstances, that result was one of the highlights of my career and I remember telling the press after that race that our team would be eating steak instead of Spam that night. It was just a joke but Bob McLean was a bit upset because he thought I was telling the world that he wasn't looking after me properly and that we lived out of the back of a van eating Spam and beans every night! Not that I hadn't done that before. Of course we didn't eat Spam every night – just some nights.

We went to a Japanese restaurant near Donington after the race with Mick Doohan, Daryl Beattie and all the team but the restaurant didn't serve Spam so in the end we had to settle for sushi. Pity! I must admit to sinking a few beers to toast our result but I was on a high for a week after that podium place so I didn't really need to drink much anyway.

Unfortunately the crowd was well down on what it had been in the late 1980s but there still was a great atmosphere and the sun was shining so it was as close to a perfect weekend as I'd ever experienced.

But for every up in racing, there's a down and mine came at the very next round in Czechoslovakia when I lost the front end of the bike and crashed out of the race. I remember that just before I crashed, I looked over my shoulder and saw British rider John Reynolds behind me. I was never in the habit of looking back over my shoulder and I don't know why I did it then but I wasn't pleased to see John there. I didn't want another British rider on another private bike so close to me so maybe that had something to do with me crashing, although I'd had problems with the front end all through practice so it's hard to say.

However if I thought that was bad, it was nothing compared to what happened at the next race at Misano in Italy. I finished in ninth place, which was okay but I had to drive all the way to Dover straight after the race to catch the ferry home at 7.30am the next morning. I bumped into my old mechanic Geoff Crust at the port and he told me that it looked like Wayne Rainey was paralysed following his crash in the race. I was completely stunned but just prayed that it was one of those wild paddock rumours which were always flying around. Surely someone like Wayne Rainey couldn't be paralysed?

I chose not to believe it for the rest of the trip home but when I got there I found out to my horror that it really was true. That had a huge effect on me because I never imagined that could ever happen to a three times world champion who was as safe and in control as Wayne always was, especially since it was such an innocent looking crash that he would normally have walked away from.

I remember waking up every morning for about two weeks after that with something lurking in the back of my mind telling me something horrible had happened and then I'd remember all over again that Wayne was paralysed. It was horrible and I felt so bad for him.

Ironically, the next race on the calendar was Wayne's home GP at Laguna Seca in America, not far from his house, and he did something there that I'll never forget. While the whole paddock was stunned and didn't know how to cope with the news, Wayne sent a fax from his hospital bed to his team. On it was a handwritten note saying something like 'Just because I'm not there doesn't mean you can stop working. Where's today's practice times?'

That message just lifted everyone. There we were trying to cope with what had happened and yet Rainey was being the strongest of all of us, cracking a joke and at the same time letting us know that he'd be all right, that he would cope. It was as if he was showing *us* how to cope and it was an incredible display of the guts we always knew Rainey had in abundance. He was the one person who was actually going through the nightmare but he still thought of everyone else in the paddock and wanted to reassure us that he'd pull through.

That accident had a big effect on me personally but it didn't affect my riding at all. The way I saw it, thousands of riders had covered millions of racing miles in safety over the years and the proportion who were paralysed or killed was very small. In fact, just as I thought it would be safer to fly after the 11 September terrorist attacks in 2001, I thought racing would be safer after Wayne's crash because the chances of something like that happening again seemed to be even more remote. It may sound like twisted logic but I suppose every racer justifies his job to himself in different ways. Racing can be dangerous and we have to find ways to live with that.

I wrote a letter to Wayne in hospital but didn't go to see him. I felt he would have more than enough visitors and it was a time for his family and very close friends so I didn't want to be in the way, even though we had been mates in the paddock.

It's not that I couldn't speak to him about it because my old friend Craig Feeney had been paralysed before I started racing and I knew what he'd gone through, but I simply didn't want to intrude or add to his problems.

Wayne came back to manage a team a couple of years later but is now out of the GP scene and living a fairly quiet life with his wife Shae and his son Rex, doing a bit of Go-Karting and some boating too. Apparently, Wayne's actually become quite religious since his accident and if that gives him some form of comfort then I'm pleased for him.

After Laguna Seca, Bob McLean flew us to his massive log cabin in Wyoming (where his neighbours include Harrison Ford) by private jet and we had a great week just chilling out in the sunshine.

Hard as it was without Wayne, the travelling Grand Prix circus had to move on and the next and last destination of the year was Jarama in Spain for the FIM Grand Prix. I qualified in seventh place, which was my best grid position of the year but that was largely due to the fact that Dunlop finally gave me some good tyres as a reward for having had a good season on a private bike. I had a pretty good race too . . . eventually. I say that because at one point I ran off the track and was down in twenty-seventh place. I think I just got too excited about the prospect of a top five finish because I really felt that was on the cards after qualifying. Anyway, at one point my brake lever was coming right back to the bar so I had to adjust it with a dial on the bar as the race went on and then clawed my way back up to eighth place at the finish.

With that, another season was over and I had finished in ninth place in the championship. This was actually better than I'd managed on the factory Yamaha France bike the year before so it was a pretty good result and I'd had a great time achieving it. It was such a difference working with a good team staffed with decent, enthusiastic people as opposed to the nightmare season I'd had with Yamaha France. But despite all that, I wasn't sure if I wanted to do the same thing again in 1994.

After the last race, Jan, Taylor and myself went on holiday to Miami for a couple of weeks with Mick Doohan and his then girlfriend Kelly for a couple of weeks and had a good time away from it all. Then after that, Daryl Beattie came to Scotland to stay with me for a week and I took him out to see the sights in Denny, which mostly meant the pubs. We hooked up with all my old mates and I knew it was going to be a big session because those boys aren't shy with the pints. I mean, I'm talking three gulps and it's time for the next round. We had just ordered the first round when my mate Wullie McKay said: 'Right, what are you for Daryl?' Daryl hadn't even touched his first pint but Wullie and the boys were ordering up the next round. Daryl just looked at me and said 'What, are we having another?' Every time he saw an empty glass he said 'Jeez mate, are we having another?'

But the Aussies aren't too shy of beer either and Daryl soon got into the swing of things. We ended up in a club in Falkirk and he was totally legless, throwing peanuts at the barmaids and just generally being loud. That's not recommended for a stranger in a small town in Scotland because you're likely to get a kicking sooner or later for being a loud mouth so I had to keep a close eye on him. Anyway, later on in the club, the DJ must have recognised Daryl because he stopped the music, turned the lights on and said over the microphone 'We'd like to welcome Grand Prix racer Daryl Beattie to Rosie O'Grady's nightclub!'

Daryl had no idea what was going on because he was so

shit-faced but he certainly won the respect of my Denny mates for his fine performance on the evening. I reckon he qualified for an honorary Denny citizenship that weekend.

We had another drunken session after the last GP at Jarama. As usual, the organisers had arranged a big knees-up that all the riders went to and the whole thing got totally out of control as per the norm, with people stripping off and dancing on the tables and whatever. It eventually got so noisy that someone pulled the plug on the electricity and the whole place was left in darkness. Jan and I were pretty wrecked anyway so we called it a night and left. As we were leaving, we spotted two very nice terracotta plant pots at the door and thought they would look much better outside our front door at home. We lifted Taylor out of his pushchair, loaded the pots into it and trundled back to the motorhome with Jan carrying Taylor.

The next day I was talking to Steve Harris who ran a team in the 500 class and I confessed to feeling a bit guilty because I'd stolen the pots. He said 'I wouldn't worry about it too much – I nicked the plants out of them!'

Anyway, as far as my racing went, there didn't seem to be much left to prove after I'd been top privateer in 500 GPs so I was at a bit of a loose end until Roc organised a demo of their 1994 machine at Paul Ricard in France.

The bike looked much smaller and more compact than the old model and it had the new big-bang engine as well so it looked very promising even before I sat on it. I loved the bike when I rode it and went faster than everyone else at the test then told Bob McLean straight away that if he was going racing again in 1994, he had to have one of these new bikes because it was brilliant. Poor old Bob was a bit worried about forking out another £100,000, which is understandable because he probably lost about seventy-five per cent of the cash he ploughed into any one year's GP racing. But I saw no point in doing another season on the old bike when this new one would just blow it away.

With Bob undecided, I was prepared to listen to Yamaha UK when they called me up about riding for them. Rob McElnea had a big crash in England riding for the Fast Orange Yamaha squad that year and had decided to retire – even though he never officially announced it to the press – maybe he's still harbouring ideas of a comeback.

Still, Rob was going to be managing a Yamaha squad under Loctite sponsorship in the UK in 1994 and he offered me a job riding for the team, which he said would be a one-man team built around me – just like Foggy had thought his Honda deal was in 1991!

It was a good offer but I didn't commit to Rob straight away and within a few days Bob McLean called and said he'd buy the new Roc Yamaha for me if I'd come and do another season of Grands Prix. The deal was done. It was time to go GP racing again.

CHAPTER THIRTEEN

It's a Boat – It'll Float

In my opinion, and I must stress that it's just my opinion, the Roc bike that I tested at Paul Ricard in France at the end of 1993 was not a sample of the privateer bikes which were for sale. I'm convinced it was a full factory Yamaha engine slotted into a Roc chassis because it was far superior to my old Roc bike and felt even better than the factory bikes I'd ridden before. It definitely didn't feel like the new Roc that Bob McLean ended up buying for me to race in 1994.

But by the time I'd found that out, I'd already signed a similar deal to do another season of 500 GPs with the team, this time under sponsorship of an engine additive called Slick 50.

The Slick 50 sponsorship deal only came together two weeks before the opening Grand Prix of the year in Australia, so it was a pretty close run thing. However, I'd had some practice at Jerez in Spain before the first race and was immediately worried about the bike because it wasn't even as good as the machine I'd ridden the year before.

As always, I had to concentrate on doing the best I could with the bike I had. I feel that once you've signed a contract, it's up to you to do your best to honour it. I was actually fastest in testing at Jerez but there were only a few works teams there so it certainly wasn't an indication of how the season was going to pan out.

Again, I was hoping for a top ten place at the end of the year but I knew that was going to be more difficult to achieve on the new bike. We had a few seizures in practice for the Australian GP and then I had to pull in after just two laps of the race with terminal clutch slip. Australia is a long way to go for just two laps of a race but that's racing for you sometimes.

The next round was in Malaysia so I took the opportunity to stay with Mick Doohan for a week, instead of flying all the way back home. I lived to regret that decision as I had the scariest experience of my life that week and it had nothing to do with motorcycles.

Mick had a new boat and he took me, Randy Mamola, Daryl Beattie and some other guys out for a bit of island hopping. It all sounded very nice and it was going pretty well until we decided to stay overnight on an island then woke up to some pretty stormy weather.

However, Mick wasn't to be deterred and he was adamant that we could sail through it no problem. We spoke to some guys on a fishing boat that was twice the size of our boat and even they were turning back for port saying it was impossible to sail. Mick still didn't care and just turned to us and said: 'It's a boat – it'll float. That's what they do.'

I wasn't convinced.

We set off to sea in a four-metre swell with Mick tacking across the waves, trying to minimise the heaving of the boat. I was absolutely terrified even at that point but I was determined not to show it to the others who all looked pretty calm about it. I'll never know if they were actually cool or just putting on a brave face as I was trying to do but believe me, I was really scared.

We didn't seem to be going forward at all because the boat was just being thrown up out of the water and slammed back down on to the waves again. Eventually, the coast disappeared from sight, which was even more worrying and then the anchor came loose and almost smashed a hole in the front of the boat, which would have put us in big trouble. Daryl Beattie and Randy Mamola held on for grim death and crawled to the front of the boat to try and secure the anchor, which was lashing about in the storm. They had no life jackets on and it looked really dangerous in those conditions so at that point I gave up thinking about looking brave and put my life jacket on. I'd rather be alive and look stupid than be drowned looking cool.

But just as I got the jacket on, a huge, heavy, oak dining table that had been securely fixed to the deck of the boat came loose and was thrown up into the air. As it came back down, it landed on my ankle causing it to swell up like a balloon. It hurt so much I couldn't move it and at that point all I wanted to do was cry and go home! I really didn't think we were going to make it back alive.

The whole trip lasted for about five hours and after my ankle got bust up, I couldn't move and I remember being desperate to go to the toilet but there was nothing I could do about it so I just had to let go there and then. But it was so hot that I dried up in no time at all. And, no, I didn't pee myself out of fear, I peed myself out of desperation!

It was terrifying and there wasn't another boat in sight if anything had happened to us. We couldn't see any coastline for about an hour but all that time, Mick seemed to know where he was going and remained totally calm about everything. He looked like he was out for a Sunday cruise. Looking at Mick was the only thing that got me through that experience. Because he never got flustered and seemed to know exactly what he was doing, it gave me confidence.

We got back to dry land safely after the storm blew itself out but that was an experience I never want to repeat. It's weird that so many people have said to me how fearless I must have been to have raced motorbikes but it's just not true. I knew what I was doing on a bike and was never afraid because I felt I was in control. Having not sailed many boats round the back streets of Denny meant I wasn't prepared for that experience with Mick. It's all about what you're used to.

I was just so relieved to get back to the relative safety of the Malaysian Grand Prix where all I had to do was race a 190mph motorcycle. It was blessed relief and a walk in the park by comparison!

It didn't last long though as I had a high speed crash on the first day of practice when my bike seized again and I landed on my ankle which was still swollen from that table landing on it. Still, crashing wasn't scary compared to that boat trip, even though it hurt a lot.

I missed the second day of practice because I was in so much pain but I remember crawling round my hotel room all day on my hands and knees just trying to keep moving. When I went to bed, I actually prayed that I would at least be able to walk on race day morning so that I would be able to get on the bike and start the race.

Someone must have been listening because I managed to get through the GP and finished in eleventh place even though I felt very uncomfortable on the bike. They were hard won points but at least I beat the three other British privateers who were again Jeremy McWilliams, Sean Emmett and John Reynolds, the same crew that raced in 1993.

I got on pretty well with those guys, particularly Jeremy

who was a really down-to-earth sort and a very hard rider. John was a bit quieter and also a very decent bloke but Sean was rather mouthy in those days. I get on well with him now that he's calmed down slightly, but back then he spent a lot of time telling everyone how good a rider he was. I remember him telling Mick Doohan that it was just a matter of time before he would be winning races. And on another occasion, while he was on his third pint, he was telling Wayne Rainey how good he was going to be. Rainey simply replied that maybe Sean should stop drinking beer and get to bed if he wanted to be that good!

It was off to Suzuka for the Japanese GP next and it turned out to be a complete fiasco as I was docked a minute for jumping the start of the race. I totally disagree with that ruling. Sure, dock a rider ten or twenty seconds, but a minute? That's just ridiculous. There's no way you gain a one-minute advantage by accidentally creeping across the start line. The punishment just doesn't fit the crime and it's almost pointless continuing the race because you're so far behind on corrected time. The same goes for the current stop-and-go penalties where you have to come into the pits for ten seconds. By the time you've slowed down and come into pit lane, waited for ten seconds, then accelerated away and joined the race again, you can pretty much forget about scoring any points. That also spoils things for the spectators if a leading rider is punished so it's a rule that definitely needs changing.

I didn't even realise I'd been docked a minute in Japan until I came in after the race and I was furious when I found out. I could have been risking my neck to gain a place in the race when in reality I was only jostling for nineteenth place and no points. I was angry with my pit crew for not telling me via my pit board during the race and I dumped my bike and stormed off to the hotel but as usual, I calmed down after an hour or so and we all made up over dinner that night. It's hard to be rational when the adrenaline's flowing so I hope teams understand that when their riders seem a bit stroppy. It's not personal . . . usually!

Things went a bit better in Spain where I finished eighth, then I had a ninth in Austria and another eighth in Germany. Those were the kind of results we were expecting and the best we could hope for really, especially as the bike was still seizing in practice on a regular basis. This was eventually traced to bad materials used to make the bike's cylinders that had been going oval-shaped at a certain temperature.

It was frustrating because the bike handled really well and steered quickly but the engine was just so slow and unreliable. If it had just been slow, I could have handled it but slow *and* unreliable is a very demoralising combination.

At Hockenheim in Germany, the bike threw me off when it seized in practice and I was starting to lose my confidence as a rider because I didn't know when it was going to eject me. I even started covering the clutch again, ready to pull it in at the first sign of a seizure and that was something I had spent ages unlearning when riding for Erv Kanemoto at Honda back in 1987.

I had a second crash in practice at Hockenheim but that was my fault. Because there are so many long straights there, I had time to notice that some clouds were moving in and I knew I'd have to get a fast lap in before it rained so I just pushed too hard and fell off. Don't listen to anyone who tells you I was rushing back to the pits to bring my washing in!

When I wasn't nursing injuries in the paddock, the daily routine was very similar from race to race. I'd get up at about 8am and have some cereal and fruit for breakfast before first practice at 10am. After that, I'd spend some time with the team discussing the bike then have a shower and relax before the afternoon practice session. Lunch would usually be pasta and fruit or anything that was easy to digest and not going to cause me problems on the bike. I didn't want to be running to the toilet halfway through a practice session, or a race for that matter!

Contrary to what some people think, you don't need to stock up on energy food right before a one-hour race as your body has plenty of resources to cope with hard work for a relatively short period of time. Some riders might load up on carbohydrates but it's probably more for peace of mind than to supply any real physical need.

The same goes for energy levels after long-haul flights. I know a lot of people who think it's dangerous to make riders fly through different time zones on eighteen-hour flights then expect them to go racing before the jet lag has worn off. But for that one hour when you're racing, your body is so pumped full of adrenaline and you're focusing so intently on the race, you don't even notice any tiredness or ill effects. After all, if a lion's chasing you though the jungle, you wouldn't notice that you're feeling a bit peckish or tired – you just run for it, and it's the same thing in a race.

If the races were more than an hour long it would be a different matter because that's when your body starts to deplete its resources, but for a normal Grand Prix distance it's not a problem. In the hot countries, you do have to drink lots of water and take on some sugar and salts just to stay hydrated but the food situation's just the same as anywhere else.

Anyway, after second practice, I'd debrief with the team again, then shower and have dinner. Having dinner is a big social thing in the paddock and the evenings were focused around that, whether we went out to a restaurant, cooked a barbecue or just ate in each other's hospitality units.

One we had eaten, we'd chat for a bit then just head back to our own motorhomes and go to bed. I rarely did any sight-seeing when I was in foreign countries because all I had on my mind was the race. That's all I ever talked about in the paddock too. I was there to race and I thought about it all day and all night.

After 8pm, I'd try and stay off the coffee so that I had some chance of getting to sleep by about 10pm but even when I went to bed, I thought about the race ahead. It's amazing how much it can help just mentally going round the track as you lie in bed. I imagined each corner with different changes to the bike and I could actually feel what difference they would make. If I had upped the gearing for one corner I could tell just by thinking about it if it was going to be too much or too little.

Similarly, if I had stiffened the rear suspension a bit then I could imagine how the bike would feel for the race. I reckon it's definitely worth a few seconds in the race just being men-tally prepared for the set-up you've chosen. It might sound daft but it really does work. The only problem was that I could have spent all night doing that so I had to tell myself that I would only do five laps or ten laps or whatever then I'd force myself to stop. I've even timed my mental laps sometimes and they've been within a second of my actual lap times!

I know some other riders did that as well so it's not as if I was a weirdo or anything. Well, maybe I am but not in that way. Another good point is that testing a 500GP bike in your bed is a lot cheaper than in reality. Maybe we should just have an imaginary world championship. It would save a lot of pain and money – and I could win it every year!

Since I'm revealing the secrets of my bedchamber, I might as well come clean and confess that there was very little nookie for me on the GP trail. Even though Jan travelled with me to as many races as possible, the GPs were so intense that I really didn't think about sex that much because I was just focused on the race ahead. But things seemed to return to normal when I came back to the UK in 1996. By comparison, the pace of life was much slower so I was fully loved up again most weekends. All the same, it just goes to prove that stress really does ruin your sex life, so avoid it if you can.

I rode at Assen with a cast on my wrist after breaking it during a test at Donington but it was hardly worth the effort since the bike went on to two cylinders after two laps of the race and I had to retire.

I finished ninth in Italy then the bike broke down again in France and by that time I was well and truly sick of it. It wasn't the team's fault, in fact, they were as upset as I was with the whole affair. The bike was just unreliable and there was nothing any of us could do about it. It was a complete dog and I ended up walking out of the pits really pissed off again in France, jumped straight into my motorhome and started driving back to the UK still wearing my racing leathers. Not very comfortable!

I was hoping for a better ride in the British GP thanks to my good luck charms Zig and Zag from Channel 4's *The Big Breakfast*.

I had received a call before the British GP from the producers of the *Big Breakfast* asking me if I'd go on and do a spot with the puppets, Zig and Zag who I happened to be a big fan of. It was back in the days when Chris Evans was still presenting the show and he seemed like a top geezer. He knew his stuff about bikes too and we got on really well.

It was funny working in the bathroom with Zig and Zag but it was really difficult not to laugh because you can see the puppeteers' faces at your feet and it's quite a bizarre sight, believe me. But it's good for the profile of the sport for bike racers to get on shows like that and I enjoyed every minute of it. I even gave Zig and Zag tickets for Donington but they never showed up.

I suppose I had to be grateful with eighth place at the British GP since at least it was a finish. I finished behind all the factory bikes but well ahead of the other privateers so I couldn't grumble but it was a big let-down after my rostrum finish the year before.

After the British, we took the bike over to Harald Bartol's workshop in Austria and did about seventy-five dyno runs in a bid to find some more torque and mid-range power as well as some more outright speed. It seemed to help a bit because the bike was going well in practice for the Czech GP and I was challenging Alex Barros and Kevin Schwantz on the factory Suzukis in the race when I had a fuel starvation problem on the last lap. I couldn't believe the luck I was having – or rather, the lack of it. As soon as we got one problem sorted we'd have another totally unrelated one. It was driving me mad.

The one good thing about that race was that Mick Doohan won the first of his five world championships there. He had shown incredible courage and determination to come back from his horrific 1992 injuries, which at one point could have ended in him having his leg amputated. But Mick didn't get to celebrate – at least at the track anyway. He was booked on the first flight out of the Czech Republic because he thought it would have been tempting fate to book a later one in case he won the title. Mick much preferred to party with his own friends anyway, away from the spotlight, so I'm sure he had a few 'tinnies' when he got home.

Needless to say, I had some more problems at the next race in America when my rear suspension linkage broke and the force of the jolt I got knocked a crown out of my teeth. It was the only one I had as well. Jeremy McWilliams ended up beating me in that race and that made me angry for a couple of reasons. It was the first time that I had ever been beaten by another privateer and it didn't help that it was by another Brit. I'm not taking anything away from Jeremy, because he rode a great race and he's a top bloke, but I had my own standards and I didn't like to let them slip.

Neil Hodgson had his first ride on a 500 Grand Prix bike at the next round in Argentina and scored a point in fifteenth place. He'd been doing 125 GPs for the previous couple of seasons so it was a big step up for him and he did a pretty good job all things considered.

I finished eleventh in Argentina then we all headed back to Cataluña for the last race of the season. I was having a great race for a change and was dicing with Alex Barros again for sixth place when my front tyre destroyed itself at half race distance. I had finally had the chance of a top four finish and was robbed of it. I was a bit nasty to the Dunlop technician after the race but within my usual one hour, I had calmed down and we all went out for a few gallons of beer in Barcelona to mark the end of the championship.

With that, the season was over and I can't say I was too disappointed: it was one of the most frustrating years of my career and I didn't think things could have gotten much worse but little did I know what 1995 had in store for me.

I was quite satisfied that I finished in the top ten of the championship because that had been my aim from the start of the season but I was frustrated because I knew I could have finished much higher if the bike had been more reliable.

The team offered me the same deal for the following season but I didn't see the point of doing another year and thought it would be better to give a younger rider a chance to learn the GP circuit. Bob McLean and Peter Clifford asked me whom I thought deserved the ride and I suggested Neil Hodgson and that's who they ended up going with. Neil's not in GPs now but he's doing a good job in World Superbikes flying the flag for Britain after Foggy's retirement in 2000.

I recommended Hodgson because of his determination which I had witnessed first-hand. His manager, Roger Burnett, asked me if Neil could come and stay with me in Scotland to train for a couple of weeks before Christmas so that he could see how hard GP riders train. At that time, I was a lot fitter than Neil (how things change.) but what really impressed me was that he never, ever gave up. Neil crawled home on his hands and knees when he had to just so he could say he finished the session and didn't quit no matter what punishment I threw at him. In fact, he was on his hands and knees a few times over those two weeks but I never broke him. He seemed to be prepared to hammer himself into the ground rather than admit defeat and I really liked that about him. Other riders I've trained with have just given up and gone home but Neil pushed himself beyond what his body was capable of and that's the kind of determination you need to cut it at the top level in racing. That's why I didn't hesitate in recommending him to Bob and Peter for the 500 ride.

As far as I was concerned, I still didn't have a ride lined up for 1995 but I wasn't too worried because I was half considering retirement. I certainly didn't want to ride a private 500 again and the UK racing scene was still pretty dire so nothing was firing me up.

Then around Christmas time, I got a call asking if I'd be interested in riding for the Dutch-based Docshop team in 250 Grands Prix. It was run by a guy called Henk van Asselt and the bikes were factory kitted Aprilias, which were supposed to be really competitive. Aprilia wanted the money up front so the team coughed up which proved to be a bad move as the bikes were absolutely useless but by the time we realised that, the money had been paid and it was too late to do anything about it.

I asked the team for £50,000 but they could only pay me £42,000, which was reasonable for a small 250 team so I signed up with them. Once I had signed, I actually got really excited about riding in 250 GPs again for the first time since 1986. My high corner speed style suited the class and I'd had years of experience riding 250s, even if it was a long time ago.

I didn't think the 250s were going to be any easier than the 500s because every world championship is tough, but I definitely thought that I was up to the job if the bike was.

My riding style was hard on front tyres on 500s but not so bad on 250s and that's all to do with different rear tyre sizes. There's so much drive through a fat rear tyre on a 500 it pushes the front too hard. But if I, in turn, tried to turn the front in hard as I was prone to doing, it wore the tyre out or caused me to crash as the front tyre broke away. The rear tyre on a 250 is much slimmer so its not pushing the front as hard and that means that I can afford to push it that bit harder.

But from the first (and only) test we did before the season started, I knew we didn't stand much of a chance. We went to

Jerez in Spain and straight away it was apparent that the bike was off the pace but an even bigger problem for me were the mechanics.

From day one there was friction between us and I still don't understand why. I can only imagine they had their minds made up about me before we even met. They seemed to think I would have a big ego having been a works 500 rider and maybe they thought they'd knock that out of me. But I think anyone who knows me will tell you I don't have an ego problem. On the contrary, I consider myself extremely lucky to have been given the chances I've been given on factory bikes and, as I've said before, I never really felt like I belonged amongst the big stars of racing.

I knew the size of the Docshop team and I wasn't expecting five-star treatment: I was there to do my best with what we had but the mechanics never seemed to believe that. They had a problem with me from the start.

Whatever the reasons, we just didn't gel at all and to make things worse, the mechanics made lots of stupid mistakes which could easily have been avoided. The first time I rode the bike the handlebars came loose because they hadn't been tightened properly and they'd also do things such as change the sprockets without adjusting the chain tension. Even an amateur garage mechanic wouldn't do that. It was pathetic.

I had made a big effort to lose weight before the season started because I thought the bike would be faster if I was lighter. But as soon as I got under ten stones I caught colds and everything else going and my health was just terrible. It was weird but I'm obviously not meant to be any lighter than ten stones so I stopped dieting. I was discussing this with Jamie Whitham at a pre-season bike show and he told me he'd been losing lots of weight without even trying. We both thought that was brilliant but we had no idea of the real reason for it at the time.

I started the season with three non-finishes. In the Australian GP, the twistgrip fell apart because it hadn't been tightened properly, in Malaysia the bike seized and at Suzuka in Japan, it just stopped in the wet conditions.

To make things worse, just after the Australian race Jan called me and said my Mum had suffered a stroke and the hospital had said she may not have long left so I flew back home instead of going straight on to Malaysia. By the time I got home, my Mum was much better and I jumped on the first flight to Malaysia, arrived at 8am and was on the bike for first practice at 9am. And after all that, almost two days spent in aeroplanes, the bike seized in the race.

We tried really hard to get some proper back-up from Aprilia and eventually they gave us a better engine for the Spanish GP at Jerez. I finished that race in eleventh place, which doesn't sound brilliant but it was quite a tight race so we were definitely making progress. Then straight after the race, Aprilia repossessed the engine for reasons of its own and we were back to square one!

Another major setback was our poor tyre supply as a private team. We were given new tyres at each GP but they weren't very good so the only other option was to use second hand rubber that had already been used by the top works riders. I sometimes used the tyres Max Biaggi threw away and, even though they were worn, they offered better grip than our brand new ones. I don't like to think of it as me using Max's hand-me-downs, but rather that he was just scrubbing in my tyres in for me!

I've spoken to Max in the paddock a few times but we've never really been friends. He came past me in practice at the first GP of the year in Australia and deliberately brake-checked me in the middle of a corner (meaning he slammed on the brakes to test my reactions). I don't know why he did it but it was probably because I'd come from the 500 class and he just wanted me to know that he was the boss in the 250 class. Biaggi definitely suffers from superstar syndrome and it makes me smile nowadays that Valentino Rossi eclipses him in both character and talent.

It's very difficult to explain to non-racers how important good tyres are to your results and as second class tyre citizens, we just had to make the best of a bad job.

With the combination of a slow bike, mechanics with chips on their shoulders and poor tyres, I began to struggle with motivation for the first time in my career. Since my first race way back in 1981, I had given racing everything I had and always tried my hardest to get the best possible result no matter what the circumstances. But midway through 1995, out of sheer desperation, I was forced to start reading self-motivation books. They were pretty good actually and I read about four or five of them that year just to try and inspire myself to keep going. I also listened to M People's song 'Search for the Hero Inside Yourself' a lot to try and keep myself sane.

I hated going into the garage in the morning and working with people who I knew didn't like me. It's not a good situation to be in as anyone who hates his or her job will be able to relate to. Any job is a big part of a person's life and it's horrible when you have to dread going to work but that was the situation I found myself in.

Back on track, we had a fourteenth place in Germany, another DNF in Italy and then a twelfth place at Assen in Holland. By that point, I told the team I wanted another mechanic and they said that was fine but I'd have to pay for him myself. It was crucial for my morale so I paid for a guy named Steve Thomson to spanner for me out of my own pocket. That's how desperate I was to have someone I could trust and get along with. He was a good guy and he came on-board in time for the French GP but everything went wrong in that race. It wasn't Steve's fault, just one of those weekends when everything that could go wrong did go wrong, such is Murphy's Law. Having had a good look over the bike, Steve agreed that it was a pile of crap and said he'd need some time to try and get it working better.

So, after the French GP he worked on the bike to get it ready for the British round which was once more held at Donington Park. It turned out to be my last ever British GP and good old Steve got the bike working better than it had done all year and I had my best of result of the season by far in sixth place.

However, just as things were looking up, I got some ter-rible news which really shocked me – Jamie Whitham had cancer. Lively, daft, young, outgoing, joker Jamie had cancer. I couldn't believe it when Rob McElnea rang to tell me and I just spent the whole night staring at the wall in my house. It was a form of cancer called Hodgkin's disease – a cancer of the lymph nodes. I had never known anyone with cancer before and for it to happen to someone as young as Jamie made it even more difficult to come to terms with. But just like Wayne Rainey had taught the rest of the paddock how to deal with his paralysis, Jamie showed the same remarkable grit when I spoke to him on the phone soon after his diagnosis. He said he had two options: he could give up and die or just get on with it. He chose to get on with it.

From that point on, Whit insisted it was no big deal and went through all the chemotherapy treatment and kept his spirits up, still laughing and joking as he'd always done. You can learn a lot from someone like that and it makes you realise just how petty many of the things are that we worry about.

Jamie had been leading the British championship from Steve Hislop at the time and, incredibly, he even tried to race between bouts of chemotherapy treatment when most other patients would have been confined to a hospital bed. He qualified well but just wasn't strong enough to race and had to concede his title hopes. It was one of the bravest displays of determination I had ever seen and I take my hat off to Jamie for the way he handled the whole affair. He's a class act.

Everyone involved in racing was relieved when, a few months later, Jamie was given the all clear and he expressed his intentions to go racing again in 1996. But little did either of us know at the time that we'd end up being team-mates in the new-look British Superbike Championship.

On the few occasions when the Docshop 250 bike went well (and I could count them on less than one hand), I became aware of just how easy a 250 is to ride compared to a 500. There's no physical effort required because they're so light and they turn really easily because the tyres are much slimmer. They just go where you want them to and I never broke sweat no matter how hard I was trying. When I got off a 500, I was usually drenched in sweat, no matter how fit I was.

The other thing I noticed was how slow they felt compared to the 500s. I remember just keeping my head under the screen watching the rev counter almost bored with how long it took to get down the straights.

Surprise, surprise, we had another DNF at Brno and a pathetic nineteenth place in Rio. Ruben Xaus, who is now a top World Superbike runner, appeared on a 250 that year and he was absolutely mad. He started coming good on the Ducati in World Superbikes midway through the 2001 season but up until that point he was an accident waiting to happen. He crashed into me at the hairpin in practice for the Argentinian GP and I tried to keep out of his way after that.

I finished eleventh in that race and it proved to be my last ever result in a Grand Prix because we didn't finish in the final round in Cataluña.

I had an unnerving experience in practice at Argentina that I don't recommend to anyone – my front brake discs shattered as I was flat out down the fastest straight on the circuit. We were using brake pads that weren't compatible with the carbon discs and they caused them to shatter, leaving me with no front brakes as I approached a corner at 150mph. All I could do was press on the rear brake and change down gears as I headed for my imminent appointment with the tyre wall. There was a lot of run-off and I had scrubbed off quite a lot of speed before I left the track but it was still one of those looking-death-in-the-face moments and it haunted me all weekend.

That incident summed up my whole year with the Docshop 250 team – it was terrible. From thirteen races, I had seven finishes and six breakdowns, which is a horrendous record and 1995 was definitely the worst season of my career. I was so relieved when it was over.

I had even begun to feel like a leper walking round the GP paddock that year. In racing, you're only as good as your last result and I didn't have any results worth speaking about all year so I felt like such a loser, like I shouldn't even have been there. I certainly felt as if I had no respect from the other riders and it was a horrible feeling. Maybe it was just in my head but that's the way I felt. I could hardly look the other riders in the eye. They all wanted to talk about racing while I did whatever I could to change the subject.

But life wasn't all bad in 1995. Jamie Whitham recovered from his cancer scare and my second son Tarran was born on October 29th and again, it was special, just as it was when Taylor was born. I don't think anyone realises how magical it is to have children until they are actually born. Wayne Rainey has a son called Rex who was born not long before Taylor and he said it was the greatest day of his life when he came along. He said winning three world championships meant absolutely nothing compared to having a child and that's coming from a man who was totally devoted to racing.

It's strange, but if Tarran hadn't been born, I would always have looked back on 1995 as the worst year of my life but now I can remember it as one of the two best years in my life – the other was 1993 when Taylor was born. Having kids makes you realise how unimportant racing really is.

CHAPTER FOURTEEN

The Dead Rat

I remember Yamaha UK's Andy Smith and Jeff Turner saying it wasn't easy convincing Cadbury's and Yamaha to back a burnt-out Grand Prix rider and a cancer victim when they were trying to persuade the money men to sign Jamie Whitham and myself.

We certainly didn't look like a dream team on paper and Jeff knew he was taking a chance in backing us for the new-look 1996 British Superbike championship. I had just had the worst season of my career in 250 GPs on the uncompetitive and unreliable Docshop Aprilia and Whitham, bald and bloated from chemotherapy treatment over the winter, had yet to prove he was fit to race after spending the last seven months battling cancer.

But races and championships can sometimes be won by taking gambles and by the end of the year, Jamie and I proved to Yamaha and Cadbury's that they had made the right choice.

The 1996 MCN British Superbike Championship saw the beginning of a new era for British bike racing. In the past, there had been so many British titles (including two separate Superbike championships), that only real die-hard race fans knew what was going on. Casual armchair viewers at home hadn't a hope. That's not the best way to attract major sponsors and expansive TV coverage, which are essential for any sport's growth.

Thankfully for everyone concerned, the Motorcycle Racing Control Board (MCRCB) took over from the Auto Cycle Union (ACU) in 1995 and got the formula and package for the British championships sorted out for the start of the 1996 season. I couldn't have had a better domestic series to return to after ten years of racing abroad.

Edited highlights from each of the ten rounds were shown on BBC TV and millions of people across the UK tuned in to watch the action. And with major sponsors like Cadbury's and Old Spice getting involved, it ensured that the financial investment in racing and the overall professionalism of the sport were taken to a new level.

There were two Superbike rounds at every meeting and at the end of the year only one man could call himself British Superbike champion but I'm sure few people thought it would be me.

Having gone from being a factory 500 GP rider to racing a private 250 in GPs, I had experienced a nightmare season in 1995 and most people probably thought I was going to ride round the British racetracks, in the twilight of my career, and pick up a few quid for my retirement fund. But I knew I wasn't going to settle for that. I still wanted to race and knew that, with a competitive bike, I could still win races.

I first started thinking about returning to UK racing in November 1995. I met Jeff Turner from Yamaha at the NEC bike show in Birmingham and we discussed it and things went from there. I had no plans for 1996 at that point but I certainly didn't feel coming back to Britain was a step backwards, especially after the series promoter and my long-time friend,

Robert Fearnall, convinced me that it was going to be a totally revamped and very prestigious championship. Anyway, I'd always planned to have at least one year in the UK when I finished GPs and at that point I was tired of all the travelling and having to ride uncompetitive bikes.

Rob McElnea was already lined up as manager for the new Yamaha team but having retired from racing himself, I think he felt it was time for me to retire too. I'd gotten on well with him in GPs but I'm sure he didn't want to sign me because he thought I was too old and had been given enough chances. He'll deny it if you ask him but I have my sources! Though to be fair to Rob, once I had signed for the team he backed me all the way, even if he would rather have had Jamie Whitham and Chris Walker as his riders instead of Whitham and myself. Jamie later told me that he tried to encourage Rob to sign Walker instead because he thought he had a better chance of beating him than he did of beating me. Fair play!

With the addition of Whitham, who was Rob's former team-mate in the Fast Orange Yamaha squad in the UK, the Yamaha Cadbury's Boost team was complete. Come to think of it, the Cadbury's link-up was a dream come true for Rob Mac as it's fair to say that he's fond of the odd chocolate bar!

Whitham felt stronger than ever for 1996 having cheated death over winter and come out the other side with an air of invincibility. He was already massively popular in UK and after fighting cancer, he understandably had the wholehearted support of the British race fans.

I had also seen my share of horrors during the off-season. My sleepy home neighbourhood near Dunblane in Scotland had been shocked beyond belief when a gunman marched into the local primary school gymnasium and shot sixteen children dead. Jan and I knew a few people directly affected by the tragedy and it was just a terrible thing to have to come to terms with.

As I said before, Whitham and I may have looked like a bit of a gamble on paper but when the first test sessions came around, we proved that we still had some fight left.

I took to the YZF750 Yamaha straight away. I was under the Paul Ricard lap record in France in pre-season tests and was on the case in shakedowns at Donington Park too. And Whitham, who was still not one hundred per cent fit, was right on the pace as well.

I remember we were both amused by each other's riding styles at first. It took me a while to get used to Jamie's style as he looked so out of control but it was great to watch; so much so that it was distracting at first. Whitham thought the very opposite of me though. He thought I didn't hang off the bike much and said I looked like Mick Grant but without the elbows!

I had ridden a really slow RC30 four-stroke for Honda in 1991 and had occasionally raced four-strokes in the Suzuka 8 hour race in Japan but this was my first full season on anything other than the screaming two-strokes I was bred on. But I still managed to clock faster times in almost every pre-season test than Jamie, who was a bit of a four-stroke specialist, and I think we both knew even back then that we would be each other's main threat for the title. We knew the bikes were up to it but I think Jamie underestimated how hungry I was for the championship because he saw me as a bit of an old man!

The Boost bikes were a hybrid of 1996 chassis parts and 1995/1996 A and C kitted engines. Or, in other words, a mixture of factory and customer engine parts that had been run by the Italian Belgarda Yamaha World Superbike team before we got our hands on them. They were as good as anything else in the championship and better than most on top speed, but they weren't full factory bikes as some people thought.

The team's budget was spent primarily on bikes and technical equipment instead of hospitality and flashy transporters. Our converted horsebox came in for a lot of piss-taking when we turned up in the paddock but it did its job and transported the kit which was all we needed.

We may not have had the flashiest transporter but we had the best team members, the best mechanics and the best overall package so I couldn't wait to go racing.

The team had a press launch in London's trendy Hippodrome nightspot and we were joined by Duran Duran singer and keen motorcyclist Simon Le Bon and his supermodel wife Yasmin. Rob McElnea made it clear there and then that he expected nothing less than a one–two in the championship and in the end, that's what he got – as well as lots of free chocolate bars!

I was also invited to appear on Cilla Black's *Surprise, Surprise* near the start of the season to present a Yamaha track day invite to a bike-racing fan in the audience. It was a bit bizarre going through rehearsals with Cilla when there was no-one in the audience! But it was good to meet the first lady of television and she had a few drinks with us all after the show.

The football legend, Geoff Hurst, one of my boyhood heroes, was in the studio too and it was great to meet him although he couldn't believe what I did for a living. He thought I was totally mad.

The first race of the season was on 31 March on Donington Park's full international circuit, in front of a twelve and a half thousand strong crowd and lots of BBC TV cameras. It was my first season in the UK since I'd won the 250 British championship on an Armstrong in 1986 and I couldn't have gotten off to a better start considering I was suffering from a stomach bug all weekend and feeling really short of fighting fit.

From second place on the grid, I was chasing Terry Rymer's Old Spice Ducati 916 when Rymer suffered fuel starvation problems on lap six and I took over the lead and held it to the chequered flag. It was a fairy tale return for me and I was enormously relieved. It was my first win since 1993 when I splashed round a wet Knockhill on my 500 Yamaha against much slower bikes. But this was the real thing and at thirty-five years old and the oldest competitor in the championship, I proved that I could ride as well as ever, and on lap record pace for good measure.

It was nice to get a pat on the back again. I knew that I was riding to the best of my ability in GPs and finishing ninth in a GP is still harder than winning a British Superbike race but you just don't get any recognition when you finish that far down the field. Grand Prix racing is the pinnacle of the sport, World Superbikes are next and I believe the British championship comes after that so it's a very good series for a domestic championship. I fully expected to come back to the UK and win and I would have been choked if I hadn't.

I had another solid result in the second leg but Whitham was less fortunate. Seconds after snatching the lead from me while braking into the Esses, he highsided on the exit in spectacular style forcing me to run onto the grass to avoid hitting him. Whitham was unhurt but the medical staff who nursed him back from cancer just a few months previously must have wondered why they'd bothered as they watched him being ejected from his YZF in one of the most spectacular crashes of the season. It was his second non-finish of the day after his gear linkage broke in race one.

My evasive action during the crash dropped me to sixth

place but I still managed to claw my way back to second behind Rymer and scored enough points to lead the championship after the first round. Things were looking good and that first win really set me up for the season.

I think Whitham knew he was in trouble after such a bad start to the season. You can't afford to drop points in such a closely fought championship. Consistency is the key and I finished off the podium just once in the twenty-race season and even when I did I still managed to net a fourth place and that's what wins championships.

But Whitham was soon back on form and took his first win of the year at Oulton Park in May. It was also his first victory since his cancer battle, which made it a really emotional event for him and the team and he thoroughly deserved it.

That weekend was the start of Whitham's full-on title charge and he followed it up by scoring doubles in the next two rounds at Snetterton and Brands Hatch leaving me just five points ahead in the title battle. At that point, Jamie and I didn't really care about anyone else and every time we pulled into the garage after qualifying or a race I'd ask 'Where's Jamie?' and he'd ask the same about me. And almost every time the answer would be 'He's second.' It was like that all season.

Knockhill was next up and I was looking forward to racing on my home track again. Whitham is popular all over the UK and Knockhill is no exception but when a Scot races at home he can rely on crowd support and it was great to have the crowd behind me that day.

I survived a crash in practice to secure pole and, on the tight and twisty Fife track where my career had begun fifteen years before, I went on to win both races and increased my championship lead in front of twelve thousand patriotic fans. Knockhill was one of the most outstanding meetings for me that year. To win at home is always special and it helped my championship hopes too so that made it even better.

As the rivalry increased between Whitham and myself, I suppose it would have been natural for us to distance ourselves as team-mates and jealously guard any set-up information that may have given the other an advantage. But the very opposite was true; the more time we spent together, the better we got on. I was full of admiration for Whit. He was a clown from the word go and kept me laughing all year long. I really learned a lot about life in the way he had beaten cancer and just shrugged it off. He was just full-on all the time and came out with the funniest expressions so naturally. For example, when we were practising at the really fast and bumpy Thruxton circuit he walked into the garage and said 'Eeh, this place is like a hideous bloody fairground ride just waiting to go wrong out there.' That sort of thing just cracked me up. He could sum up in one sentence what I'd been thinking about all day but could never express so perfectly.

He was a top practical joker too, was Jamie. I remember one time that year when someone put a dead rat in Rob McElnea's briefcase thinking Rob would find it the same day which wouldn't have been too bad. But Rob went off to Japan and forgot to take his briefcase so by the time he got back the rat had thoroughly decomposed and was absolutely stinking! To this day Rob doesn't know who planted that rat but Jamie has to be prime top suspect although Jim Moodie's name has cropped up in connection with it too.

Whitham's then girlfriend, and now wife, Andrea, became good friends with Jan so the whole team atmosphere was of one big happy travelling family where racing just happened to be part of the holiday.

I had no doubts that Whitham would be my chief rival for

the title I wanted to win so badly. But we continued to swap information throughout the season and there was never any tension between us no matter how close the racing was on the track and no matter how close the points situation became.

Swapping information with a team-mate helps both riders. If you get your bikes working better then you've got a better chance of pulling away from everybody else so all you have to worry about is beating your team-mate. If you don't help each other to make the bikes faster then you're going to have to worry about the rest of the field too. That always seemed like simple logic to me but some other riders never got it.

I knew James would be quick over the season but I was still pretty confident I could beat him overall. We both tried to force ourselves to hate each other to gain a psychological edge but we were too busy laughing all the time so it just didn't work. Another good thing was that we also made lots of room on the track for each other so it was always safe out there. That wasn't always the case with my team-mates and things were very different when Steve Hislop joined the Boost team in 1998.

The Cadbury's Boost team couldn't have had it any better as Jamie and I were battling for the title all year and we grabbed all the headlines and publicity at every round. But that didn't mean we were having cash thrown at us to make sure we gained every possible advantage over the other teams.

Rob McElnea was on a tight budget and he made us use knackered old tyres when some other teams were using fresh stuff all the time but we just had to get on with it. In fact, when I joined the GSE Ducati team in 2000, I couldn't believe the number of tyres we got through. Every time I turned my back someone fitted a new tyre and I almost felt guilty about how many we were using.

I had a good laugh mid-season when I attended a school reunion back home at Denny High. It was just like being back in the playground except that we were all holding pints of beer. I was even asked to come back the following year and give a speech about my career, which I was nervous about at the time but it went really well. I took along a Boost bike and enough Boost bars to feed everyone and it seemed to go down very well. The school usually invited past pupils who had become doctors or lawyers so it was a bit of an honour for me as a bike racer and definitely an unexpected one.

Another unexpected development that happened mid-season wasn't so welcome: I lost my driving licence for the third time. This time it was for doing 106mph on the M9 in Scotland in my Honda NSX, which for me was quite slow really. I lost my licence for four months which was something I could have done without as I had to blag lifts from everyone else for a while.

Still, after my Knockhill double, Whit racked up another four wins at Cadwell Park and Mallory Park to put him five points clear but I was still unfazed. Towards the end of the season I was thinking about the championship more than individual races and I thought I was going to come out on top at the last round at Donington so I wasn't too bothered about James having a five point lead. In fact it gave me someone to chase which can actually be easier than leading a championship.

But as it turned out, Whitham's lead didn't last long. Neither of us relished the dismal, damp conditions at Brands in the penultimate round and we left the wet-weather heroics to Terry Rymer and his Ducati. The second race was notable for me because it was the only time all year when I failed to stand on the rostrum as I finished fourth.

However, I was lucky to race at all at Brands: it was so misty during the morning warm-up session that I missed the chequered flag and did an extra lap of the course by mistake. The clerk of the course said I would be excluded from the races but then backed down and said I could race but I'd get no points. I told him there was no way I was going to race for no points and he seemed to panic because that would have ruined the championship (and depleted the crowds at the final round) so he said I could race if I paid a £400 fine. I paid it but it was a ridiculous situation that could have completely spoiled the whole year.

But as Whit and I dried out our leathers after Brands and emptied our waterlogged boots, we were aware of the scenario we had just set up for the final round at Donington Park. I had beaten Jamie in both races so we were tied on three hundred and forty-nine points and there was only one round to go. It was scheduled for 13 October and it had to be unlucky for someone but it promised to be a great finale for the championship.

Perhaps most sympathy should have been reserved for Rob McElnea as he was in a win/win and a lose/lose situation at the same time. Since no one else was close enough to clinch the championship, our team was guaranteed to lift it either way, whether it was Jamie or myself who came out trumps. On the other hand, Rob had to deal with both of us in the run up to the event, knowing he would have to console one of us come the afternoon of the thirteenth.

What made the situation even more tense was the presence of a Boost bike in the garage all weekend with a number one on it. Jamie and I knew that by Sunday evening, it had to belong to one of us but which one?

It would be hard to imagine two riders wanting a

championship more than Jamie and I did for our own different, but really quite similar, reasons. I felt I had to win because
I needed to prove I could still cut it after some dismal years
in Grands Prix, while Whitham had a point to prove to show
he was fully fit after his cancer scare and ready to go world
championship racing again.

But despite the high stakes involved, we remained close
friends. We didn't even avoid each other in the week leading
up to the final round as most riders would have done. In fact,
the weekend before Donington we raced at Bishopscourt in
Northern Ireland on the Saturday and at Knockhill in Scotland
on the Sunday so we spent a lot of time together and laughed
a lot as usual. Looking back it was pretty risky racing in two
events so close to the final of the championship but it meant
some extra wedge in our back pockets so we couldn't turn
it down. After all, we're talking about a Yorkshireman and a
Scotsman here!

Back home and alone in the house I felt the pressure more
keenly than I admitted in public. There was a bit of tension for
sure but if I caught myself thinking about it I just went out
and ran for miles. Every time it was hurting I thought 'It's only
hurting because I'm going to win it.' There was definitely a bit
of a psychological build-up but for me but it just wasn't an
option not to win.

Incidentally, I recommend running to anyone struggling
with motivation for whatever reason. When I come back from
a forty-five minute run, I feel I can take on the world!

Whitham had a bit of bad luck early on in the season and I
just kept the pressure on all year so I went to Donington
totally confident that I was going to win. I didn't think he was
likely to chuck it away or do anything silly but I thought that
he thought I might just have the edge at Donington because

I'd always gone well there and it was one of my favourite tracks – I was banking on that really. If it had been at Cadwell or Mallory then things might have been different.

The two Donington races were classics with plots, sub-plots, everything to play for and a spoiler in the shape of former GP rider Sean Emmett. The weekend didn't start off too well for me as I crashed at Goddards in practice. But I dusted down my leathers, re-focused myself and eventually came back to grab pole position by two-tenths of a second from Jamie.

I knew that my one Achilles' heel during the season had been my poor starts and lack of confidence in pushing cold tyres. So in between bouts of manic running to erase the thought of the title from my tortured mind, I watched my starts on videos to see where I could improve. It seemed to work as I got off the line well in the first race in front of fifteen thousand spectators and grabbed the lead at McLeans on the first lap, pushing my tyres quite hard.

For Whitham, it was a disaster as he dropped back to third after a poor tyre choice and virtually watched his title hopes disappear. Rob McElnea had persuaded him to use a harder compound rear tyre than the one he'd used in practice, knowing that it would be sure to last the fifteen laps. The downside was that his bike didn't handle so well on the harder tyre and his race was lost. I remember he said later that he should have had the bollocks to stand by the tyre choice he had made but Rob talked him out of using the same rubber as me because his riding style was harder on tyres than mine and Rob reckoned he'd wear them out. It's not that it was Rob's fault (in fact he was apparently close to tears after that race because he felt he'd let Jamie down), it was just a gamble that didn't pay off and racing is all about those sort of choices.

Whitham reverted to the softer tyres, the same as mine, for

race two but it was too little too late. He gave it his all and won the race but I did what I had to do and finished second, securing the title by just four points after a season-long duel. As a final mark of how closely matched the two of us were all season, we both set identical fastest laps of 1'35.78 in that final race.

At the time, I remember there were arguments regarding the presence of Sean Emmett who had recently quit 500 GPs to focus on Superbikes. Emmett finished second in the first leg, splitting Whitham and myself and some people argued he shouldn't have interfered with the championship in a one-off ride but I disagree. If I'd had to beat Jamie in the second leg I would simply have taken more chances and upped the pace to beat him so Sean's result still wouldn't have mattered. As it was, second place was enough to win the championship so I settled for that.

Whitham's disappointed fans pointed out that if Emmett had also finished second in the second leg, the title would have gone to Jamie because he would have tied on points with me and with ten wins to my five, would have taken the title.

But even Jamie didn't see it that way and he took such a disappointing defeat with grace. He was gutted and I was sorry for him but one of us had to lose. It was as simple as that.

I'm still impressed to this day with Whitham's gracious handling of defeat. If I hadn't won the title that weekend I'd have been devastated but Jamie handled it really well. He had to stand and have pictures taken with me straight after the race and he still played with his band that night at the end of season party rather than sulking in his motorhome. I admired him so much for that and I take my hat off to him. I didn't feel guilty about beating him after his cancer battle because when you're sitting on the grid you can't think about anything like that. I knew how much I needed to win to put me back on the map again and I did it.

However, Jamie had his revenge in a roundabout sort of way later that evening. Proving that our friendship remained intact even after such a fierce contest, we got drunk together and let our hair down at the evening's party hosted in a marquee on Donington's infield. Unaccustomed to drinking any considerable amount of alcohol during the season, this was our big chance to let rip, toast my victory and commiserate Jamie's defeat.

As we both peed against the outside of the marquee while slightly the worse for drink we spotted a van left unattended with the keys in the ignition and the engine running. The temptation was too much. Such was our level of communication after a whole season of working together, neither of us had to say anything as we looked at the van and then at each other. The decision to take it for a drunken lap of Donington was taken without a word being spoken.

But as soon as I jumped in the driver's seat, I felt a hand on my shoulder and looked round to see two of the biggest security guards I have ever seen in my life getting ready to haul me out of the van. They started to give me such a kicking and obviously didn't know who I was or didn't care. As far as they saw it, I was just some pissed-up bloke trying to nick their van. Whitham legged it and said to me later he felt it was pointless for both of us to get a kicking when it could just be one of us. But he did run and get assistance from some people he thought could help me like Jim Moodie. By the time he rallied help though, the guards had realised who I was and started apologising.

I suppose Jamie must have taken some consolation in me getting a kicking after I'd beaten him. But I'd gladly have agreed to take a kicking if it meant winning the championship. No problem.

I took the incident in good humour but had to cancel a photo session organised for the following day because my face was such a mess of cuts and bruises!

In 1996, I ended up as the only rider to score points in every single round of the championship and looking back, I rate the first of my three British Superbike titles as the most satisfying because it was such a relief to win it. I felt I had put a decent season together and beaten some very good riders and the excitement of going into the final round on equal points was really special. It was a very enjoyable year.

I would probably have retired if I'd been getting beaten regularly but I was only off the podium once during the whole year. Aside from the results, I was also at home with my family during the week, the team was great and I got on just great with Jamie.

I can say now that I definitely tried harder in GPs than in BSB. I wasn't going to come back to the UK and lay it on the line at dodgy tracks like Cadwell Park but I knew when I decided to ride in the UK that I wouldn't have to ride at one hundred per cent. Looking back, the hardest I ever had to ride was maybe ninety-five per cent. I told Jan not to worry about me getting hurt because I knew I wasn't prepared to take risks and I didn't think I'd need to take them to win the championship. After all, I was hoping to grow old in one piece.

If there's such a thing as a perfect season then 1996 was probably it for me. I mean, ideally it would have been better to have had a perfect season in the world championships but that wasn't to be and if my first year back in BSB proved one thing to me, it was that I didn't miss the GPs at all.

I was happy to be back home.

CHAPTER FIFTEEN

10 Downing Street

I suppose bike racers lead pretty strange lives when you think about it. There's a big contrast between racing seasons and off-seasons and the same can be said for the differences between weekdays and weekends.

During the week away from the racetrack, the vast majority of racers are unrecognisable to the general public. Partly, this is because when we are on television or seen in pictures we're clad from head to foot in protective gear so only keen race fans know what we actually look like. The other reason is that bike racing simply doesn't enjoy as high a profile as other sports like football or Formula One car racing.

There are exceptions to this of course – Italian super-star Valentino Rossi was forced to move to London from his native Italy to avoid the round-the-clock attentions of the bike-mad Italian public and press. But he is an exception. Even multiple world champions like Eddie Lawson and Kenny Roberts are free to walk down the streets unnoticed in their native America because Grand Prix road racing just isn't big news over there.

But come the weekend, when tens of thousands of race fans throng to circuits around the world, the first thing they want to do is get a glimpse of the riders and maybe grab an auto-graph or have a picture taken. This is when racers become public figures and, whether they like it or not, they become the centre of attention not just for the fans present, but for all the pressmen, sponsors and TV camera crews. And that's not to mention the millions of fans watching on television around the world. In a nutshell, during the week bike racers are normal blokes at whom no one looks twice and yet we come under the spotlight at weekends and are afforded all the adulation of pop stars. It's weird.

This double life thing is even more pronounced during the off-season, which typically runs from October until March. Not only does the weekly attention from fans and the media cease, but riders are no longer able to get their regular fix of adrenaline by racing bikes. And racers who have signed a con-tract don't have any fixed job to do to while away the weeks and months until it's time to go racing again. So what do we do for five months when we're not racing? Watch TV? Do the ironing? Shop for new leathers?

My off-season routine was probably typical of most racers. I never seemed to be sitting still yet it's hard to remember exactly what I did looking back on it now. There were lots of functions to attend especially when I'd won a championship. I had to go to bike shows, speak at dinners, go to dealer open days and chat shows and all sorts of stuff. Aside from that I spent my mornings training, whether it was running, training in the gym or riding my motocross bike. I suppose I'm quite sad because I always trained on my own but I always enjoyed it. I felt it was part of the job and never got into the routine of training with a football team or a rugby team, which some other riders do.

A lot of riders have to find a novel way to train to try to

make themselves do it. Joining a club or a team seems to make it more acceptable for them but I never felt that it should be nice or easy. I'd do it on my own and attach a heart-rate monitor so I knew exactly when I was working hard and when I wasn't.

I did have one novel training experience in the winter of 1996 when I went to Cape Town in South Africa with my family and Jonny Towers from AGV helmets to train for three solid weeks. They have really good facilities over there and athletes travel from all over the world to use them. It's also a good country for training at high altitude so we had a good, if physically demanding time.

But usually, if there was nothing to do on any particular morning back home I'd take the kids to school and then train until lunchtime. It's a routine I've had since my time in Grands Prix but I don't think everyone in British Superbikes has a routine like that – I know for a fact that many don't and knowing that gave me a psychological advantage. I felt that I needed to train and come race weekend, I needed to feel that I'd put the effort in and deserved my place on the grid. I looked at other riders and knew they'd done a lot less than I had and that made me think I was more prepared for the job ahead than they were. And I could never cheat myself by not training because I'd have felt too guilty.

On Christmas Day, for example, I'd train because I thought no-one else would and that would make me feel better. Then after dinner, I'd think 'What if someone else *did* train like me?' and I'd go out and train again just in case. So I always ended up training twice on Christmas Day.

Even at GP level not everyone was putting in the same amount of work as me when it came to training. Mick Doohan became a renowned fitness freak with a training regime bordering on the psychotic but it wasn't always the case. The first time he saw me in 1989 I was running round the Hockenheim circuit in the evening. Mick was eating his dinner in a hospitality suite overlooking the track and wondered what the hell I was doing. I told him that I always ran round the tracks at night and something must have clicked because after that, he started doing it too.

He really got into running and we trained together a lot over the next few years. But he wasn't doing any training when he started GPs. He had no concept of it. But he went back home that winter and started training with triathletes and he just got totally addicted to it. He eventually took it to ridiculous extremes and I'm sure he won't mind me saying that! But you can't argue with the results even though he admits that winning is eighty per cent psychological and twenty per cent physical. Knowing he was fitter than the opposition gave him a mental strength and he had many riders beaten before a wheel was turned in anger. Whatever works for you on a Sunday afternoon, when that flag drops, is all that matters and it varies between riders.

Even though I wasn't racing a bike I never got bored during the winter. I would always take a couple of days off training each week and I'd always take holidays around Christmas time when the kids were off school. I somehow just managed to fill my time and catch up on all the things I couldn't do during the racing season.

But no matter what I did in winter there were always aches and pains when I finally got back on a bike. In the first session out on the bike after several months away, the sheer speed always amazed me for a while because I'd forgotten what it was like. Then the day after I'd be a bit sore because I was using muscles I didn't even use in the gym, but on the second

On my way to third place on the Yamaha France YZR500 at Jerez in Spain, 1992. One highlight in an otherwise unhappy year.

Take that Mick. Soaking Mick Doohan and Wayne Rainey on the podium at the 1992 Spanish GP.

Fog up ahead, but not for long. Hunting down Carl Fogarty at the 1993 British Grand Prix on my privateer Valvoline Yamaha. I overtook him on the line for third spot.

Celebrating with Luca Cadalora and Wayne Rainey on the Donington podium in 1993. I did a bit more celebrating that night too.

Best privateer
again on the Slick
50 Yamaha in my
last season in
500 GPs.

One more race to
go in the British
Superbike
championship in
1996. On the
podium at
Donington with
my team-mate
and good mate
Jamie Whitham.
I won the title in
that last race.

Prodigy's Keith
Flint was a good
luck brolly dolly
at Brands Hatch
in 1997. I set
pole, won both
races and lifted
my second
championship.

Being stalked by the Stalker, Chris Walker, at Brands Hatch in 1997.

Brands Hatch, 1997. Title number two but the T-shirt was from the year before apart from a hastily drawn-on number 2.

Brno, Czech Republic, 1998. Testing Simon Crafar's Yamaha YZR500cc Grand Prix bike for the Red Bull team, which is run by my old employers Peter Clifford and Bob McLean.

Leading my team-mate and arch rival Steve Hislop on the Boost bikes in 1998. He pushed me hard all year and it's fair to say we had a few run-ins that season.

Title number three but no, I haven't only got three fingers. My hand was just a bit stiff from being injured. To the left is my former team boss Rob McElnea (purple shirt) and my wife Jan.

Leading factory Kawasaki rider Akira Yanagawa on my Virgin Yamaha at the Donington World Superbike round in 1999.

BBC reporter Suzi Perry chats with me and my Virgin team sponsor, Richard Branson, at Donington World Superbikes, 1999.

Left: My final race, Donington Park in October 2000 with Neil Hodgson, my INS/GSE Ducati team-mate and British champion that year.

Below: I really did think this was my last ever race …

… until I was persuaded to ride a farewell race on the Clarion Suzuki at Knockhill where my career took off 20 years before.

Below: They think it's all over and this time they're right. Despite offers to return to racing, my British Superbike comeback at Knockhill in August 2001 really was the end. I think.

Left: Signing off. Saying goodbye to my Scottish supporters was the perfect way to end a 20 year career.

Right: Scots Wha Hae: with the famous statue of Robert the Bruce, King of Scots, at Bannockburn, site of the Battle of Bannockburn.

Making an honest woman of Jan at last. On our way to Airth castle on our wedding day, 15th November 1991.

I've told them not to go motocrossing through the bedroom! My sons Taylor (front) and Tarran on Taylor's fourth birthday. The little Yamaha PW50 was his present that day but they both now ride bikes.

day of testing everything was usually back to normal and I'd be ready to go again.

The most crucial part of the off-season was obviously setting up a ride for the following year if I hadn't already signed a contract. Despite the success I enjoyed with the Boost Yamaha team in 1996, it was by no means certain that I'd automatically sign up for the team again in 1997. But as the reigning champion, my bargaining power had increased considerably from the year before when I was a relatively unproven commodity on a Superbike.

I received a couple of offers to return to international racing but I opted to stay at home and defend my title. It was just a matter of deciding which bike I'd be sticking the number one plate on.

Kawasaki's Colin Wright approached me to talk about the 1997 season and made a good financial offer but it wasn't just the money I was interested in. The success of the championship in 1996 had encouraged greater manufacturer support and that meant there were better bikes on the grid. Both Kawasaki and Ducati had '96 spec WSB machines and I wanted assurances that Yamaha would have better bikes too. That was the only real stumbling block in keeping my signature from a Yamaha contract.

Kawasaki's offer was very attractive so I asked Yamaha to match it and they said fair enough. I was assured that the Yamaha team was going to be bigger and better for the new season so it looked like it was going to be good to stay home in the UK rather than go back to racing abroad.

The money was certainly better as my earnings in 1997 leapt up to £120,000 including sponsorship and prize money whereas I'd bagged around £70,000 all-in the year before.

The bike kept the same chassis but we had '96 spec factory

WSB engines and that's what finally convinced me to sign for Yamaha again.

On paper, the 1997 season looked harder than the year before because there were John Reynolds, Steve Hislop and Sean Emmett on Ducatis, Kawasaki had Terry Rymer and Iain MacPherson and Suzuki had Jim Moodie and Matt Llewellyn. They were all good riders but I was still confident that I could win the title again.

My new team-mate was Chris Walker, a talented former motocrosser with a bit of a 'bin it or win it' reputation and it was that reputation that gave me a psychological advantage over him. I knew Chris was a big talent and that he was hungry but I also knew he was inexperienced. I thought he'd be fast at times but I didn't think he'd be able to put a whole season together.

As usual, before the season started, I mentally evaluated all my opponents so I could pinpoint the ones that I thought would give me the most trouble. Most of the riders who had moved teams would be at a disadvantage because it usually takes a year to settle into a new team. Reynolds, for example, was new to the championship having raced abroad for the last few years so I thought he might struggle. And Emmett was going from a peaky, two stroke-500 to a torquey, lazy V-twin Ducati so I thought he might struggle too.

On paper the opposition may have looked stronger but I realised there were weak points to every rider once I sat down and really thought about it. I was on the same bike and in the same team as the year before and I knew we worked well together so I had an advantage straight away.

I don't know if every rider analyses the opposition like that before a season starts but I always looked for riders' weak points. Even so, I tried not to screw around with anyone else's mind like some people in GPs do. Wayne Rainey, as much as I liked him, had to beat his team-mates at tennis or swimming or anything they did together to try to out-psyche them and Christian Sarron was the same. Wayne Gardner liked his mind games and Carl Fogarty was just as bad too – he didn't mind using the press to upset everyone but it seemed to work for him.

Anyway, I went well in pre-season tests, posting the fastest times at Paul Ricard in France and at Snetterton in Norfolk. The new YZF750 engine and new suspension parts worked well and I knew it was going to take a very determined rider to beat me. I felt well up for the double.

The season kicked off at Donington Park again on 13 April and I got off to an even better start than the year before by winning both races but it could very easily have been a different story. After setting pole, I crashed on oil but was luckily still fit enough to race and my two wins were the first of five doubles that season.

I felt I was riding better than ever and already people had me down as odds-on favourite to lift the title. Chris Walker was fast at times but lacked a bit of consistency when it came to stringing laps together. But personally we got on great. I first met Chris on the GP trail in 1995 when he had a couple of wild card rides on a 500 Yamaha and we clicked straight away. He even came up to Scotland to go jet skiing and motocrossing with me when we were team-mates.

At Oulton Park, Walker scored a good win in race one but went on to justify his crash or win reputation by highsiding at over 120mph in the second race. In contrast to Chris's all-or-nothing approach, I cruised to safe third and fifth places and kept my championship lead.

In May, it was back to Donington Park for a round of the

World Superbike Championship where I proved I could still cut it with the fastest Superbike riders in the world even on a year-old bike and a comparatively small budget. I was quite happy with my seventh and eight places and I even managed to beat my old team-mate Jamie Whitham – who was by then a full time WSB rider with the Suzuki factory team – in both races.

Back on BSB duties at Snetterton, Walker and I scored a win apiece to put us first and second in the championship. An eighth and a fourth at Brands Hatch was all I was prepared to risk in the dodgy conditions but I won both races in the next three rounds at Thruxton, Oulton and Mallory and racked up enough points to give me a very healthy seventy-four point title lead. And it's a good job I did because my home round at Knockhill almost ruined my championship hopes.

However, before the Knockhill round, it was off to Brands Hatch for the second British round of WSB. Competing against world championship teams with huge budgets and the very latest factory bikes is tough going for a domestic team but I rode to third place in the first leg despite being as low as eleventh at one point so I was well chuffed. But simply out-riding other competitors isn't always enough to score points at world level: too much is at stake and every last point is jealously fought and squabbled over, both on the track and off it. Even world championships have been won in courtrooms.

I was chucked out of third place for a fuel infringement, which made no difference whatsoever to the performance of my bike. We were told the BSB control fuel was the same as WSB stuff but apparently it was 1.5 octanes higher than the limit so I was disqualified. But I got to stand on the podium, I kept the trophy, kept the money and I'm still in most of the result sheets so it didn't really make much difference.

The real problem was that I beat John Kocinski on his Honda on the last lap and he was grasping at points for the championship. It was Honda that really forced the issue. The WSB organisers admitted that I hadn't had any advantage and the company who supplied the Boost team with fuel even apologised and fought my corner but it was decided that rules were rules and my points were never officially reinstated.

Points or no points, I was still quite satisfied with my ride. I had taken on the best Superbike riders in the world on an inferior machine and beaten all but two of them. But more trouble awaited me at Knockhill.

I was caught up in a collision with Jim Moodie and Sean Emmett in the first race and broke my ankle in what was my first race crash since returning to the UK in 1996. But between races, I went knocking on Terry Rymer's motorhome door to borrow one of his extra large racing boots to fit over my swollen and strapped-up ankle. I didn't have any painkilling injections but I shoved as many painkilling tablets down my throat as I could, put ice on the ankle then pulled on Terry's big boot and went out and won the second leg. It felt great to do something special at Knockhill. It was always good racing in Scotland but I was always expected to win so hopefully I didn't disappoint the spectators, even though I didn't win both legs.

However, I still wasn't out of trouble. After finishing seventh in the first round at Cadwell Park, I fell in the second race and broke my radius, which is the largest bone in the wrist. The only consolation was that there was a three-week break until the next round at Brands Hatch, which I thought would allow me just enough time to recover. I worked out as much as I could over those three weeks to make sure I was as strong as I could possibly be under the circumstances and by the time Brands came around, I was confident I would be okay to ride.

I also had a special cast made for the races to allow me to grip the handlebar.

At Brands, I was joined on the grid by a pretty unusual 'brolly dolly' – rock star Keith Flint of Prodigy. Flint is a massive bike fan who has even taken time out of his recording and touring schedule to race in clubman events. He took my wife's place on the grid because she had to stay at home in Scotland to look after the kids and he seemed to really enjoy himself. He certainly proved to be good luck for me as I set pole position, won both races and scooped the championship too.

It's good for the profile of bike racing to attract celebrities like Keith and actor Ewan McGregor, who's another big bike racing fan. Speaking of Ewan, I think I owe him an apology. He was introduced to me in the paddock once just before a race but I had my race face on and was concentrating so hard that I didn't realise who he was. I thought he was a footballer and just muttered 'Hello' at him because my mind was elsewhere. It could have been Elvis Presley standing there and I wouldn't have noticed! But I've met Ewan again since so hopefully there's no hard feelings.

With my wrist strapped up in a custom cast, I think I had already surprised some people by setting pole position but it was even better when I won both races and secured enough points to lift the title for the second year in succession. All I really needed to do at Brands was stay in touch with Chris Walker since he was the only man who could still mathematically win the title. But when Walker crashed out of race one he blew his chance and I suppose I could have just cruised round for fun after that. But grabbing two wins just for the hell of it was the best way to end my most dominant year of racing to date, even if it meant I couldn't sleep that night because I was in so much pain from my broken wrist. Your body produces endorphins during physical activity which act as natural pain-killers so I didn't feel too bad during the day but at night when I was trying to sleep, all the pains came back again.

It was a great year for me. I had led the championship from the very first round at Donington, won thirteen races and scored five doubles over the season.

If there had been just one weekend in between the Cadwell and Brands races instead of three I don't think I could have won the title at Brands but in the end, it was really satisfying and things couldn't have worked out any better.

In 1997, I felt more confident on the bike and it was maybe a little easier to win the series than in 1996. I didn't think there was anyone who could beat me in the UK at that time and even at the Brands WSB round there weren't many riders who I felt were stronger than me. Pier Francesco Chili and Scott Russell beat me in the first race and in the other leg my gearshift broke so who knows what could have happened?

It's a truism that you either want to race more than anything or you don't and in 1997 I still wanted to race more than anything which is why I didn't retire with the title. After having such a successful and fun season I thought 'Why knock it if I can have some more fun next year?'

And winning over the last two seasons had turned my career round from an enjoyment point of view. It had been soul-destroying finishing so low down in GPs on an uncompetitive bike.

Chris Walker was the perfect replacement for Whitham in the team; from the very first day he made me laugh too. I think to a certain extent Chris knows how to make people laugh and it may be a conscious effort to do that but it certainly worked for me and we also swapped info all season and I enjoyed the experience of bringing him along a bit. I think he

learned a little bit of riding from me and certainly a bit of training. I enjoyed passing that along although I never wanted him
to beat me. He made me slightly nervous at times because he
was definitely fast but I managed to keep the pressure on him
all season and it told in the end.

When we trained together I remember his annoyance that
I was fitter than he was despite him being a fair bit younger
than me! That really wound him up but it did encourage him
to work at his fitness and he's really fit now – probably a lot
fitter than me since I retired!

Walker and I may have had a great team for 1997, but the
Boost bikes weren't always the fastest out there although they
were probably the most reliable and had a good overall bal-
ance. There were no tracks where they really struggled like
some of the other bikes did but the big advantage was that we
didn't have to mess about too much with settings from track to
track because we had a good basic set up from the year before.

With a second title in the bag, I faced another winter with
all the duties that go with being British Superbike champion.
One of the most pleasant was picking up my trophy for
winning the MCN Man of the Year award. The ceremony was
very flashy and I was particularly pleased because the award
is voted for by ordinary bike racing fans and not big industry
figures.

Over all my years in racing, I was delighted in general that
I was allowed to do what I wanted to do and even got paid
for it. To actually think that people respected me for it is
something else.

I don't know how much the new Prime Minister, Tony Blair,
appreciated my racing efforts but he still invited me to a party
at 10 Downing Street along with lots of other British sports-
men. Jamie Whitham and Carl Fogarty were there too and

Cherie Blair opened the door and invited us in to have some champagne and canapés. It was all going fine until speedway star Gary Havelock got a bit carried away with the old champers. He was completely pissed and kept farting all the time so Foggy and Whit sneaked off because of all the looks we were getting. I stayed with Gary, not wanting to leave him on his own but then he started having a go at Lennox Lewis saying his mates could take him on no problem.

Lewis was pretty cool about it – I suppose he's used to all that stuff – and Gary ended up crawling along to his van which was parked at the end of the street and slept off the drink overnight in the back of it. Top bloke!

At the end of 1997, I was forced to close my shop, On The Edge, which I ran with some friends, as Motorcycle City bought out the premises that I was leasing. I had opened the shop, which sold just bike clothing and accessories, in Tamworth in 1992 but its closure didn't mark the end of my retail involvement as I'm still a director of Allan Duffus Motorcycles in Scotland.

As far as racing went, I think I rode better in 1997 than I had ever ridden, certainly in the UK and maybe even in my whole career. But I knew that I would have to ride every bit as hard in 1998 if I wanted to make it a title triple. I felt that twice was nice but three times would really underline the fact. It was definitely my ambition to do the hat trick in 1998 as no rider had won three before and I knew this would be something special.

CHAPTER SIXTEEN

The Mackenzie Shuffle

My campaign for a third straight British Superbike title produced some of the fiercest battles I'd ever been involved in and my arch enemy was one of my own countrymen – Steve Hislop.

Hislop was my nemesis throughout the season and he pushed me harder than anybody else had since I returned to the UK race scene three years before.

But before the racing got underway, I had to go through the usual bargaining process of setting up a new deal. As a double BSB champion, I had several good offers for 1998, one of which was a big money deal to race in America. Vance & Hines Ducati approached me at the end of 1997 and expressed some interest but I didn't really pursue things much farther. Some of the circuits in the States are a bit dodgy so there would have been a greater risk involved if I'd been riding hard and as I didn't want to go there and just cruise round for the money, I decided against the idea.

I was racing because I enjoyed it and I didn't want to race, even for big bucks, if that wasn't going to be the case. I didn't have millions in the bank but I wasn't exactly on the breadline either, so with Yamaha being keen to keep me it just sounded like more fun staying in the UK and working with a team that I liked and worked well with.

But the atmosphere in our pit lane garages during '98 wasn't as light-hearted as the last two years had been with Jamie Whitham and Chris Walker as team-mates. Everything changed when Steve Hislop joined the squad.

Like Walker before him, Hislop had agreed to ride without being paid. Yamaha didn't have the budget for two riders so whoever took the second ride, was doing it because the bike was good enough to win on and to most riders, that's more important than getting paid. Once you've really proved yourself, the money soon starts coming in.

Hizzy relied solely on personal sponsorship deals with helmet and leathers companies and prize money (£1000 for a race win and an extra £1000 bonus from the team) for his income. To this day, Steve complains that he doesn't make much money from the sport which is very unusual for some-one of his pace and talent.

I was being paid pretty well that year so I couldn't complain. I netted about £130,000 that season after I'd included my own personal sponsorship deals and prize money. I suppose that was just one more incentive for Steve to try to beat me; he probably wanted to prove to Yamaha that he was worth a decent salary and the way he rode that year, I think he certainly proved that.

But Hislop is a complex rider. On pure road courses like the Isle of Man TT where he made his name he was virtually unbeatable but on short circuits he tended to blow hot or cold. With a good set up, Steve was as fast as anyone, but if things weren't quite perfect, he had been known to throw in the towel. For example, he finished last in one of the races at Thruxton in 1997 and was booted out of his Ducati team.

But just two rounds later he was back on the podium on a Kawasaki!

I didn't know Steve very well when he joined the team and I still don't. Of course, we still speak to each other but we've never been real 'let's go for a pint' type of mates. I don't know if he's got any really close mates and I never really knew where I stood with him.

But if I made one mistake in 1998, it was underestimating Hizzy as a threat for the championship. Deep down, I thought I was just going to clear off and win the title again after having such a dominant year in 1997. But Steve was always close to me in testing and when the races came along he was still right up there with me and I really had to dig deep to beat him.

Before the season got underway, I was invited to Australia and Malaysia to help test the Red Bull Yamaha YZR 500cc Grand Prix bike. As far as I was concerned, the test would offer more valuable time on a bike as well as being a chance to escape the Scottish winter climate for a few weeks. But it was also good to be invited as it seemed to show that people still valued my set-up abilities on a GP bike and I actually signed a deal to test for the team (which was run by my former employers Peter Clifford and Bob McLean) all season.

Back in the UK, I was honoured with the Jim Clark Memorial Award by the Association of Scottish Motoring Writers and was expected to attend a ceremony at the world famous Gleneagles Hotel. But even though I was flattered to be chosen for the award, I already had a sports dinner to attend where myself and Falkirk Football Club manager Alec Totten were to give talks as former pupils of Denny High School so I felt I couldn't disappoint the organisers of that. The writers had to throw a hasty afternoon tea party to give me my accolade instead.

Getting back to business, the 1998 Boost bikes featured a lot of new factory parts to bring them up to World Superbike specification. We had new engine and suspension parts and new exhaust systems which all helped but with eleven other factory bikes on the grid and a bunch of former Grand Prix and World Superbike racers riding them, it looked like being the toughest BSB season ever. But that would all be good for the spectators and the armchair viewers at home were getting a better deal too. There was a lot more television coverage than ever before with footage being beamed to around fifty countries worldwide including extended coverage on BBC Grandstand.

The first race in any championship is rarely indicative of how the overall season will unfold and the opener at the Brands Hatch Indy circuit on 29 March was no exception with me and Hislop only managing to place sixth and seventh respectively. But we were both on the pace in the second leg and ended up taking first and second places. I won the race after I had made some suspension changes from the first leg but Hislop had fired an early warning shot for the title. I knew he meant business.

The real drama didn't begin until the second round at Oulton Park in Cheshire. Hizzy and I began what would eventually become a running battle both on the track and in the motorcycling press. I was fourth and Hislop was ninth in the damp opening leg but Hizzy came out with all guns firing in the second race and claimed his first victory of the season. Sounds simple enough on paper but I was less than pleased about the way he did it.

I was leading on the last lap and thought a win was in the bag until Hizzy just barged past me in the last corner. I suppose that's what I was used to doing to other people in GPs but it just particularly rattled me for some reason. I wasn't impressed with it at all.

With the luxury of hindsight, I'm glad Steve did that because it really fired me up and I couldn't wait to get to the next race to beat him. I felt he'd started something serious and I was ready to play ball if that was the way he wanted it. Whatever I had to do to keep my title, I was prepared to do it.

The next round was at Thruxton and that was the first time we actually made contact. I won the first race quite comfortably but in the second there was a bit of pushing and shoving and I forced my way past Hislop and got the result. Our team boss, Rob McElnea, was still smiling at that point because Steve and I were still finishing races up front but that was soon to change.

To be fair, Hislop shrugged off that move at Thruxton and said he accepted it but I was starting to feel there was a real needle between us as the battle for the title heated up. I think Rob Mac was behind Steve at that race because he was the underdog and he probably thought it was about time that someone started beating me.

But there's only so long that racers can get away with planting desperate moves on each other. Things were bound to get out of control sooner or later and sure enough, at Snetterton, they did.

When you're riding for a team, the overall good of the team is supposed to come before any individual rider's ambitions. In other words, the worst thing a rider can do is knock his own team-mate off the track but that's exactly what I did to Hislop at Snetterton in the second race after he had won the opening leg.

Steve led into the last chicane and I was second but I turned a secure one–two for Cadbury's Boost into a third and fourth for the team and needless to say, I wasn't the most popular person in the garage after the race. I admit now that it was probably my fault but at the time, I dug in and fought my corner. Hislop obviously wasn't happy and told the press that there was no gap for me to go for and I shouldn't have made the move, which I suppose was fair comment.

But I had to make moves like that to get past Stevie because of the way he rode. Every time I tried to pass him he leaned on me so I had to grit my teeth and force a way through whereas a rider like Jamie Whitham always allowed me plenty of room and I did the same for him. When you lean on somebody it holds you both up and that means other riders can catch you up.

Steve had done that a few times so I knew that at Snetterton I would really have to shove my way past but it all went pear-shaped and we both ran off the track, though fortunately we stayed on the bikes. I didn't like having to do that kind of stuff but Hizzy set the rules (the rules being that there were no rules) back at Oulton and I was prepared to play by them even if it got dangerous because I really wanted a third championship title.

Rob McElnea was fuming over the incident at Snetterton and it was the first time I'd ever experienced any friction in the Boost team. I'm sure Rob thought my little mishap made a mockery of him, the team and the sponsors, losing first and second places as I did and the fact that I never apologised to him probably didn't help. But it's not like I tried to knock Steve off; it was just a racing incident and I can't really be sorry for that.

So for the first time in three years there was a bad atmosphere in the team and I even fell out with Rob over that for the first time since we'd known each other way back in the early 1980s. We didn't speak for a week or so and up to that point we had spoken to each other every day. But once we'd had a bit of space and time to cool off, we soon made up. Racing's not worth losing friends over and Rob was, and is, a very good friend.

Incidentally, I had a bit of a stalker during my years with the Boost team. A girl always used to stand just outside the garage at every meeting and stare at me but never spoke to me. She looked perfectly normal but I could tell something wasn't quite right, if you know what I mean. Then one weekend, she turned up with a Niall Mackenzie replica leather suit exactly the same as mine in every detail right down to the sponsors' patches. The only difference was that instead of 'Mackenzie' on the back she had 'Miss Chief.' That got me worried a bit. How much mischief was she going to get up to? I used to say hello to the girl but whenever I did she started shaking and looked nervous. It was very strange.

But that was an exception. As a rule, I don't get recognised that often except at bike shows and stuff because any time I'm on the telly I have a helmet on so nobody knows what I actually look like! I do get lots of letters from bike racing fans though and some of those have just been addressed to 'Niall Mackenzie, Scotland' so it's quite amazing that I ever got them. On one occasion, I got a letter from a family in England saying they'd cheered me on at the British GP the year before but couldn't afford to go to the next one so could I send a signed postcard? I was more than happy to oblige and the following year I sent a signed T-shirt when the same family requested one of those. But I had to stop responding the following year as things started getting a bit cheeky.

They told me they couldn't afford to go to the GP again as usual and couldn't afford a satellite dish to watch it on TV either so would I be kind enough to send them the money to buy a satellite dish so they could cheer me on at home! I thought 'You've taken that too far. What's next? My bike? My car? My house? A holiday in the Maldives?'

Needless to say, I had to decline the request. Much as I appreciate all the support I've had over the years, I can't afford to buy everyone a satellite dish!

My ten point lead over Hislop going into the next round at Donington was turned into a seven point disadvantage after I crashed in the first race due to a wrong tyre choice. After that, Hizzy was leading the championship but I didn't have a problem with that because I thought he would crack while leading the series. Before Donington, all he had to do was follow me and play catch up so I thought he would feel the pressure more being in the lead and that was fine by me.

I remember at that point Steve said that the next three tracks, which were Knockhill, Mallory and Cadwell, would suit him perfectly but that prediction came to nothing when he fell off in the first leg at Knockhill and I went on to win both races there.

I knew Steve was going to struggle in the first race at Knockhill when he came into the garage in a panic because his girlfriend had messed up the carpet in his motorhome with her muddy boots. Rob Mac was trying to calm him down but he was stressing so much, I knew he'd have a poor race. That kind of stuff really seemed to affect Steve.

However, in the second leg he was with me for the whole race and broke the lap record on just about every lap – mostly because he'd got his motorhome cleaned up and Rob had sorted him out.

Two wins at Knockhill put me back in the championship lead and then it was back down south to Mallory Park where, unusually, I was the only Boost rider to get on the podium all weekend with a second place in the second leg.

In the first race I got tangled up with Aussie Troy Bayliss (who went on to become the 2001 World Superbike champion) when he crashed in front of me at the hairpin and I remounted to finish seventh. Steve finished sixth and seventh in the two races. For a team so used to scoring firsts and seconds it could have been viewed as a disastrous weekend. But for me, the real battle was with Steve and I came away from Mallory with a bigger lead than I had going in (forty-one points as opposed to thirty-one points) so I, for one, counted the weekend a success.

Cadwell Park was next up and I've never been a fan of the circuit, particularly the tight woodland section where there's about as much run-off as you'd find at the Isle of Man TT. I had even more reason to feel nervous after my title-threatening crash there the year before and I still had bad memories of my big crash in 1986 when I broke my leg.

But it was Hislop who fell to the Cadwell curse in practice at the same Barn corner that had claimed me one year before. He dislocated some bones in his wrist joint, broke a bone in his wrist, and suffered some tendon damage as well as breaking some bones in his foot. That sounds bad but I've known riders who have came back from similar injuries pretty quickly. Even so, Steve now looked to be out of contention for the championship with the next round at Silverstone being just one week away.

Unbelievably, I had *another* two crashes at Cadwell. First I was highsided at Mansfield Corner in practice and knocked out, then I crashed *again* at Barn corner in the first race. This time it was Chris Walker's bike that literally flew into my path and resulted in one of the most horrific looking crashes of my career. My gear lever skewered its way through my left foot as the Yamaha and I went end over end. I was completely upside down at one point facing the Tarmac and wondering when I was going to land. Houston, I have a problem.

Hislop's hopes must have been given a new boost (pardon the pun) when he saw Walker and I crash, but I managed to make the restart after having six stitches hurriedly sewn into my foot. I finished fifth in the restart and seventh in the next race to keep my championship hopes alive so I was pretty pleased with that.

A disappointing second and sixth at Silverstone for me meant my old team-mate Walker, who had won three races on the trot before arriving at Silverstone, was now in with a very slim chance of the championship – there were fifty-seven points between us with a hundred still to play for.

Hislop, incidentally, didn't turn up at Silverstone and didn't score any brownie points with the Boost team for being absent. When he got busted up at Cadwell, I thought he'd still be back at Silverstone to ride, or at least try to ride, but he didn't turn up. I felt that I had come back from worse injuries before and it was a surprise to both Rob and myself when he didn't show. Rob wasn't too impressed.

But when Hizzy did show up two weeks later at Brands Hatch, he was on good form winning the first leg from John Reynolds on the Ducati while I trailed home in fourth place just behind Walker.

Even though Walker finished in front of me again in the second leg with a second place to my third, I had done enough to win the championship for a third time. With just fifty points left to play for and a fifty point gap between us, Walker couldn't have matched my podium record even if he won both of the last two legs and I had failed to finish them both. I had done the triple and I was very happy. It was a perfect ending to a very tough year.

There was also a happy ending to the feud between Hizzy and myself too. Since he had no chance of taking the championship, he rode shotgun for me at Brands, keeping the rest of the pack off my tail. He did a sterling job, making his YZF wider than a bus, and I went to see him in his motorhome later and thanked him for helping me. I gave him a Kevin Schwantz book as a peace offering and we shook hands so I hope that stuff's all behind us now.

Compared to the way in which I won the title in 1997, winning the 1998 crown was a relatively subdued affair but I felt the achievement was actually greater. I'd had to dig deeper than ever to beat Steve Hislop and I think I proved I was still prepared to have a dog fight if it came down to it.

Winning the treble was a great achievement for me and ironically, I still owe some thanks to Hislop for helping me do it. He said a lot of things to journalists during the season and they learned to wrap him round their little fingers. He would come out with just the kind of quotes they wanted whereas I usually preferred not to say anything, and when I read what he said about me, it really wound me up.

I realise now that it only served to make me faster and more determined to beat him so in the end it worked in my favour. If he'd been my best mate all season and never wound me up he might well have won the title that year because he rode really well. But as it was, my whole year focused around beating him and in the end I managed it.

I don't suppose it's the first time a rider has been inspired to victory because of an arch-rival, as Kenny Roberts and Barry Sheene or Valentino Rossi and Max Biaggi would tell you. But Scottish riders are usually renowned for sticking together in paddocks whether they're in the same team or not. Steve and I just weren't like that and I'm still not sure why. I don't think it was a case of in-house Scottish rivalry with each of us determined to prove ourselves as Scotland's best racer. It was just a battle at every race to win and it could have been anybody I was racing, from England, Australia or wherever. I had been really confident of winning at the start of the year but Steve was such a fly in the ointment; a bloody inconvenience giving me such a hard time. But it's better to have a worthy rival than to beat a lame field.

Deep down, I think Steve had a bit of a chip on his shoulder because he felt he was every bit as good as the likes of Foggy, Whitham and myself. But in a way he'd been left behind in the UK while we'd gone on to do other things at world level.

Despite everything, the intense rivalry between us ended on a humorous note at an end of season party in Scunthorpe thrown by Rob Mac who could by then afford to breathe freely again. Jamie Whitham pronounced Hislop guilty of dirty riding and punished him with a custard pie in the face. It seems only fair that I should have suffered the same fate for my move at Snetterton but Whit was acting as judge and jury so I couldn't argue with him, could I?

I had another interesting experience post-season when I was invited to the BBC Sports Personality of the Year awards, as I had been every year when I'd won the championship.

But that year I had one of my 'What the hell am I doing here moments?' when I found myself up on the dance floor alongside boxing legend George Foreman!

I was doing the Mackenzie shuffle on the dance floor (not a graceful sight) all by myself and then Foreman got up and started doing his bit too, about as gracefully as me I might add. Then, Olympic athlete, Michael Johnson joined in and that was when I totally lost the plot. What was a little bloke from Fankerton who raced motorbikes doing on the dance floor with legends like that? I couldn't believe it but I was chuffed to bits and just kept grooving while all the time reminding myself that the big bloke next to me actually fought Muhammad Ali in the all-time classic 'Rumble in the Jungle' fight in Africa in 1967 when I was just a boy. It was totally bizarre but I wasn't complaining. I would have been happy to dance all night.

I suppose I should have been thinking about retiring after winning a third straight title but I didn't really give it much serious thought and Jan certainly never put any pressure on me to quit. Jan wasn't the sort of person to sit at the side of the track worrying anyway as she'd never known anything different since we'd met back in 1985. Even so, I might have considered retiring if I hadn't seen a photo of Yamaha's new R7. As soon as I saw the first picture of that bike I just knew I had to ride it. It looked like it had been built for me and I knew there and then that I'd have to do at least one more season. Well, you would, wouldn't you?

CHAPTER SEVENTEEN

Like a Virgin

Cadbury's Boost had been a great, high-profile sponsor and it was a bit of a blow when they withdrew their support for the Yamaha team to concentrate on other projects.

As far as we were concerned, we had delivered the title for the last three seasons so we had done everything that could have been expected of us. But it had always been a three-year deal with the company and when that time was up they decided to spend their money elsewhere which was their decision and fair enough. It was an amicable split but a disappointing one, certainly from my point of view, as I had to start paying for chocolate bars again.

But the fact remained that the Yamaha team had no title sponsor for the forthcoming 1999 season although, to be honest, I didn't worry about it initially because I thought that as the number one team, we'd have no problems in finding a replacement sponsor. How wrong I was.

By the time December came around, there was still no movement on the sponsor front although I had a really good offer of £80,000 from Suzuki and Kawasaki also showed an interest so I was pretty sure I would get something sorted out. But I told both of those teams that I really wanted to ride for

Yamaha again on the new R7 and didn't want to commit to anyone else before I knew what they were doing.

Yamaha never actually admitted it, but I think it would have suited them if I'd just gone away after the 1998 season. Going racing was a big hassle for them at that point as they had too many other things going on at the time and they didn't have the budget to go racing without a major sponsor. I'm sure Yamaha would have been happy to take a year out and re-focus their efforts again in 2000 but I really wanted to ride their bike and I wasn't about to go away.

By the time I suspected their lack of enthusiasm though, it was too late to sign for any other team because all the positions had been taken. It was Yamaha or nothing. So from December onwards, Rob McElnea and I turned into bike racing's equivalent of double glazing salesmen spending every day on the telephone trying to find some cash. We asked everyone we came into contact with if they'd like to back our team. Yamaha said they would supply the bikes and a team transporter if Rob and I could find the sponsorship so ultimately it was down to us if we went racing again. I started dreaming up loads of mad ways to fund a season and although I didn't mention it to Jan, I even considered funding the team myself. I was just so desperate to race that R7.

Rob and I approached lots of companies and presented them with all these ideas as to how they could fund the team and benefit their business at the same time. Many said yes, they were interested, but nothing actually came of it all. People are very good at promising cash but not so hot on delivering it.

We spent the whole winter knocking on doors and phoning around and it wasn't much fun but eventually Rob struck gold. He was talking to someone from the Virgin Limo Bike Service and managed to put Yamaha in touch with Richard

Branson's right hand man, Wil Whitehorn, who then ran the idea past Branson himself. Branson's usual policy is to go with the underdog and he didn't really see a triple championship-wining team as underdogs, but given our desperate circumstances (the racing season was only one week away when we signed the deal), he decided to make an exception. The whole affair was sealed in just twenty-four hours and the Yamaha team became the Virgin Yamaha Team and we couldn't have hoped to land a better sponsor. A global brand recognisable to everyone is a major boost for any sport and Branson's support couldn't have come at a better time. If it had been one week later, Yamaha would not have supplied the bikes because they made it clear that they wanted to do a full season of racing or nothing at all so we had to be ready for the first round.

The first thing to do was publicity photos at Richard Branson's house in Oxfordshire and it was a mad rush for me to get back from a Yamaha R7 road bike launch in Spain. He only had half an hour to do the shoot then had to rush off to meet the Home Secretary of Nigeria.

Branson's son, Sam, was into bikes and knew who I was so it was all very pleasant and Richard's house was surprisingly modest. But then, he does have houses all over the world.

Richard Branson is just as everyone describes him – a genuine, nice bloke whom you'd never imagine to be so powerful and I'm sure if he'd had more time he'd have sat and chatted with us for ages. He came along to a few races that season with his son and was always really friendly and supportive and he also invited the team and myself to a Virgin garden party that year.

My contract was with Yamaha rather than Virgin and I signed a deal to ride in a one-man team with the new R7 in the traditional red and white Virgin colours. Together with my personal sponsorship deals and prize money from the year, I made about £140,000, which I felt was reasonable for a British championship ride.

It was a huge relief when things finally came together and I wasn't too worried about the fact that we had no time to go testing before the season started. After all, how could a bike that looked as good as the R7 be anything else but a missile?

I should have been more cautious as Yamaha's World Superbike team was struggling to get the bike working properly and they had far greater resources than we did as well as a very good rider in Noriyuki Haga.

The chassis on the R7 was really good and probably the best thing about the bike but the engine initially felt like a 600cc machine instead of a 750. It was seriously slow. The team really didn't want to hear that at Brands Hatch for the opening BSB round because we had no time to test it to make it faster.

The fuel injection system was a bit of a mystery as it was the first time we had run an injected bike. The bike had no trick parts, it was just one of the many standard R7s made for racing throughout the world and certainly nothing like the special WSB machines. The factory shared technical information with us but that was about it.

Our season kicked off with a seventh place and a non-finish at Brands due to a fuel-pipe splitting. It was a shock to see how fast the GSE and Red Bull Ducatis were that year and how slow my bike was in comparison. Even in that first round I realised I would have been quicker on my old Boost YZF750. I wasn't used to being beaten in the UK either and I must admit it upset me a bit but I was determined to get the bike sorted out and get up to race speed before too long.

Having said that, we opted to wheel out the old YZF painted in Virgin colours for the next round at Thruxton to allow for crankshaft problems on the R7 to be sorted out. They had broken twice in practice at Brands and we thought they might go in the race at Thruxton so we took the safe option while the factory sorted things out.

I pulled out of the first round at Thruxton with a misted visor then I was sixth in the second leg but couldn't understand why I was off the pace and that really got to me. It was only when Rob Mac rang me on the way home and said they'd stripped the bike and found a problem with the shock, that I could relax again knowing it wasn't my riding which was at fault.

We decided after Thruxton not to use the YZFs again because it would be wasting development time on the R7 so from that point on, for better or worse, I rode the R7. We scored a fifth and sixth at Oulton, obviously still off the pace but whenever I was upset with my results, all I had to do was look at the bike and see how gorgeous it was.

At least the team and I were still enjoying themselves so no one got totally demoralised even though we had all been used to winning for so long and now had to cope with defeat. Everyone tried their best to make it happen and we were grateful to have a team at all considering we had come so close to not having anything for 1999.

The faster pace of the World Superbike riders meant we finished even farther down the field in twelfth and tenth at the Donington WSB round and then it was off to Snetterton for the next BSB round where I had another two mediocre rides to sixth and seventh.

Throughout the season we struggled with the black art of fuel injection. It would work really well in some practice sessions and then be awful in others, which we just couldn't understand. It turned out to be so sensitive that even different weather conditions and temperatures were affecting it so we could never find a good setting that worked well everywhere. It was very much trial and error all year long – and most of the trials led to errors!

After another DNF in the first leg at Donington I knew I wasn't going to retain my British title. You can get away with a couple of non-finishes over a season and still win titles but that was my fourth and that's just too many against good competition. I finished fifth in the second leg and from that point on, I was just looking for some decent results and had to forget about retaining the number one plate.

A bit of friction crept into the team mid-season when Rob told me off for having bad starts. His attitude was that we didn't have a competitive bike and I wasn't helping matters by getting slow starts, which I suppose was fair enough. But at the same time it's hard to give it everything as a rider when you know your bike's not up to the job and I was struggling and taking chances just to score sixth places.

The bike was good enough for a couple of fast laps in practice and I did qualify on the front row at some rounds but we could never seem to get a good set-up for a whole race distance. With really soft tyres on, I could carry a lot of corner speed and if the track was clear I'd put in a fast lap. But the bike's biggest Achilles' heel was getting out of slow corners and over the length of a race that cost me a lot of time. I had to open the throttle really early to get any drive and as soon as the tyres had gone off, the bike just slid everywhere. The Ducatis were so good out of the slow corners that I lost a bike length to them every time, which is why I finished behind them all year.

After two more fifths at Silverstone, I crashed at Oulton Park in the first leg, which didn't help my cause. I had qualified well and got away with the leaders but then clipped John

Reynolds as I passed him and ended up running off the track and hurting my shoulder. It was a stupid crash and although I rode the bike back to the pits I couldn't move my shoulder enough to race in the second leg so we added a did-not-start to our comprehensive list of did-not-finishes.

Next, it was off to Brands Hatch for the second British round of the World Superbike Championship and it was the best meeting of the year for me. I was in the top four in every practice session and the only reason we could come up with to explain that, was the hot weather. Because the temperature remained constant, the fuel injection worked better than it had all year so the bike felt really good. I was actually fastest in the morning warm up before the race but all my qualifying efforts were in vain when it rained for Superpole (where riders get one flying lap to try and improve on their grid position) and I dropped back down to the third row.

I was still well up for the race though and running in fourth spot in the first leg until my tyres just destroyed themselves. Most of the Dunlop riders had a similar problem – Pier Francesco Chili's rear tyre chunked so badly that the bits of rubber flying off it smashed his rear seat unit. I ended up in eighth place when I knew I could have been on the rostrum so I was really disappointed but there was still another race to go.

In the second leg, I used harder tyres, which just weren't very grippy, and I ended up seventh. But problems aside, I was motivated by the fact that, when my tyres held out I was on the pace with the fastest Superbike riders in the world and I thought I was going to have a great end to the season.

So I headed off to Scotland for my home round at Knockhill where I was hoping I could get some decent results. I suppose a fourth place and a second place should have been satisfying after the poor results I'd had earlier in the season but I still wasn't happy considering all those years when I had won there.

Even so, it was our first rostrum of the year and at one point I was actually in contention for a win but then I ran off the track and lost too much time. Another mistake I made was thinking the race was over when there was still a lap to go. I had been checking my on-board lap timer and according to it, the race was over so I slowed up and started waving to the crowd. I couldn't understand it when they didn't wave back and I wondered why they were all staring blankly at me. Then I remembered there were two warm up laps at Knockhill because the track's so short and that's why my timer said the race was finished! Needless to say, I had to get my head down after that but I still managed to secure second place.

After my experiences with him in 1998, I wasn't too chuffed when Rob McElnea announced that Steve Hislop would be joining the team as a second rider at Cadwell Park. I think Rob felt I needed a kick up the backside and he thought that bringing Hislop into the team would have the desired effect. I felt that we were struggling to run one rider on an uncompetitive bike without spreading our resources by running a second rider. This was just at the point where I thought we could have a cracking end to the season too.

The team now had to cobble together a third bike so instead of having two good bikes, I had one good and one average bike because my other good bike was given to Hizzy.

Rob Mac said he wanted to build up a picture of a two-man team for 2000 to attract more cash from Virgin but I felt it worked against us. Yamaha did give me the option to block a second rider but I said no, it was okay, because I knew if I blocked it it would have looked very petty of me, so I just went along with things and kept my mouth shut.

It was also annoying that I did all the development work while Steve reaped the benefits: the bike he rode at Cadwell was a very different machine from the one I started the year with so he had a much better bike to ride from the start.

By that time, there was a bit of friction building up between Rob McElnea and myself. Good friends that we were, we had been used to getting results and it had been a very frustrating year for both of us which started to tell in the paddock. It was nothing major but we were in a way asking each other why things weren't happening and we didn't really have any answers. I was struggling to get what I wanted from the bike but I think Rob blamed me and didn't think I was trying hard enough.

Anyway, I had the same old gut feeling driving into the Cadwell Park circuit that I got most times – that I'd be leaving in an ambulance. It was almost a dead cert that it was going to happen. Even recently in a test for a monthly magazine I had that feeling going into the circuit and sure enough, I left in an ambulance again after yet another crash.

Cadwell could be good fun in a club race but the level of competition in the British Superbike championship was now so high that you couldn't afford to back off anywhere. However, the woodland section of Cadwell is not a place where you want to be riding flat out but that's what you have to do if you want to win.

With all that in the back of my mind, I had a couple of steady rides to ninth and seventh places and looking back it's possible that I was subconsciously affected with all that was going on in the team and maybe wasn't as focused as I could have been.

Troy Bayliss eventually won the BSB title in 1999 and I was genuinely pleased for him. As a person, he reminded me of

Mick Doohan in many ways. He's the same sort of down-to-earth, genuine Aussie bloke. We got on well straight away; he's got no ego whatsoever and he always gives one hundred per cent when he's on the bike. He always made me laugh when he said: 'I'm only racing so that I can feed my wife and kids.' That was the side of Troy that appealed to me. He's a real family man with no time for pretentiousness and in his view, racing is just a fun way of making money for his family, so good on him.

Speaking of Mick Doohan, his career came to an abrupt halt in 1999 when he crashed at the Spanish GP in Jerez. It was a real loss to the because his career had ended before he was ready. Five world championship victories is absolutely incredible but I really believe Mick could have won eight straight titles if he hadn't been so badly injured at Assen in 1992 and missed so many races.

He had a fifty-three point lead back then and looked certain for the title that year. In 1993, he probably would have been dominant again if he'd not been recovering from those injuries. Then in 1999, I think Mick would have beaten Alex Criville for title number eight if he hadn't suffered his career-ending injuries, as he'd already proved many times before that he could beat Criville and Alex was his only real opponent that year. It wasn't to be but Mick was one of the best, if not the best bike racer ever. The statistics speak for themselves. He had one hundred and thirty-seven 500cc GP starts between 1989 and 1999, fifty-four wins, ninety-five podiums, and fifty-eight pole positions as well as winning those five world titles.

But the public always got the wrong impression of Mick Doohan and usually saw him as some sort of machine with no emotions. Sure, he could appear like that when he was racing because that was his way of focusing and keeping the media at arm's length. Away from the track when the pressure was off though, he was a top bloke. He was really just one of the lads and so normal that it would shock people who were only used to seeing the professional side of him.

I remember being at a post-race party at the German Grand Prix in 1990 when Mick was still quite new on the scene and at that point, he hadn't become deadly serious about training or anything. He was as big a party animal as anyone else back then. That night he was crawling about under the tables with his pants round his ankles which was proof that he's as human as the rest of us – until he gets on a bike, that is!

My next race that season was at Brands Hatch and Steve Hislop got pole position but by that time I was used to the idea of having him in the team and it didn't really bother me.

I finished both races in fifth place, which meant I had finished fifth six times that year, but when we went to Donington for the last round, I equalled my best finish of the season with a second in the first leg. I actually led the race for a while which was the first time I'd done so all year. It was a wet race too and it was unusual for me to do well in the rain, but it seemed to level the competition so it was a chance for a good result.

Having said that, I remember thinking at the time that lots of riders seem to get good in the wet as they near the end of their careers. Roger Burnett was one example and I wondered if it was some kind of omen telling me to retire.

Things didn't work out so well in the last leg though as I finished my miserable season in seventh after I collided with Suzuki's James Haydon and was forced off the track.

So, that was the end of my nineteenth season of racing and, as usual, I started sniffing around for possible rides for the year 2000. I was pretty sure I wouldn't be with Yamaha again after the reception I got from the team when I finished second at Donington. One mechanic came over to see me and said well done but the rest of the team didn't bother. Things weren't as they used to be in the team and I realised that was a sign to me to get out. I knew Rob was very keen to have Hislop in his squad the following year and I didn't really want to ride with Steve again after our unhappy season in 1998.

I told a TV interviewer after the Donington race that I would ride again in 2000 if I had a bike and team capable of winning the championship. It must have come out a bit wrong though, because I just meant that I needed a better bike and a team that I felt believed in me as a rider and had a better budget. I mean, the Virgin Yamaha team was still operating out of a horsebox and the budget was peanuts compared to some of the other teams. However, Rob wasn't very happy with my little speech and phoned me up to tell me so in no uncertain terms. I just repeated what I said on TV – give me a decent bike and a team with a decent budget and I feel I can win the title again. As a team, Yamaha had been simply overtaken by others with bigger budgets and eventually, money starts telling in results.

I finished seventh in the 1999 championship which was obviously a bit of a comedown from the previous three years but if I could have chosen anyone to pass on my number one plate to, it would have been Troy Bayliss. He'd really committed himself by moving his whole family over to England and learning all the tracks and he got his just reward for all his efforts. One of my mechanics, Adrian Marsh, made a Virgin number one trophy for Troy and we all signed it and wished him the best for the future. He really deserved it and went on to even greater heights two years later by adding the World Superbike crown to his collection.

About one week after Donington, Colin Wright, who was

Troy's manager in the GSE Ducati team that year, called and asked if I wanted to ride for him since Troy had signed a deal to race in America in 2000. The prospect of riding for a well-funded team like GSE on a Ducati that I knew was capable of winning the championship was immediately tempting. Suzuki also expressed some interest and to be honest, if they could have given me a contract there and then I'd have signed with them because I liked the team and was more accustomed to riding four-cylinder bikes. But they asked me to wait a week or so and I had to make a decision so I went with GSE Ducati.

I had finally left Yamaha and lost my Virginity all in one stroke.

CHAPTER 18

Evil Twins

I know it makes me sound very old, but the year 2000 marked the start of my third decade in racing.

As the '80s gave way to the '90s and the '90s gave way to the new millennium, the tapes in my motorhome had changed to compact discs and I was no longer listening to Simple Minds and the Human League but was rocking to Travis and Prodigy.

The Mackenzie mullet was thinning and the stretch jeans had given way to loose fitting combat trousers but one thing that never changed was the racing. That still involved getting on a bike and riding it as fast as I could, week in, week out and I was certainly up for doing that again in the first season of the new millennium.

It was all quite exciting being part of a new team again after four years with Yamaha especially as the GSE Ducati team set-up was far more lavish. I didn't really make more money than the year before but there was just a greater feeling of money being spent on things like the transporters and hospitality units that were all top notch. Even the tyre budget was better than Yamaha's so we weren't scrimping and scraping and trying to make tyres last. I'm not knocking the Yamaha team because they did a great job with limited resources – they just needed more resources.

Darrell Healey's GSE squad, on the other hand, set completely new standards in the British Superbike paddock and there was no expense spared. For once, I could go to my home round at Knockhill with the best set-up in the paddock and a flashy, big truck – a big change from the days when I turned up in a CF Bedford van.

I had signed up two weeks after the last round of the 1999 season and was really looking forward to 2000. I rode the Ducati for the first time in November of '99 at Donington but it was that year's bike rather than the new model. It was really just for the benefit of the press and to give me an idea of what to expect for the coming season and I didn't expect to set any fast times in the middle of an English winter.

Ducati's are deceptive bikes to ride because they don't feel very fast. You don't rev them like you rev two-strokes or four-cylinder bikes so there's no mad rush of screaming top end power; it's all about lazy, short-shifting through the gears and that was a big change to what I'd been used to over the last twenty years. All the power is at the bottom of the rev range but the chassis was nice and Ducatis had been winning pretty much everything in Superbikes both at British and world levels for the last few years so I was really confident for 2000.

Having said that, I disagree with people who think that twins have an advantage over four-cylinder bikes. No one complained when the fours were winning everything and if one manufacturer builds an exceptionally good bike like Ducati has with the 998, then I think it's up to the others to raise their game and try to beat it.

And it's not like the fours were being completely outclassed.

In 2000, Noriyuki Haga very nearly won the World Superbike Championship on a four-cylinder Yamaha and Chris Walker came so close to winning the British title on his Suzuki so, with the right rider, I think four-cylinder bikes can still be competitive with the twins.

At the start of the 2000 season I had no idea that it would be my last year in racing. I had decided a long time before then that I would never plan my retirement – I would just stop when I wasn't enjoying racing anymore, even if that meant quitting in the middle of the season. If I'd planned to have one last year, I don't think my heart would have been in it because I would just have been waiting for the season to end.

The 2000 season was a tough year for me for a number of reasons. I struggled to get the best from the bike because it was so different and maybe the age factor was starting to creep in meaning I couldn't adapt as quickly as I might have done years before. Also, although I wasn't aware of it at the time, it seems you just reach an age when you're not as fast any more or maybe just not prepared to take the same risks as younger riders and that's when it's time to call it a day.

I certainly could never blame the bike or the team for my under par performances in 2000. As far as I was concerned, both were the best in the paddock as Neil Hodgson proved by going on to win the title. Things just didn't happen for me that year.

One key moment of the season came at Cadwell Park when I crashed there (again) after my throttle stuck open at 140mph. I was sitting next to the tyre wall thinking 'No matter how safe I try to make this racing lark, accidents like this will still happen.' That's when I started thinking about my wife and kids and whether I should be racing at all and I'd never thought like that before. I always told myself that if I started thinking like that I should quit so that's when the seeds were sown for my retirement.

I've spoken to lots of retired riders and they all say the same thing – one day, for no apparent reason, you just start thinking about the risks and at that point you need to get out. In twenty years of racing I'd never thought about the dangers or even thought I was in any great danger. I don't know why that mental attitude just changes overnight but it does and that's when it's time for a rider to retire.

Anyway, my final season got underway at Brands Hatch and it wasn't the best of starts – a sixth place in leg one then a non-finish in the second race. I had qualified on the front row and felt good about the races but the front end of the Ducati just didn't give me much confidence in the opening race and when I tried to push it harder in race two, I lost the front and crashed out.

I had a debrief with the team after the crash and they said if I wasn't happy with the bike we'd go testing and get it sorted out. That's the kind of attitude you need to win championships and it was great to have that kind of support.

I suppose everyone remembers the 2000 BSB championship because of the incredible battle between my GSE team-mate, Neil Hodgson, and Chris Walker, who was riding for Suzuki that year. I liked both riders so I had to sit on the fence when it came to supporting one or the other but, ultimately, I suppose my allegiance was to my team and I was always chuffed when Neil did well. Deep down, I felt that Hodgson had a slightly better bike than Chris, so Chris was a bit of an under-dog and seemed to be the crowd's favourite too.

Walker was doing things on a four-cylinder bike that no one else was even getting close to doing so I really admired him for that but Hodgson had a poor start to the season and still managed to turn things around so he was worthy of respect too. That was another thing which led to my decision to retire – I realised I was pleased for Neil when he got results and I shouldn't have been thinking that. I should have been concentrating on my own results and seeing him as another threat when it came to scoring points. You should never be happy when your team-mate's doing better than yourself!

I was an old dog trying to learn new tricks on the Ducati and it didn't work out. I kept changing everything round trying to find a feel that suited me and I never quite got there. With hindsight, I should have left the bike as it was and learned to ride it before I started changing everything but that's easy to say now.

I got a fourth and fifth at Donington Park then had a particularly bad weekend at Thruxton with a seventh place and a DNF because of a misted visor. A few days after that, Colin Wright, the team manager summoned me to his office and pulled a real surprise on me. He said we should set up the hospitality at the next race at Oulton Park, have an all-night party and announce my retirement from the sport! I was gobsmacked – if I hadn't been sitting down I'd have fallen down.

He said he had done everything he could for me as far as the team and the bikes went and I still wasn't getting the results so maybe I should just pack it in. I told him there was no way I was going to retire just like that, and suggested he should let me race at Oulton to see how things went.

I don't know if Colin was using some sort of reverse psychology on me by trying to get me fired up and angry but I don't do all that mind game stuff. I went well at Oulton but I'd have done that anyway; things just came together better at that round than they had done before. It wasn't reverse psychology that made me faster – I just had a good race. I know Colin's used similar tactics with Neil Hodgson too but I'd rather stay away from all that.

I remember being very careful with my responses during that meeting because if I'd agreed to retire, there was still a question of outstanding wages to consider. I felt there was a lot more to the conversation than there appeared on the surface. The rest of the season was fine with Colin but I didn't like that incident at all. I don't think there was any need for it.

As it turned out, I had my best ride of the season at Oulton and stood on the podium in third place after the second leg. After that, Colin told me to forget all about our little chat and never mentioned it again!

Incidentally, that was the only podium finish I had all year and the very last one of my career.

Oulton was also the start of the real battle between Walker and Hodgson as they collided and Walker crashed out of the race. It was the beginning of a series of very hard on-track battles, as well as some off-track verbal abuse and threatened legal actions, but it made the series great to watch.

Snetterton ended up being a nightmare for Neil Hodgson and myself thanks to some over-zealous officials. I fell off in the morning warm-up and Neil gave me a lift back to the pits while the session was still underway. That seemed totally innocent to us and it has been done a thousand times before but the organisers took a different view and decided to make an example of us because the rule-book stated it was illegal.

Usually, riders just get a warning about doing things like that but Neil got a £1000 fine and had six points added to his racing licence and I was fined £500 and given four points.

Poor Neil was also given a suspended one-race ban that was later lifted. The whole thing was absolute nonsense and we had to pay the fines out of our own pockets too! Not good.

Hodgson was a different rider in 2000 to the one he'd been in previous years. He'd always struggled with concentration before so while he was capable of putting in a handful of quick laps, he found things difficult over a full race distance. In 2000, he sorted all that out. He'd also gotten himself into top physical condition and was prepared to race very hard for results when he had to. He seemed to have left behind that 'comfort zone' of a top ten finish that he used to talk about and was now only happy winning races. Neil had obviously made a mental decision over the winter to do whatever he had to do to be competitive and I don't see any reason now why he can't win the World Superbike Championship if his bikes are reliable and fast enough.

Certainly, I couldn't have asked for a better team-mate. We shared everything we learned about the bikes and from about halfway through the season I'm sure he didn't see me as a threat for the title and I was pleased whenever he did well, so there was a really good atmosphere in the garage. Neil and I socialised together away from the track quite often and found we shared the same sense of humour and Jan and Neil's wife Kathryn got on really well too so although my results were very average in 2000, it was an enjoyable year from that point of view.

But that year will always be remembered by most bike fans as the year that the great Joey Dunlop was killed while racing in Tallinn, Estonia. The British Superbike series was at Silverstone when the news came through and everyone in the paddock and the crowd was simply stunned. Like Wayne Rainey, Joey had seemed invincible and so safe on a bike and people just didn't expect brilliant, safe riders like Wayne and Joey to ever get seriously hurt or killed. I didn't know Joey that well but the few times that I did have a drink with him have become precious memories. He was unique and there will never be another racer quite like him.

After Oulton, it was time for Knockhill again and I thought I'd struggle there on the Ducati but when we tested at the track a few weeks before the race I was faster than Neil Hodgson so my fears appeared to be unfounded. The Ducati loved the tight, twisty circuit because of all the torque it makes out of slow corners so after setting pole position in practice, I was a lot more confident for the races.

The first race was run in wet conditions and I didn't do as well as I'd hoped. I was actually quite happy about the rain because I'd been going well in the wet that year but when I let the clutch out on the start line, my back wheel started spinning like crazy and I was going nowhere. I had my feet up on the pegs and my body all tucked in but the scenery wasn't moving and the bike was just banging off the rev limiter.

By the time I initiated some forward motion, everyone else had obviously mastered the art and was long gone. I played catch up for the whole race but in the end I ran out of laps and lost out on third place by just thousandths of a second. If I'd made a decent start, it should have been at least an easy second for me, if not a win. If my auntie had balls she'd be my uncle I hear you say . . .

The second leg was worse for me as I high-sided the Ducati at Clark Corner on lap twelve, chewed on some Scottish soil (it's good stuff) and my race was run. I actually made a good start and was catching Walker and Hodgson when I just got caught out and went down, probably just through trying too hard. My only consolation was setting a new lap record which, at the time of writing this, still stands.

Still, at least I had been on the pace all weekend from practice through to the races themselves; I just didn't have much luck when it really mattered. But I still thought I could have a strong finish to the season as I was getting more used to the Ducati.

Cadwell Park was next on the agenda and, as I said earlier, I had a big crash in practice that led to my first thoughts of retirement. My braking point for the entry to the Gooseneck was always when the engine hit the rev limiter in fourth gear but when I tried to throttle off and squeeze the brakes on that occasion the bike was still flat out on the rev limiter! No fun, I can assure you and a very effective laxative!

I got over my little incident in time for the first race and didn't have any serious injuries so thoughts of retirement left my head – but they were to return before the day was over for altogether different reasons.

I was on the pace of the leaders in leg one and was on for a good finish until James Haydon crashed in front of me and cost me some time. But I was quite happy with the fourth place that I eventually got especially after having such a big crash in practice.

By the time we were out on our warm-up lap for the second race, it was wet and I touched a white line while the bike was leaned over and fell off again. I had never crashed on a warm-up lap in my life so I can only think it was the Cadwell curse having a laugh at poor old Spuds Mackenzie once more. I certainly felt a bit of a plonker.

The result of it all was that I had to ride back to the pits, jump on my spare bike and start the race from the pit lane after everyone else had got away. That meant I was starting the race about ten seconds down on the leaders but I still thought I could pick up a few points so I got stuck in and started carving my way through the field.

On the last lap I could see that there were blue flags out (to warn riders they are about to be lapped) but I thought they were to warn the riders in my way that I was coming through. Unknown to me, Hodgson and Walker were just about to pass *me* and I moved right over in front of my own team-mate, Neil Hodgson, forcing him to take evasive action which allowed Walker through for the win. Going into the Cadwell round, there had only been one point between Neil and Chris so every point was crucial and there I was, getting in the way and preventing Neil from increasing his championship lead. I didn't feel too clever about that one but then I wasn't exactly used to being lapped either so I was really a bit of a novice at it.

Even so, I felt so embarrassed by the incident that I offered my resignation to the team on the spot. In fact I asked them to shoot me as well for good measure but they kindly declined both my offers. I apologised to Neil as soon as I could and thankfully, he was really cool about the whole thing. I knew I might have cost him the championship because it was so close but he told me not to worry about it. Colin Wright and Darrell Healey were great about it too but I still felt bad and thoughts of retirement resurfaced. This time, they didn't go away.

After a ninth and a seventh at Mallory Park, I prepared myself for the last round at Donington Park because it was going to be a bit special for me: it was to be my last race after twenty years in the sport. I had finally decided to call it a day.

I actually made my mind up ten days before the race and there were several reasons for my decision. One was that I was on arguably the best bike in the championship and still wasn't getting very good results. Another was that I was about to turn

271

forty and I'd been racing for twenty years and they were all nice, round figures so it just seemed like the timing was right. The last round was also at Donington Park which was one of my favourite circuits so even the venue was suitable.

I was actually lying in bed with Jan back in Scotland when I made the decision. We'd been mulling it over and she said she was keen for another season's racing if I was. However, I'd been toying with the idea of retiring since that crash at Cadwell and finally thought 'I've had enough'. So I told the GSE press people and news got out just in time for the last race of the season at Donington on 8 October, 2000.

Shortly after I made the announcement, I was driving up to Scotland and was listening to the Steve Wright in the Afternoon show on Radio 2 (it's an age thing). Every hour, the show broadcast the news of my retirement and by the time I got to Scotland, it had just about sunk in that I had really made the decision.

I didn't get all emotional about things on race weekend because, at the end of the day, I was still there to race and I was too busy stressing out and concentrating on setting the bike up to be getting all nostalgic. People kept saying that it must be an emotional meeting for me but to be honest, it felt like any other weekend. The only thing that niggled me though, was that I had been on the front row all through qualifying until the last minute when Australian Anthony Gobert (on the Virgin Yamaha for a couple of races), knocked me back onto the second row. I had really wanted to start my last race from the front row of the grid but just missed out.

I ended up having two average rides with a fourth and a sixth but I really enjoyed the whole weekend. My team won the championship after Chris Walker's Suzuki blew up in the final race when he was in a championship-winning position.

Everyone felt sorry for him but at the same time I was happy for Neil winning – they both rode brilliantly that year but someone had to win.

I also had a win with my own little team in the 250 British championship, which gave me more cause for celebration. At the start of the season, my fellow Scot Callum Ramsay had no bike to ride and Colin Davies, my former mechanic, had no job to go at the time to so I bought them a bike and a truck, brought a few sponsors on board and they won the championship. It really was that simple.

I suppose I could have built on that team but to be honest, I didn't really enjoy the experience of being a team owner. I really couldn't be bothered with all the hassle. I dipped my toe in the water and found it too hot so I just pulled the plug.

I ended my final season in fifth place overall and the crowd over the weekend were great, giving me cards, flowers and all sorts of gifts. I couldn't have asked for a better send off and a good moment was getting my own back on the Ducati after the second race. I held it on the rev limiter doing burnouts for ages just and generally gave it a good thrashing. There was nothing wrong with the bike, as Neil Hodgson proved, but I just never clicked with the twin-cylinder bikes so it felt good to give it a bit of a kicking.

I had a brilliant night out in Castle Donington with the team that night and we had a treble celebration for my retirement, Neil's first British Superbike title and my 250 team's title.

When I woke up the next morning, slightly hungover, I was aware that my life had changed completely. No more waiting for the phone to ring with offers of another ride, no more testing schedules, no more hanging around in airports thousands of miles from home every weekend. Instead, all I had to think about was pottering around the garden, playing football with the kids on a Saturday morning and upsetting shop assistants by unecessarily unfolding clothes while shopping with Jan. Well, that's what I thought retirement was going to be like, but I couldn't have been more wrong.

CHAPTER NINETEEN

Pipe and Slippers

When the fact that I had retired from racing actually sunk in, it felt the same as the day I left school.

I had no plans (apart from a holiday to Mexico with Iain and Kristeen MacPherson), no expectations and nothing urgent to do but the feeling of excitement was intoxicating. There was a whole, new world out there for me to explore without the heavy commitment of racing to worry about. Having said that, I also had no idea what I was going to do with myself. I knew I'd still want to go to a racetrack now and then to keep in touch with the sport but there was no risk of me becoming a bit of a sad anorak just hanging around the pits with nothing to do!

The first thing I got round to was selling stuff I didn't need anymore like my motorhome and the bike and truck from my 250 race team. Jan and I had moved to Ashby de la Zouch in Leicestershire at the beginning of 2000 so there was plenty to do on the new house. Lots of people have pointed out that I commuted from Scotland to go racing for twenty years then only got round to moving down to England closer to all the racetracks and airports when I'd retired! True Mackenzie logic at work there.

But the real reason was that Jan had lived in Scotland for fifteen years and although she liked it there, she wanted to be closer to her family. I suppose it was my turn to move across the border. I still drive up to Scotland regularly though and I still have my mum's house there now that she's in a nursing home so we've got the best of both worlds. I will always have a property in Scotland as there's a strange magnetism that always draws me back there.

It was nice not having to think about the next racing season and all the associated sponsorship deals and things that I'd normally be thrashing out over winter. Some riders have managers do deal with all that but I always did it myself and it was a bit of a slog.

At the same time as I was enjoying my new stress-free life, I wasn't making any money so I had to think about what I could do job-wise as well although as a racer, I never made any money over winter anyway so it still felt the same.

I should have had a substantial financial windfall when I retired but I got misled on a pension scheme. I had paid hundreds of thousands of pounds over a period of fifteen years into a pension which was arranged by someone I once considered a friend and I was led to believe there would be some handsome returns upon retiring but the whole thing proved to be a big mistake. This so-called 'friend' was making big commission out of selling me a pension plan which was unsuitable for my needs.

But within a couple of weeks of retiring from racing the phone started to ring with job offers. Eurosport offered me a job commentating on World Superbike races, that I accepted and I was also asked to commentate on ITV Digital's British Superbike coverage with Jonathan Greene.

I still do all the WSB rounds alongside my co-commentator

Jack Burnicle and mostly that means flying round the world again although occasionally, we commentate from a studio booth in London or Paris. It's good fun though and I enjoy doing it. It's also a good way of keeping in touch with people in the paddock who I'd not see otherwise.

Next, Suzuki asked me if I'd like to get involved with testing their GSX-R750 British Superbike and help out their riders John Crawford, who is another Scot and a good friend of mine, and young Karl Harris who looks set to have a bright future in racing. I accepted that offer too and I'm testing for them this year on the Suzuki GSX-R1000s, this time with John Reynolds and Karl.

There's not much I can teach someone as experienced as John Reynolds so I offer Karl any advice I can and it's good trying to bring someone along. I've got great faith in him because he's got a very natural talent on a bike. Some people have to really work on their riding but he seems to know instinctively what to do and that's rare. Hopefully he'll go a long way and I can continue to help him.

I do about ten tests a year with the team and attend all the BSB rounds that don't clash with my WSB commitments, so it works out well. And the GSX-R1000s are so much fun to ride that they make me feel like making a comeback again! Only joking.

Another call I received was from some people putting together a new bike magazine to be called *Two Wheels Only* or *T.W.O* for short. I knew most of the guys involved in it and they asked me if I'd like to be their road test editor. I thought 'Me – a bike journo? Yes please.' Finally I could crash bikes with impunity and blag lots of free kit too!

I do a couple of tests each month and whatever new bike launches I can fit in and I really enjoy riding so many different types of bike from cruisers to Supermotos after spending so many years on race bikes. Not so sure about long, cold, wet trips to South Wales in the middle of winter though . . .

All of this happened within a month, and suddenly my diary was filling up again. It looked like the pipe and slippers would have to wait a while. A few people, including Rob McElnea at Yamaha and Paul Denning at Suzuki, asked me if I had definitely stopped racing for good just so they could tick me off their potential rider list for 2001. I told them I had and wasn't going down the Frank Sinatra comeback road.

I've spoken to other riders who retired too soon and they can't get the bug out of their system but I was comfortable with my decision and quite happy in all my new roles.

Other, more bizarre offers came along too like at the end of 2000 when I was invited to appear on the kid's Saturday Morning TV show, *Live and Kicking* which I'd seen often as my own kids watch it. The circumstances leading to my invite were a bit strange though. Apparently, a kid e-mailed the studio and said that one of the crew members looked like Niall Mackenzie. When the presenters realised I was a bike racer (or used to be) they thought it would be a laugh to get me on the show to see how much I looked like one of their crew members. So they showed some footage of me on-screen then lined me up with the crew guy and a few others. The TV audience had to call in and guess which one was the real Niall Mackenzie and wouldn't you know, they got it wrong! So, apparently, I don't look anything like me, which is always good to know.

I took my son Taylor along to the studios and he loved it. He got autographs from everyone on the show including tennis player Greg Rusedski, S Club 7, singer Billie Piper and presenter Katie Hill so we both had a lot of fun.

As 2001 rolled around, I realised I was really enjoying my new life. I still got to ride interesting bikes and go on flashy bike launches with *T.W.O* magazine, still travelled a lot to commentate for Eurosport, and also got to test proper race bikes on track with Suzuki. But there was one thing that continued to niggle me – I felt I hadn't said goodbye properly to my beloved Knockhill circuit and all the Scottish supporters who had cheered me on for twenty years. So when Suzuki said I could race their bike if I wanted to I started thinking about Frank Sinatra again.

I had always promised the owners of Knockhill that I'd do something there to mark my retirement but we were thinking more in terms of a few parade laps to say goodbye or a chat show or something. There were certainly no plans to race again. But when the idea of a farewell race cropped up, I was very tempted. Coming out of retirement was the oddest way of marking my retirement that I could think of so that appealed to me and I also wanted to end my story at Knockhill where it really all began so a final race seemed the perfect way to do it. I had a deadline of five weeks before the race to make up my mind and by the time that came around, I was itching to go just one more time. I said yes.

But the easy life of retirement had left me below par in the fitness stakes and if I was going to race again and have any chance of doing well, I had to get back in shape. I didn't want to go there and just wobble round at the back of the field waving to the spectators.

I was still training a few times every week but not as much as I had done when I was racing so I stepped up my exercise programme again to try and get into the best possible shape for event.

Obviously, I realised I wasn't going to be as race-sharpened as the championship leaders who had been riding all year long but I was still hoping not to disgrace myself.

As the event approached, I also fell back into my old habit of not being able to sleep properly and that made me realise how well I'd been sleeping since I retired. Oh, the joys of growing old!

I managed to sneak in a secret practice session at Knockhill two weeks before the race just to blow the cobwebs away and reacquaint myself with the circuit.

For race day itself, I was in second position on the grid after posting the second fastest time to John Reynolds in a wet Superpole session the day before. It would have been nice to set pole at my farewell race but it wasn't to be.

Race day dawned on 12 August with typically Scottish drizzling rain but as the morning wore on, conditions improved and it eventually dried out enough to attract a crowd of more than twenty thousand people, which equalled the best crowd a bike race had ever drawn at Knockhill. I hope at least some of that was down to me.

I opted to run number eighty-eight on my bike as it was the number I wore in my first race at Knockhill in March 1981. I even managed to squeeze into the very same set of leathers I wore back then and kicked about the paddock trying to look twenty years younger. It was great chatting to all the spectators and signing autographs and during the lunch break I did a few demonstration laps on a Yamaha RD350LC just like the one I started my career on. In the paddock there was a display of some of the bikes I'd ridden over the years including the Boost Yamaha, the Virgin Yamaha and the 250 Armstrong that I now own.

But there was more serious business to attend to as race one approached and from the moment I went out on track for the warm up laps, the crowd were brilliant, all waving and blasting their air horns. Those same people had voted me the Scottish rider of the year eight times at the Scottish Motorcycle Show and I had always appreciated their support. They were the reason I decided to race again in the first place.

In the first leg I had a really good battle with my Clarion Suzuki team-mate John Crawford and eventually beat him for fifth place by just over two-tenths of a second. Then in the second, and for me my very last race, I went one better by finishing fourth ahead of Michael Rutter. A podium would have been good to cap off a great weekend but I was still pleased with my results considering I hadn't raced in almost a year.

After that race I tossed my helmet into the crowd to show my appreciation. It was one of three I lobbed over the fence that weekend including an old AGV from my early racing days. Then, secure in the knowledge that I didn't have to worry about race bans anymore, I wheelied my way back to the paddock with no helmet or gloves on, parked up the bike, and that was that. It was all over. That whole weekend was more enjoyable than emotional for me and I'll always remember it but I certainly won't be doing it again! In fact, I remember telling everyone in the press office after the race that they had my permission to shoot me if I ever tried to race again!

Despite all the fun I had, there were a few things that reminded me of the downside of racing: sleepless nights, aches and pains from riding, the stress and nerves of race day. The whole experience served to remind me that I'd made the right decision to retire.

I had a few beers that night and that's something I can do now whenever I like without having to feel guilty about it. The same goes for food; I can eat the odd bit of junk food with no worries whereas before I'd have to run it off. I still run about twenty miles a week and still go down the gym regularly because it's just something I can't shake off but the nice thing is knowing that I don't have to do it if I don't feel like it.

When I was signed to a race team, I felt that they owned me to a certain extent because they were paying me to perform to the best of my abilities. Most teams I rode for gave me one hundred per cent so I always felt a responsibility to do the same so I must admit it's nice not to be owned by anyone now.

My racing days may have ended with the Knockhill outing but I got an interesting offer to go testing in Malaysia in October of 2001. Sauber Petronas, famous for their Formula One car racing team, had decided to build a bike to go GP racing and asked me if I would fly to Malaysia to test it then do a few demonstration laps at the Malaysian GP at Sepang. I had only been retired for a year and there I was back in Grands Prix . . . well, sort of.

British firm Harris Performance Products, who have years of experience in GPs and WSB, built the chassis for the bike and it was co-owner Steve Harris who called and first told me about the project. That was back in April and he couldn't tell me who the manufacturer was then, although he assured me it wasn't Royal Enfield!

I wasn't too sure at first because any firm making a bike for the first time can make mistakes and I didn't want to run the risk of injuring myself on an untried machine. The last thing I wanted to be in my retirement years was a guinea pig for some mad bike designer!

But when I was eventually told it was a Sauber Petronas Engineering (SPE) project, I was a lot more comfortable with the idea. I met Paul Fricker from Sauber at Brands Hatch and he showed me some computer designs and details of the bike and it looked impressive.

From that point onwards, I received a weekly update on what was happening with the bike but obviously the project was top secret so I had to keep quiet about it for a long time despite increasing attention from the media.

Once the bike was unveiled things became a lot easier and it has actually been a fascinating project to be involved with as it's the first time F1 technology has been directly applied to bike racing.

The GP-1, as the bike was tentatively called, was easily the most powerful motorcycle I'd ever ridden. It was about 10mph faster than anything I'd ridden, and I reckon it could easily crack 200mph. I spent two weeks in Malaysia testing it and also rode it for one flying lap at a press launch at Sepang. At the circuit we had secret garages away from the main paddock area to work in and it was all real cloak and dagger stuff. The plan was for me to do one flying lap of the track while the press were gathered round the unveiling of the static bike.

It all sounded very dramatic but it called for clockwork precision as I was to start from the far end of the circuit and had to be passing the pits at just the right time to surprise everyone. I was a bit worried about the bike breaking down or having problems which would not have looked too clever but it all went smoothly and the awesome sound of the engine, which was more like an F1 car than a bike, must have impressed the gathered media. It certainly impressed me.

Since that debut, things have become a bit confusing. The original plan was to build a great engine that could be leased to other Grand Prix teams but there was speculation that Sauber Petronas Engineering would run an official team themselves. That didn't happen for a number of reasons and the bike was not entered for the inaugural four-stroke GP series in 2002.

Then came the revelation that Carl Fogarty was going to run a modified version of the bike in the 2002 World Superbike Championship and that caused a lot of excitement in the press too. But in yet another twist, Sauber then withdrew from Foggy's project after it initially looked like they were going to build the bikes. So Foggy took the Petronas money to another engineering firm headed by former GP racer Eskil Suter to build a bike for him.

But before Foggy's riders, Troy Corser and James Haydon, can go racing, seventy-five road going versions of the FP1 (Foggy Petronas 1) bike will have to be completed as well as the race bikes, and that's going to take time. No one really knows when the team will make its racing debut or how competitive the bike will be.

To complicate things further, Sauber still has a link-up with Harris Performance Products and they're continuing development on the bike with the intention of leasing it to GP teams eventually. Only time will tell how all this pans out but I'm still in talks to test the GP version of the bike so I'm hoping it all comes together at some point. It would be a shame to come this far and then see the whole project fold.

I was probably busier than ever in 2001 because I also fronted up the European Superbike school alongside WSB rider Pier Francesco Chili. It was good fun but I had too many date clashes with other commitments so I had to cut back my activities somewhere. The school still operates and Chili's still involved but it's run in France and Spain now and no longer has dates in the UK.

Instead of the European school, I will be instructing at the Niall Mackenzie Track Days at Donington Park in 2002. There's eighteen dates to do so I'll still be getting lots of track time and hoping to discover some new talent.

All in all, it's a pretty hectic schedule for me but I'm very grateful that I can still make a good living out of doing what I love – riding bikes and talking about bikes. It's all I've ever known and it's never felt like a proper job and that's the best way to get through life as far as I'm concerned. Doing all the things I'm doing now also means I can still get the buzz of riding fast bikes without the negative aspects of racing such as stress and getting hurt on a regular basis.

Speaking of getting hurt, I feel very lucky to still be in one piece after so many years of racing. I don't even have any injuries that give me grief as so many ex racers experience, although I can probably expect some arthritis in my later years with all the bones I've broken!

So many of my friends and colleagues have not been so lucky and have paid the ultimate price for pursuing their passion. The only thing that gives me comfort about that is the knowledge that they wouldn't have had it any other way. Racing bikes is a kick like nothing else on earth and once you've been bitten by the bug, it's very hard to let go.

I don't have any regrets about my career either. Sure, I would have done some things differently but so would everyone in any line of work – it's all part of growing up and learning from your mistakes. And anyway, for every poor decision I made, I made plenty more good ones.

If there's one achievement I'm most proud of though, it's that I still feel more or less like that same lad from Denny, even though my accent's not as strong as it used to be.

Some riders like to shout about their careers and talk about themselves all the time while others prefer to keep their heads down and let their riding do the talking. I like to think I fall into the second category. It's not that I'm not proud of what I've achieved because I am, it's more to do with my upbringing.

In small town Scotland you learn from an early age that if you puff your chest out too far, you get hit over the head with an Irn Bru bottle so I prefer just to keep my head down and get on with things.

I also like to think I've not made too many enemies over the years and if I can be remembered in racing circles as a normal bloke then that's fine by me.

As far as results went, a Grand Prix win may have eluded me but I've still beaten all the top riders of the last two decades fair and square at some time or other. Names like Mick Doohan, Wayne Rainey, Eddie Lawson, Freddie Spencer, Kevin Schwantz, Randy Mamola and Wayne Gardner are now legendary and although I never managed to beat them to a world title, I've finished ahead of them all in individual races and I'm proud of the fact.

Just for the record, I'm also the only rider ever to have got onto the rostrum with all three modern Japanese V4 bikes: the NSR Honda, the YZR Yamaha and the RGV Suzuki.

Standing at the side of a racetrack now and watching the action is a bizarre experience for me. It's as if I never raced myself – as I if I'd never been there and did that very same thing. You're so focused when you're racing that afterwards you hardly realise you've done it. For twenty years of my life it seems I wasn't fully registering what I was doing.

But there's one thing that's even weirder than that. When I watch a pack of race bikes screaming past at full speed with the riders jostling and elbowing each other for space before they haul their bikes over into the approaching corner at near impossible angles, I think to myself that they're mad – that they must have something missing. I simply can't believe I ever did that. But that's when I'm wearing my jeans and T-shirt and standing in the sunshine with my cool box and sandwiches peering through the fence. When I'm getting ready to go out testing with Suzuki or Sauber and start to pull on my racing gear, it's a different matter and something very strange happens: I feel like Clark Kent going into a phone box or, more likely, Mr Benn going into his magical changing room and coming out the other side as a medieval knight or a World War Two fighter pilot. It's the smell of the leathers, the tight, secure feel of a crash helmet against my face, the action of slamming down the black visor and climbing on the bike and grabbing the bars. Suddenly the fear seems to go and I'm happy to push a 180bhp Superbike to its limits and bring it back again. I no longer feel like that insignificant little bloke standing at the side of the track marvelling at the mad racers hammering into the corners at 140mph. I'm one of them. I'm Niall Mackenzie. And I love that feeling.

Career Results

1981

Venue/Race	Class	Place
Carnaby	500/P	3rd
Knockhill	500/P	2nd, 1st
Knockhill	500/P	3rd
East Fortune	500/P	2nd
Knockhill	500/P	4th
Knockhill	500/P	1st
Silloth	500/P	4th
Knockhill	500/P	4th
Knockhill	500/P	1st, 2nd
	Pro-Am	5th
Knockhill	500/P	1st, 3rd
Knockhill	500/P	6th
Knockhill	500/P	1st, 1st
Carnaby	500/P	4th, 4th
Knockhill	500/P	1st
Croft	500/P	1st
Knockhill	350cc	3rd
	500/P	1st, 2nd
	1000cc	6th, 5th

East Fortune	500/P	2nd
	1000cc	16th
Croft	500/p	5th
Knockhill	350cc	10th
	1000cc	6th

Cumbria Club champion
Scottish 500cc Production Championship: 2nd

1982

Venue/Race	Class	Place
Silloth	250cc	1st
	350cc	2nd
Knockhill	250cc	3rd
	500/P	1st, 2nd
	1000cc	1st
Donington Park	Pro-Am	14th
Knockhill	250cc	6th
	500/P	1st
	1000cc	2nd
East Fortune	250cc	5th
Cadwell Park	250cc	1st, 1st, 1st, 1st
	500/P	3rd, 3rd, 1st, 1st
	1000cc	4th
Knockhill	250cc	2nd
	1000cc	1st
Donington Park	250cc	18th
Knockhill	250cc	1st
	500/P	2nd, 6th
	1000cc	1st
Donington Park	Pro-Am	2nd

Knockhill	Pro-Am	1st
	500/P	1st
	1000cc	9th
Knockhill	250cc	4th
	500/P	1st
Ingliston	500/P	2nd
Knockhill	500/P	4th
	1000cc	7th
Cadwell Park	250cc	3rd
	500/P	1st
Donington Park	250cc	17th
	Pro-Am	12th
Knockhill	250cc	1st
	500/P	1st, 2nd
	1000cc	1st
Knockhill	250cc	2nd
Carnaby	250cc	4th, 2nd, 3rd
	1000cc	2nd
Brands Hatch	250cc	23rd
	Pro-Am	10th

Scottish 500cc Production champion
Knockhill Club champion

1983

Venue/Race	Class	Place
Donington Park	250cc	16th
Donington Park	Pro-Am	2nd
Brands Hatch	Pro-Am	9th
Donington Park	250cc	DNF
Beveridge Park	1000cc	1st

Donington Park	Pro-Am	12th
Snetterton	Pro-Am	1st
Knockhill	250cc	1st
	350cc	1st
Donington Park	Pro-Am	1st
	350cc	4th
	Pro-Am	1st
Knockhill	1000cc	3rd
Hockenheim	Pro-Am	4th
Brands Hatch	Pro-Am	DNF

Yamaha Pro-Am Championship: 2nd

1984

Venue/Race	Class	Place
Donington Park	350cc	2nd
Thruxton	250cc	5th
	350cc	2nd, 1st
Cadwell Park	250cc	4th
Knockhill	250cc	1st
Donington Park	250cc	17th
Oulton Park	250cc	1st
East Fortune	350cc	1st
	1000cc	1st
North West 200	250cc	5th
	350cc	2nd
Knockhill	250cc	1st
	250cc	1st
Mallory Park	250cc	2nd, 2nd
Donington Park	250cc	3rd, DNF
Le Mans	250cc	7th
Snetterton	250cc	4th
	350cc	1st

Donington Park	1000cc	5th
Silverstone	250cc	28th
Anderstorp	250cc	DNF
Iwello	250cc	3rd, 2nd
Cadwell Park	350cc	1st
Knockhill	250cc	2nd
Donington Park	350cc	1st
Darley Moor	1000cc	4th
Brands Hatch	250cc	1st
	350cc	1st
Calafat	250cc	1st, 2nd, 2nd

Circuit Promoters 350cc champion

1985

Venue/Race	Class	Place
Cadwell Park	250cc	2nd, 2nd
Kyalami	GP250	24th
Brands Hatch	250cc	2nd, 3rd
Mallory Park	250cc	1st, 1st
	350cc	1st
Jarama	GP250	DNF
Brands Hatch	350cc	1st
North West 200	250cc	3rd
Hockenheim	GP250	DNF
Mugello	GP250	DNF
Salzburgring	GP250	14th
Raalte	250cc	5th
Rijeka	GP250	16th
Donington Park	250cc	DNF, 2nd
	350cc	1st
Assen	GP250	14th
Spa Francorchamps	GP250	DNF

Snetterton	250cc	1st, 1st
	350cc	1st
Le Mans	GP250	14th
Silverstone	GP250	DNF
Anderstorp	GP250	10th
Oulton Park	250cc	1st, DNF, 2nd
	350cc	2nd
Misano	GP250	DNF
Schwanenstadt	250cc	1st
	500cc	4th
Thruxton	250cc	1st, 4th
	350cc	1st
Carnaby	250cc	2nd
	350cc	1st, 1st
Cadwell Park	250cc	1st
	350cc	1st
Knockhill	250cc	1st
	1000cc	1st
Brands Hatch	250cc	1st
	350cc	1st
Jarama	250cc	3rd, 3rd
Calder	250cc	3rd
Oran Park	250cc	4th
	350cc	1st

British 250cc champion
Circuit Promoters 350cc champion
GP250 Championship: 28=

1986

Venue/Race	Class	Place
Cadwell Park	250cc	1st, 1st
	1300cc	3rd, 4th

Donington Park	250cc	1st
Brands Hatch	250cc	3rd, 4th
	1300cc	1st, DNF
Oulton Park	250cc	1st, 1st
	1300cc	1st
Salzburgring	GP250	DNS
Rijeka	GP250	DNS
Donington Park	250cc	1st, 1st
Assen	GP250	12th
Spa Francorchamps	GP250	8th
Donington Park	250cc	2nd
	350cc	DNF
Paul Ricard	GP250	21st
Mallory Park	250cc	1st, 6th
Silverstone	GP250	10th
	GP500	7th
Anderstorp	GP250	11th
	GP500	7th
Misano	GP250	DNF
	GP500	8th
Thruxton	250cc	1st, 4th
	1000cc	2nd, 3rd
Schwanenstadt	250cc	1st
Silverstone	250cc	2nd, 2nd, 1st
Knockhill	250cc	1st, 1st
	350cc	1st, 1st
	1000cc	1st
Oran Park	1000cc	DNF

British 250cc champion
1300cc British Championship: 6th
GP250 Championship: 21st
GP500 Championship: 10th=

1987

Venue/Race	Class	Place
Suzuka	500cc	1st
Suzuka	GP500	DNF
Jerez	GP500	4th
Hockenheim	GP500	7th
Monza	GP500	10th
Salzburgring	GP500	3rd
Rjeka	GP500	DNS
Assen	GP500	DNF
Le Mans	GP500	7th
Suzuka	WEC	DNF
Donington Park	GP500	5th
Anderstorp	GP500	5th
Brno	GP500	5th
Misano	GP500	7th
Jarama	GP500	6th
Goiania	GP500	8th
Buenos Aires	GP500	7th

GP500 Championship: 5th

1988

Venue/Race	Class	Place
Suzuka	500cc	1st
Suzuka	GP500	4th
Laguna Seca	GP500	3rd
Jarama	GP500	5th
Jerez	GP500	7th
Imola	GP500	11th
Nürburgring	GP500	9th
Salzburgring	GP500	DNF
Assen	GP500	5th

Spa Francorchamps	GP500	11th
Rijeka	GP500	DNF
Paul Ricard	GP500	DNF
Suzuka	WEC	DNF
Donington Park	GP500	4th
Anderstorp	GP500	4th
Brno	GP500	6th
Goiania	GP500	4th
Fuji	500cc	4th

GP500 Championship: 6th

1989

Venue/Race	Class	Place
Suzuka	GP500	6th
Phillip Island	GP500	DNF
Laguna Seca	GP500	5th
Jerez	GP500	3rd
Misano	GP500	DNF
Hockenheim	GP500	DNF
Salzburgring	GP500	DNS
Rjeka	GP500	12th
Assen	GP500	8th
Spa Francorchamps	GP500	10th
Le Mans	GP500	7th
Silverstone	GP500	4th
Anderstorp	GP500	4th
Brno	GP500	6th
Goiania	GP500	9th
Donington Park	750cc	2nd, 3rd
	F1	2nd
Knockhill	1000cc	1st, 1st, 1st

GP500 Championship: 7th

1990

Venue/Race	Class	Place
Suzuka	GP250	13th
Laguna Seca	GP250	14th
Donington Park	250cc	DNF
	F1	1st
	WSB	13th, 4th
Jerez	GP500	8th
Misano	GP500	5th
Nürburgring	GP500	3rd
Salzburgring	GP500	5th
Rijeka	GP500	3rd
Assen	GP500	5th
Spa Francorchamps	GP500	12th
Le Mans	GP500	6th
Donington	GP500	5th
Anderstorp	GP500	5th
Brno	GP500	4th
Hungaroring	GP500	7th
Phillip Island	GP500	5th
Sugo	500cc	2nd
Johor	500cc	1st

GP500 Championship: 4th
GP250 Championship: 33rd

1991

Venue/Race	Class	Place
Daytona 200	750cc	9th
Donington Park	WSB	7th, 7th
Mallory Park	1000cc	16th, 12th
Brands Hatch	1000cc	17th, 13th, 15th

North West 200	1000cc	6th
Donington Park	F1	1st, 3rd
Brainerd	WSB	15th, 14th
Brands Hatch	F1	5th, 3rd
Suzuka	WEC	22nd
Donington Park	GP500	7th
Mugello	GP500	5th
Sugo	F1	4th
Sugo	WSB	DNF, 6th
Le Mans	GP500	12th
Shah Alam	GP500	6th
Tskuba	F1	3rd
Cataluña	500cc	5th, 5th, 5th

GP500 Championship: 17th
WSB Championship: 23rd

1992

Venue/Race	Class	Place
Suzuka	GP500	7th
Eastern Creek	GP500	DNF
Shah Alam	GP500	DNF
Jerez	GP500	3rd
Mugello	GP500	8th
Cataluña	GP500	7th
Hockenheim	GP500	DNF
Assen	GP500	7th
Hungaroring	GP500	14th
Magny-Cours	GP500	6th
Donington Park	GP500	DNF
Interlagos	GP500	9th
Kyalami	GP500	8th

| Brands Hatch | 250cc | 2nd |
| Kirkistown | 250cc | 2nd, 1st |

GP500 Championship: 11th

1993

Venue/Race	Class	Place
Eastern Creek	GP500	10th
Shah Alam	GP500	8th
Suzuka	GP500	13th
Jerez	GP500	7th
Salzburgring	GP500	11th
Hockenheim	GP500	9th
Assen	GP500	8th
Cataluña	GP500	6th
Mugello	GP500	8th
Donington Park	GP500	3rd
Brno	GP500	DNF
Misano	GP500	9th
Laguna Seca	GP500	8th
Jarama	GP500	8th
Donington Park	WSB	DNF, 4th
Knockhill	1000cc	1st, 5th

GP500 Championship: 9th

1994

Venue/Race	Class	Place
Eastern Creek	GP500	DNF
Shah Alam	GP500	11th
Suzuka	GP500	19th
Jerez	GP500	8th
Salzburgring	GP500	9th
Hockenheim	GP500	8th

Assen	GP500	DNF
Mugello	GP500	9th
Le Mans	GP500	DNF
Donington Park	GP500	8th
Suzuka	WEC	11th
Brno	GP500	9th
Laguna Seca	GP500	10th
Bol d'Or	WEC	DNF
Buenos Aires	GP500	11th
Donington Park	WSB	22nd, DNF
Cataluña	GP500	8th
Albacete	500cc	4th

GP500 Championship: 10th

1995

Venue/Race	Class	Place
Eastern Creek	GP250	DNF
Shah Alam	GP250	DNF
Suzuka	GP250	DNF
Jerez	GP250	11th
Nürburgring	GP250	14th
Mugello	GP250	DNF
Assen	GP250	12th
Le Mans	GP250	19th
Donington Park	GP250	6th
Brno	GP250	DNF
Rio	GP250	19th
Argentina	GP250	11th
Cataluña	GP250	DNF

GP250 Championship: 18th

1996

Venue/Race	Class	Place
Donington Park	BSB	1st, 2nd
Thruxton	BSB	3rd, 1st
Donington Park	WSB	DNF, 13th
Oulton Park	BSB	2nd, 3rd
Snetterton	BSB	3rd, 2nd
Brands Hatch	BSB	3rd, 3rd
Brands Hatch	WSB	11th, DNF
Knockhill	BSB	1st, 1st
Cadwell Park	BSB	2nd, 2nd
Mallory Park	BSB	3rd, 2nd
Brands Hatch	BSB	2nd, 4th
Bishopscourt	1000cc	3rd, 3rd, 2nd
Knockhill	1000cc	1st, 1st, 1st, 1st
Donington Park	BSB	1st, 2nd
British Superbike champion		

1997

Venue/Race	Class	Place
Donington Park	BSB	1st, 1st
Oulton Park	BSB	5th, 3rd
Donington Park	WSB	7th, 8th
Snetterton	BSB	1st, 2nd
Brands Hatch	BSB	8th, 4th
Thruxton	BSB	1st, 1st
Oulton Park	BSB	1st, 1st
Mallory Park	BSB	1st, 1st
Brands Hatch	BSB	3rd (Disqualified), DNF
Knockhill	BSB	DNF, 1st
Cadwell Park	BSB	7th, DNF

Brands Hatch	BSB	1st, 1st
Donington Park	BSB	1st, DNF
British Superbike champion		

1998

Venue/Race	Class	Place
Brands Hatch	BSB	6th, 1st
Donington Park	WSB	DNF, 6th
Oulton Park	BSB	4th, 2nd
Thruxton	BSB	1st, 1st
Snetterton	BSB	2nd, 4th
Donington Park	BSB	DNF, 1st
Oulton Park	BSB	2nd, 2nd
Brands Hatch	WSB	6th, 10th
Knockhill	BSB	1st, 1st
Mallory Park	BSB	7th, 2nd
Cadwell Park	BSB	5th, 7th
Silverstone	BSB	2nd, 6th
Brands Hatch	BSB	4th, 3rd
Donington Park	BSB	4th, DNF
British Superbike champion		

1999

Venue/Race	Class	Place
Brands Hatch	BSB	7th, DNF
Thruxton	BSB	DNF, 6th
Le Mans	WEC	DNF
Oulton Park	BSB	5th, 6th
Donington Park	WSB	12th, 10th
Snetterton	BSB	6th, 7th
Donington Park	BSB	DNF, 5th

Silverstone	BSB	5th, 5th
Oulton Park	BSB	DNF, DNS
Brands Hatch	WSB	8th, 7th
Knockhill	BSB	4th, 2nd
Mallory Park	BSB	7th, 7th
Cadwell Park	BSB	9th, 7th
Paul Ricard	WEC	DNF
Brands Hatch	BSB	5th, 5th
Donington Park	BSB	2nd, 7th
Knockhill	1000cc	1st, 1st

BSB Championship: 7th

2000

Venue/Race	Class	Place
Brands Hatch	BSB	6th, DNF
Donington Park	BSB	4th, 5th
Thruxton	BSB	7th, DNF
Oulton Park	BSB	DNF, 3rd
Snetterton	BSB	5th, 5th
Silverstone	BSB	6th, 4th
Oulton Park	BSB	6th, DNF
Knockhill	BSB	4th, DNF
Cadwell Park	BSB	4th, 17th
Mallory Park	BSB	9th, 7th
Brands Hatch	BSB	8th, 4th
Donington Park	BSB	6th, 4th

BSB Championship: 5th

2001

Venue/Race	Class	Place
Knockhill	BSB	5th, 4th
(Farewell race)		

KEY TO ABBREVIATIONS

GP500 = 500cc Grand Prix World Championship

GP250 = 250cc Grand Prix World Championship

WSB = World Superbike Championship

BSB = British Superbike Championship

WEC = World Endurance Championship

F1 = Formula One

Pro-Am = Yamaha Pro-Am Challenge

P = Production Class

DNS = Did not start

DNF = Did not finish

Index

Docshop team 199
Doohan, Mick 96, 286
  1989: 117, 125
  1990: 134
  1992: 159, 166
  1993: 176, 177
  1994: 196
  boat 188–9
  fitness 225–6
  retirement 175, 258–9
Downing St party 234–5
Ducati 228, 263
  GSE team 261, 262–3
Dunblane 127, 209
Dunlop, Joey 46, 268–9
Dunlop, Robert 71

E

Emmett, Sean 190, 191, 220, 228
energy levels 193
European Superbike school 284
Evans, Chris 195
experience 72

F

Falco 87
Fankerton 3
fans 223–4, 242–3
Fearnall, Robert 60, 128, 209

Feeney, Alan 27
Feeney, Craig 10, 27, 28, 31
Feeney, Wullie 27, 32
Fleming, Pim 7, 22
Flint, Keith 232
Fogarty, Carl 109, 137, 138, 284
  1991: 144, 145
  1993: 178–9
  1997: 229, 234
Foreman, George 247
Fowler, Geoff 40
Fricker, Paul 282
fuel injection 252, 253–4, 255

G

Gardner, Wayne 286
  1986: 69
  1989: 117, 123, 125
  1990: 140
  Mackenzie's start story 2
  racing, starting 1
  retirement 175
  team-mate 77–8, 86, 91, 92, 93, 107
Goddard, Peter 150, 170
Grands Prix 141
  British 88–9, 108, 123–4, 177–80
  teams 151

Towers, Jonny 225
truck race 128
Turner, Jeff 207, 208
Tuxworth, Neil 144, 148, 149
Two Wheels Only 277–8, 279
tyres
  bike set up 120, 124, 137
  changing 22
  choice 219
  cold 89
  importance 202
  lifespan 178
  problems 255
  radials 81
  sizes 199
  supply 201, 215

V

Vance & Hines Ducati 236
Virgin Yamaha team 251, 260

W

Wakai, Noboyuki 174
Walker, Chris 151, 245, 265, 266, 271, 272
  team-mate 228, 229, 232, 233–4
Whitehorn, Wil 251
Whitham, Jamie 137, 138, 145, 200, 203–4, 206, 247
  1997: 230, 234

team-mate 207, 209, 210, 212, 213, 214, 216, 218, 220–1
Wimmer, Martin 34
Wood, Russel 148
Woods, Jim 104
World Superbike Championship 144
Wright, Colin 227, 261, 266–7

X

Xaus, Ruben 204–5

Y

Yamaha 150, 227, 228, 236, 237, 249, 250
  FS1E (Fizzy) 9
  R7 248, 252, 253
  RD350LC 13, 16, 32, 33, 35
  TZ250 28, 29
  TZ350 20–1
  YZF750 210, 252
  YZR 286
  YZR500 113, 114
Yamaha Cadbury's Boost team 209, 211
Yamaha France team 152, 153, 154, 155, 156, 157
Yamaha Japan 155